THE POWER OF X

ENTER

THE 10 GODS

八字十神入門篇

The Power of X - Enter the 10 Gods

First Edition July 2011

The author can be reached at:

Mastery Academy of Chinese Metaphysics Sdn. Bhd. (611143-A)
19-3, The Boulevard, Mid Valley City,
59200 Kuala Lumpur, Malaysia.
Tel : +603-2284 8080
Fax : +603-2284 1218
Email : info@masteryacademy.com
Website: www.masteryacademy.com

Published by JY Books Sdn. Bhd. (659134-T)

INDEX

PREFACE TO THE POWER OF X

As I was writing this preface, I realised that it has been almost 4 years since my copies of ***The Destiny Code*** and ***The Destiny Code Revealed*** were published. I am long overdue on having finished this book, which is the continuation of *The Destiny Code Revealed.*

The truth is that this book, or rather, this series of books on the 10 Gods, *The Power of X* series, has been a work-in-progress ever since I finished the second title. The matter of finding an appropriate manner in which to introduce to students of BaZi the subject of the 10 Gods (or the 10 Essential Stars of BaZi Astrology) has been something that has proven to be quite a challenge. Indeed, it required a considerable and formidable detour, in the form of a different 10 Gods book, namely my recently released ***The Ten Gods – An Introduction to the Ten Gods in BaZi***, before I was able to really settle into a presentation of the 10 Gods which I felt would be worthy of the many readers of the Destiny Code titles around the world.

For avoidance of doubt, throughout this text '10 Gods' is used to refer to the subject matter, whilst 'The Ten Gods' refers to the textbook.

Readers may be wondering what is the difference the *The Ten Gods* and the *Power of X* series? Well, the former is really more a combination of textbook-practitioner tome, and was written with students who have undertaken the BaZi Mastery series in mind rather than laypersons. It is a highly technical text and presumes the reader has existing BaZi knowledge and some measure of professional practice. By contrast, the latter, a sub-series, is really designed for the layperson and, although it makes use of some common material from *The Ten Gods*, is an entirely different type of book altogether.

The *Power of X* series has been designed for individuals who are unable to attend a professional BaZi class and for laypersons who enjoy and relish the challenge of DIY BaZi. All the books in this sub-series will contain walk-throughs and guided formats as well as appropriate worksheets to help you learn and master the 10 Gods. The analysis methods and techniques have also been selected to ensure a maximum amount of relevance to the layperson, and as always, attuned to help readers gain insight into the key questions in the area of Career, Relationships and Wealth.

Nonetheless, serious students of BaZi and new practitioners who have read *The Ten Gods* may find the more guided approach in the *Power of X* series complementary to its hard-edge technical style.

Readers may also be wondering – why a sub-series within the Destiny Code series? BaZi as you will all know by now, is a subject that exists on both a macro and micro level. There are times in which the overall perspective (or the BaZi image) is relevant and there are situations where a detailed approach (looking at individual aspects of the chart) is warranted. The Destiny Code titles are very much in the vein of 'big picture' perspectives, looking at BaZi and BaZi analysis in a broad and introductory fashion. By contrast, the sub-series are very specifically focused on a very important aspect of BaZi analysis, namely the 10 Gods.

Where appropriate, a subject may be dealt with on a macro level, through more Destiny Code series. But where apropos, a sub-series is useful because it helps isolate the subject and enables the break-down into manageable bite-chunks of what is a very, very large topic indeed. And as you will learn from Chapter 1 of this book, the 10 Gods is a topic of immense depth and breadth and even *The Ten Gods* textbook does not in any way claim to be definitive about the subject.

Truthfully, BaZi enthusiasts and practitioners could go on and on about the subject of the 10 Gods – it seems infinite in its reach and extent and that is because it is in many ways, the center of the BaZi universe. So in this respects, I have no idea at this time, how long the *Power of X* series will run. But as long as readers out there continue to enjoy reading these books and find value in the information, knowledge and analysis methods shared, I will continue to write and share my own expanding and growing understanding of this fascinating subject with them.

Joey Yap
July 2011

Author's personal website : www.joeyyap.com

Academy websites : www.masteryacademy.com | www.baziprofiling.com

Joey Yap on Facebook : www.facebook.com/joeyyapFB

Email : JY10G@joeyyap.com

THE ULTIMATE BAZI DESTINY CODE COLLECTION

BaZi – The Destiny Code (Book 1)

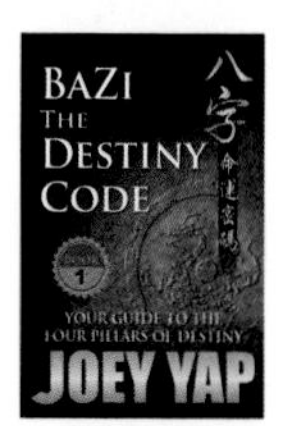

This is an ideal introductory book on BaZi or Four Pillars of Destiny, written in an easy-to-read style with helpful illustrations.In this comprehensive book, delve deeper into BaZi beyond the conventional Chinese Astrology readings. Learn about the Ten Heavenly Stems, Twelve Earthly Branches, special relationships between the Five Elements, the technique of plotting a BaZi chart and simple, quick analysis techniques for deciphering your Destiny Code.

BaZi – The Destiny Code Revealed (Book 2)

Elevate the knowledge gained through **BaZi – The Destiny Code** with this comprehensive volume, taking a step further into BaZi chart interpretation through an understanding of the Key Elemental relationships that affect the Heavenly Stems and Earthly Branches.

Enter the 10 Gods (Book 3)

YOU ARE HERE

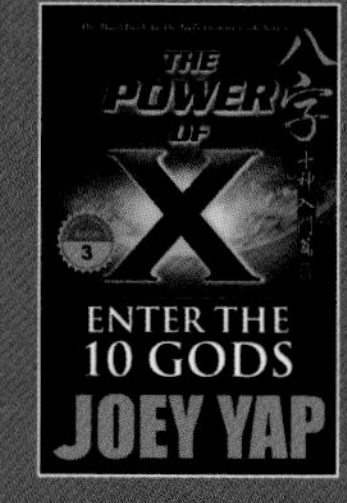

Get acquainted with the 10 Gods to strengthen your technical foundation in BaZi chart interpretation in terms of career, wealth and relationship. Find out how the 10 Gods present in a BaZi chart influence and shape a person's character, which is a composite of attitude, mindset, perceptions, actions and choices.This book aims to put your knowledge into practice and to improve your BaZi reading skills towards the professional level.

The Ten Gods: An Introduction to The Ten Gods in BaZi

THE TEXT BOOK

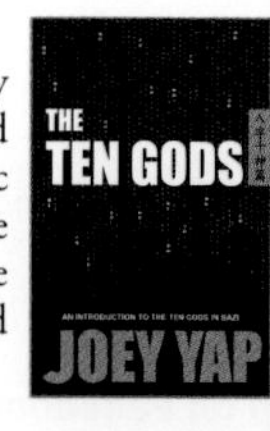

The Ten Gods are an integral and core component of the study of BaZi. This book presents a one-of-a-kind reference designed to provide a thorough and extensive introduction to the specific subject matter, the Ten Gods in BaZi. It has been written with the novice and intermediate students of BaZi in mind, bringing the necessary understanding for anyone seeking to master BaZi beyond the beginner level.

These titles are available at the Mastery Academy Online Store at

www.MasteryAcademy.com/eStore/eStore.asp.

DO THIS FIRST

Print your Free BaZi Chart to facilitate your learning process as you use this book.

To plot your BaZi Chart :

www.masteryacademy.com/regbook

Here is your unique code to access the BaZi Calculator:

AMYH1879

The following steps will guide you to plot your BaZi Chart with ease.

Step 1 : Upon access to the site, key in the required information – Name, Gender, Hour, Day, Month and Year of Birth - as per instruction.

Step 2 : Your BaZi Chart will be generated accordingly. A sample is illustrated below.

Step 3 : Print your BaZi Chart.

Step 4 : Begin CHAPTER 1.

Sample: This is how your BaZi Chart will look like

Chapter 1
A New Beginning

My first two books were written with a specific goal of introducing the English speaking public to the subject matter of BaZi. My purpose was to demystify many of the misconceptions about BaZi. The goal was to show the public that BaZi was not all-superstitious fatalistic mumbo-jumbo, but a substantive, metaphysical science that enables people to make real change and achieve their goals in life. Both *The Destiny Code* and the *Destiny Code Revealed* were also written with a view to giving the layperson an opportunity to dabble and get their feet wet with this exciting and intriguing field of study.

The time for getting your feet wet is over.

As we move into the subject of the 10 Gods, we are venturing into hard-core territory as far as BaZi. This is not to say that what you read about in *The Destiny Code* and the *Destiny Code Revealed* was somehow… fluff. Indeed, much of the material contained in those two books is as much necessary technical foundation, introducing readers to the basic fundamentals of the BaZi chart and concepts such as the Luck Pillars. Many of you would no doubt have realised that the broad techniques you learned in the first book, notably, how to discern the Favourable and Unfavourable Elements of a chart and technical information you would have picked up from the second book about the Day Masters and chart interactions (such as Clashes, Combinations, Harms, Destructions and Punishments) offer you limited insight and accuracy and a very elementary understanding of the person's Destiny Code.

The reality is that no decoding of a person's Destiny Code can be done with any degree of accuracy without adding the filter of the 10 Gods into the decoding process. The 10 Gods is the heart and soul of BaZi in many ways and it is through the 10 Gods that BaZi's power of forecasting and capacity for results-orientated solutions can be harnessed and utilised. Forecasting and solutions are an integral part of successfully utilising the strategic benefits of knowing BaZi – what is the point after all in knowing if one does not act on that knowledge?

The 10 Gods in essence, take decoding your Destiny to a different level. A higher level. A level of greater accuracy and deeper insight.

You might well be wondering at this point – what is so amazing about the 10 Gods anyway? And if it's such an important subject, why wasn't it in the first two books?

What are the 10 Gods?

The 10 Gods are not really Gods in the divine sense. For the avoidance of ambiguity, there is nothing 'godly' about the 10 Gods. There is nothing spiritual or religious about this subject, nor do the 10 Gods relate to anything spiritual or religious in any way.

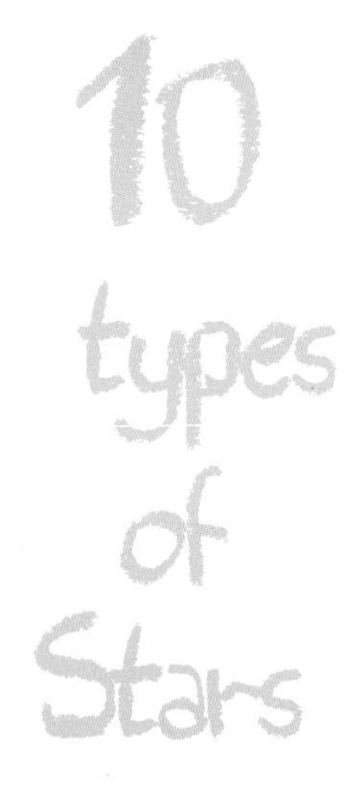

The 10 Gods (十神 *shi shen*) are essentially names given to 10 types of Stars. It must be recalled that BaZi is a form of Chinese Astrology and as such, it ultimately is referencing Stars in the cosmic system. Chinese Philosophers prefer the term 'God' (神 *shen*) to the term 'Star' (星 *xing*) purely for dramatic and literary purposes. It simply sounds better to say 'God' than to say 'Star' and certainly is more poetic as well for the purposes of the written script. For all intents and purposes, the two words are interchangeable within the vocabulary of Chinese Metaphysics and BaZi, and are not meant in any way to be a reference to any religious or spiritual beings.

These 10 Gods (or Stars) are identified throughout my BaZi books using the following Western names. Note, these Western names represent my preferred transliteration of the Chinese names. These terms will not be uniform across different English language books on this subject. In case of doubt, always check against the Chinese words to be certain. It is important to recognise that some of these names are a little dramatic or outrageous, but they by no means are meant

to convey any implication of 'good' or 'bad' to the individual Stars. Chinese Metaphysics, with the concept of Yin and Yang at its core, has a fundamental tenet that nothing is ever entirely 'good' or 'positive', nor is it permanently 'bad' and 'negative'. All Stars have a positive and negative side, and can exert both these sides.

The 10 Gods (in no order of preference) are:

- Direct Wealth Star 正財星
- Indirect Wealth Star 偏財星
- Direct Officer Star 正官星
- 7 Killings Star 七殺星
- Direct Resource Star 正印星
- Indirect Resource Star 偏印星
- Hurting Officer Star 傷官星
- Eating God Star 食神星
- Friend Star 比肩星
- Rob Wealth Star 劫財星

As you will see when you get to Chapter 3 of this book, the 10 Gods is the language in which BaZi uses to define the entire universe and world in which we live in.

Read that again. *Entire. Universe.*

There is not a single object, person, relationship, situation, circumstance, challenge, obstacle, goal that cannot be connected or tethered to or defined by a 10 God. That the whole world and universe, including things that have yet to exist, can be represented by 10 concepts, is a testament to the simple yet profound power of the 10 Gods. Hence, I have chosen the name '*The Power of X*' for this series of book that focuses exclusively on the 10 Gods and will serve as your bridge into the 10 Gods. The phrase '*The Power of X*' to my mind captures both the expansiveness of the 10 Gods, and yet the compact nature of the concept.

(Conspiracy theorists may also note that 1 and 0 represent the binary code, which is the basic building block and foundation of all advanced mathematics and computer programming. 1 and 0 can also be said to be representative of yin and yang. Make what you want of that!).

Why not just start with the 10 Gods then?

In my previous two books, I have already offered readers a little taste of the 10 Gods, an appetiser as it were. Thus, you already have some awareness of the 10 Gods and some of the 10 God terminology may even be faintly familiar to you. You might accordingly be wondering why such an important subject was not discussed right at the onset? Why were readers only offered a taster?

Just like a medical student must first spend two years learning advanced chemistry and biology before they can actually start learning any real medical diagnosis skills, accordingly, before you can learn to analyse a chart and propose solutions to problems, you first need to know the essentials of what makes up a BaZi chart. It is not possible to discuss the 10 Gods without first familiarising a person with the Day Masters, the 10 Stems, the 12 Earthly Branches, the Luck Pillars and the chart interactions of Clash, Combination, Harm, Destruction and Punishment. Indeed, as you will find out in Chapter 2, which covers the technical essentials, understanding of the 10 Gods also requires first a requisite understanding of the 5 Elements cycles (Production, Weakening and Control cycles) and an ability to wield the elements to determine the Five Factors.

Once you have the basics of BaZi down to pat, only then can you proceed to the next step, which is to gain a thorough understanding of the underlying technical and theoretical foundation of the 10 Gods and a basic comprehension of the 10 Gods. That is the goal of this book, to serve as bridge into the veritable *smorgasbord*-like subject of the 10 Gods.

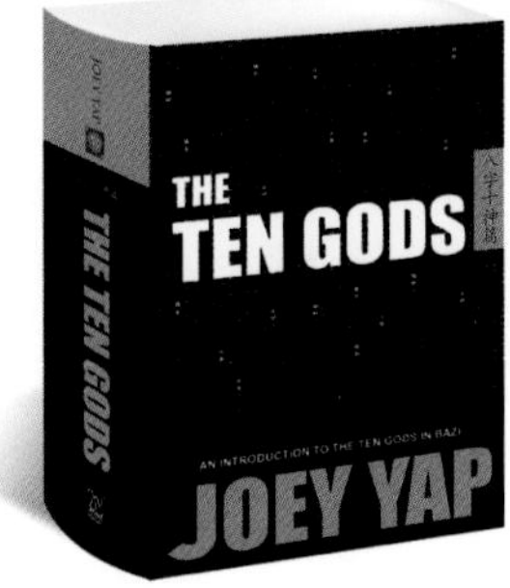

Another reason why the 10 Gods was not broached in detail in the first two books is because it is quite frankly, a huge bottomless pit topic. One book cannot conceivably do the topic justice. Trust me, I tried with my BaZi practitioners textbook, ***The Ten Gods***, and even after 500 pages, that book isn't anywhere near covering the topic of the 10 Gods in anything beyond an introductory manner. I constantly remind my students that metaphysics is a living, breathing topic, and thus, is ever continuously organically evolving. This is the reason behind the decision to cover this topic as a series rather than a stand-alone book.

In the *Power of X* series, which will focus exclusively on the 10 Gods, you will find that we will move increasingly away from a very broad style of analysis and increasingly into analysis that aims to obtain very specific information and insight about a person, via their Destiny Code. This is very important because specificity of timing, outcomes and events is part of the inherent advantage BaZi affords when it comes to strategising for success in the battle called *Life*.

With the information and analysis techniques and methods that will be shared with you in the *Power of X* series, you will gradually develop a greater accuracy in your reading of BaZi charts. By the end of the 2nd book in this series, you should not only be able to read your own chart and those of your close friends and family members accurately from a character standpoint, but you will also be able to seize up total strangers from just their BaZi chart.

As you learn to put the pieces of BaZi puzzle together, incorporating the information from the first two Destiny Code books, you will start to slowly learn how to utilise BaZi to forecast outcomes or events. And once you have the capacity to analyse and forecast, learning how to develop solutions is just a matter of practice and developing elasticity in the way you perceive and wield the 10 Gods.

Take a breath, take a moment

Before you begin your journey into the 10 Gods, first take a moment to reflect on an important question.

WHAT DO YOU WANT TO KNOW?

You might be wondering: why is it relevant or important to know what it is that I want to know?

Allow me to briefly digress as I explain this.

I have taught BaZi to students from all cultures and backgrounds around the world, from Down Under to the Canada to Poland and India. I've also met many of the readers of my BaZi books, at book signings and events around the world. Students and readers alike all exhibit a great enthusiasm and passion for BaZi. And they all also express the same puzzlement: How is it that they don't seem to be able to read their own charts (or that of others) despite having done a number of classes and read my books and those of others (including Chinese books) on the subject?

The answer to their conundrum is very simple: people expect the chart to function like an oracle and miraculously reveal to them the past, present and future in some kind of eureka moment. There is almost this expectation that like the movie, 'The Da Vinci Code', the 8 characters of their Destiny Code will just unscramble and reveal THE ANSWER.

Before you begin your journey into the 10 Gods, first take a moment to reflect on an important question.
WHAT DO YOU WANT TO KNOW?

Often when this question is posed to me, I ask the following question: so what is it that you want to know about yourself from the chart?

And the answer, invariably, is one word. EVERYTHING.

Unfortunately, 'Everything' is not a dish that is available on the BaZi menu. This is not to say that you cannot find out 'Everything' about someone or yourself from your BaZi chart. Of course you can. The BaZi chart contains a comprehensive map and code of your life after all. Theoretically, 'Everything' is there. But 'Everything' is one of those words that actually means *nothing*. When someone says they want to know 'Everything' about themselves, this indicates an absence of reflection about what is important and significant to the person in their life. If someone says they want to know EVERYTHING about themselves, this means that they have no idea about ANYTHING about themselves. What is worse than a person with a problem? A person who doesn't know what their problem is or who doesn't know what they want.

Now once I sat these students and readers down and explained that they must start from a position of knowing what they want, they GET IT.

In order to gain an effective answer about someone or something, you must first know what it is that you want to know (or what is it that you don't know). Do not approach decoding your Destiny Code or that of another person's in a thoughtless unconscious and unaware manner – that is a guaranteed path to being stuck in Metaphysical purgatory. Approach the subject from a considered, conscious and reflective standpoint. The best way to do this is to start by asking yourself

What is it you want to know?

So before you read any further, I'd like to ask you to take a moment or a few minutes to jot down in a notebook, a list of questions that you have about yourself. (Let's start with you first before we get on to other people's business). Write down what are the things you want to find out about yourself through your BaZi chart. Make your questions as specific as possible and as clear as you can with details. For example, maybe you want to start a business. Then your question would perhaps be:

I want to start a business. Am I suited to do this? (Hint: it might be a good idea as well to list down the potential businesses you are thinking of starting)

Perhaps you have high financial aspirations but don't seem to be able to achieve them. Then your question might be:

Why do I never seem to have enough money? Why do financial opportunities constantly elude me?

Maybe your issues are less about your professional life and more about your personal life. So maybe your question might be:

Why can't I meet someone?

These are just sample possibilities and you should list down as many of your questions as possible. Of course, this is usually the part where most people get cold feet because it requires some thought and reflection into possibly their deepest fears or most private concerns. Still, if you can't ask yourself the hard questions, then why are you trying to learn more about yourself through BaZi? Remember, we are not here just to learn about the Good and the Nice, but the Bad and the Ugly about ourselves. Only when we acknowledge our flaws and the errors of our ways, can we actually take the steps needed to rectify or minimise the effect of those flaws. So be honest with yourself as you write down your questions. But at the same time, let your dreams and ambitions fly forth. For something to be in the realm of the possible, first it must exist and so put down as well those aspirations and goals that you have. After all, if you don't ask if they are possible, how will you ever know if they are? There may even be some questions in which you already have the answer, but you are curious to know what perspective is offered by your BaZi. Go ahead and put those questions down too.

After you've written down your questions, review your questions. Below each of those questions, write the same question but this time, start your question with the word 'HOW'.

For example, let's say your concerns revolve around financial matters and you've written your question as follows:

Why do financial opportunities constantly elude me?

Underneath this question, write the same question but using 'HOW' as your kick-off point.

How do I gain more financial opportunities?
How do I increase my financial opportunities?
How can I change myself to improve my financial circumstances?

I would also recommend you add a goal or a call to action below the question, like the ones below.

I want to achieve financial independence.
I want to own 4 properties.
I want to be able to buy my own home.

Why the additional question and the call to action or goal-setting? The re-phrasing of the question in the context of 'how' and adding a goal or call to action is to focus your perspective on the positive in each situation. Turning your question on its head by converting it from 'WHY' (which if you think about it, is very woe-is-me in tone) into a 'HOW' (which is more pro-active in tone) serves as a reminder that knowing your Destiny is only half the equation. After all, the whole purpose of awareness is ultimately to act upon it in the form of change, right? Acting upon the knowledge you have obtained from your BaZi is what truly makes the difference when it comes to making effective use of BaZi knowledge.

The rephrasing of the question from WHY into HOW is also designed to shift you from an emotional reaction to a logical reaction. Both logic and emotion are important here in terms of creating effective change – emotion after all, is a very powerful driver in life but equally, it can also be destructive if it is unleashed unchecked, namely, without the control of logic. Think of one as the Yin and one as the Yang, and both are needed to achieve equilibrium.

You can also only act upon knowledge if you focus your mind on a solution (ie: How do I achieve something) rather than just the reason (ie: Why does the challenge exist), although of course, the reason does have to come first. So after you understand WHY from your BaZi chart, turn you mind to figuring out HOW, both through the use of your chart and through common sense.

The addition of a call to action or goal is designed to make you think about what you want to achieve in more precise terms and to provide you with a greater sense of focus as you give thought to the what action you need to take or what solutions you need to implement.

If you are interested in using BaZi to learn more about those around you, it is important also to utilise this approach. Before any analysis of another person's BaZi chart, start by asking yourself what is it that you want to know about this person or defining the problem that this person is facing.

Think of one as the Yin and one as the Yang, and both are needed to achieve equilibrium.

Some of the questions that you have written down for yourself will be answered by the time you get to the end of this book. Others may require a little more understanding of the 10 Gods, which you will gain as you progress through the *Power of X* series. In particular, you may find that the solutions and actions that you need to take to answer the 'How' questions or achieve your goals may not be immediately apparent. However, in some instances, you will find that at the end of this book, you have the answer to the 'Why' version of your question and armed with that insight, the 'How' part just naturally falls into place.

In time, some of the questions may change or alter as you learn new things about yourself with the added layer of clarity that comes from understanding the 10 Gods. Thus it is important to keep revisiting the broad issue of WHAT DO I WANT TO KNOW throughout your BaZi journey because as your knowledge grows, your perspective may well change and thus, your goals, aspirations and dreams will shift tangibly as well.

Onward!

Chapter 2
Deriving the Ten Gods

Before you can start to understand what the 10 Gods are all about, you need to be able to understand how they are derived. It's often difficult for BaZi students to understand why there is a need to know the technicalities – there is often an understandable eagerness to get on with the business of analysis of a chart and a decided impatience with the niggling details.

The reality is that without a good technical foundation, your ability to engage in truly accurate analysis of a BaZi chart will always be limited. Once you start exploring and delving into the 10 Gods, a strong technical foundation is required in order for you to not only comprehend analysis but to actually expand your understanding of the 10 Gods. Without a strong grasp of the technicalities, which are heavily rooted in the Five Elements, you will not only find it difficult to progress to a higher level of knowledge, but will be stuck with at best, a superficial understanding of the 10 Gods. This is certainly insufficient for any accurate forecasting skills, and further, will limit your ability to then be able to develop or provide solutions to problems that are indicated in the BaZi chart.

The Five Elements: The Heart of the 10 Gods

The first step to deriving the 10 Gods begins with the Five Elements, notably the Production, Control and Weakening Cycles.

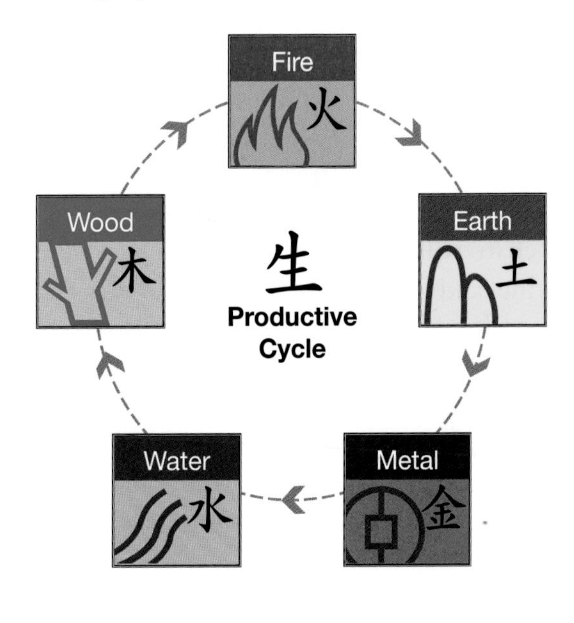

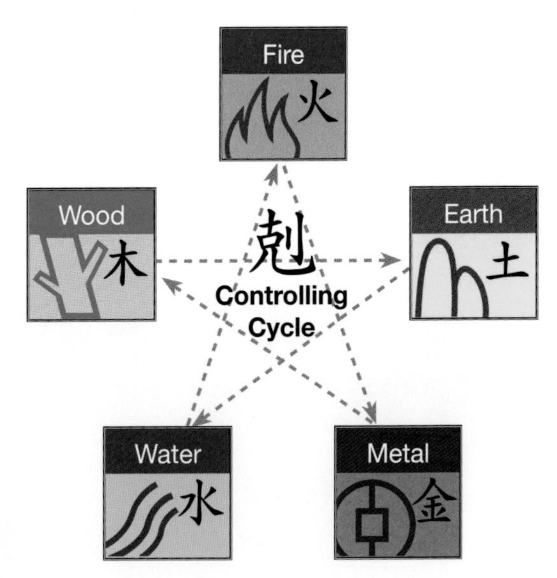

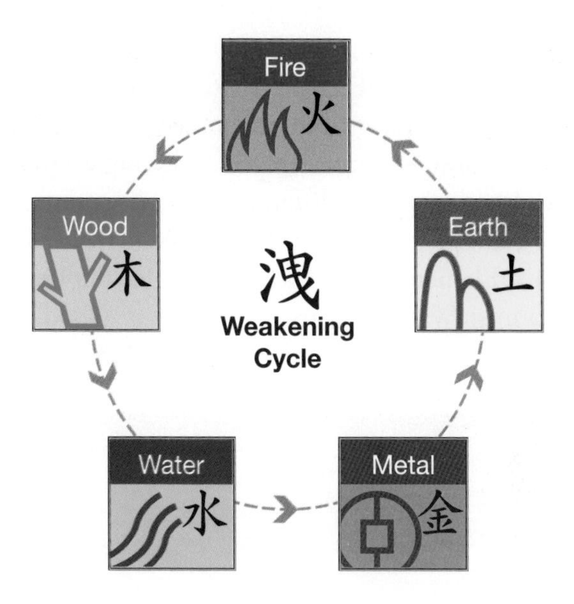

From the Five Element Production, Control and Weakening Cycles, we know that every one of the five basic Elements (Wood, Fire, Earth, Metal and Water) has

- An Element that Controls It (termed the 'Influence Element')
- An Element that it Controls (termed the 'Wealth Element')
- An Element that It Produces (termed the 'Output Element')
- An Element that Produces It (termed the 'Resource Element')
- An Element that is the same as It (termed the 'Companion Element')

Collectively, Influence, Wealth, Output, Resource and Companion Elements are known as the Five Factors. I won't delve too much into the Five Factors as they have been adequately introduced in Chapter 7 of *The Destiny Code*. The most important thing to grasp is that each of the Five Elements has a different element representing its Five Factors. For example, Wood's Influence Element is Metal, whilst Fire's Influence Element is Water. Similarly, Earth's Output Element is Metal, whilst Water's Output Element is Wood. The following table captures this concept for easy understanding.

Self Element	官殺 Influence Element (Controls the Self Element)	財星 Wealth Element (Controlled by the Self Element)	印星 Resource Element (Produces the Self Element)	食傷 Output Element (Produced by the Self Element)	比劫 Companion Element (same as the Basic Self Element)
木 Wood	金 Metal	土 Earth	水 Water	火 Fire	木 Wood
水 Water	土 Earth	火 Fire	金 Metal	木 Wood	水 Water
火 Fire	水 Water	金 Metal	木 Wood	土 Earth	火 Fire
金 Metal	火 Fire	木 Wood	土 Earth	水 Water	金 Metal
土 Earth	木 Wood	水 Water	火 Fire	金 Metal	土 Earth

In order to develop an effective understanding of the 10 Gods, it is essential to commit to memory the Five Factors of each of the Five Basic Elements. So before you move on to the next section, you should be able to confidently state which Element (Wood, Fire, Earth, Metal, Water) represents the Five Elements for each of the Elements.

From the Five Factors come the 10 Gods

Once you have done that, we can move to the next stage, which is deriving the 10 Gods. By this stage, you know that each of the Five Elements (木 Wood, 火 Fire, 土 Earth, 金 Metal, 水 Water) has a Yin and Yang variant. Thus, Wood can be either Jia 甲 Wood (Yang Wood) or Yi 乙 Wood (Yin Wood), Fire can be either Bing 丙 Fire (Yang Fire) or Ding 丁 Fire (Yin Fire), Earth can be either Wu 戊 Earth (Yang Earth) or Ji 己 Earth (Yin Earth), Metal can be either Geng 庚 Metal (Yang Metal) or Xin 辛 Metal (Yin Metal) and Water can be either Ren 壬 Water (Yang Water) or Gui 癸 Water (Yin Water).

Element	陽 Yang Variant	陰 Yin Variant
木 Wood	甲 Jia Wood	乙 Yi Wood
火 Fire	丙 Bing Fire	丁 Ding Fire
土 Earth	戊 Wu Earth	己 Ji Earth
金 Metal	庚 Geng Metal	辛 Xin Metal
水 Water	壬 Ren Water	癸 Gui Water

Accordingly, each of the Five Factors will also manifest in a Yin and Yang variant. Thus, there is a Yin and Yang variant of the Influence Element, the Resource Element, the Wealth Element, the Companion Element and the Output Element.

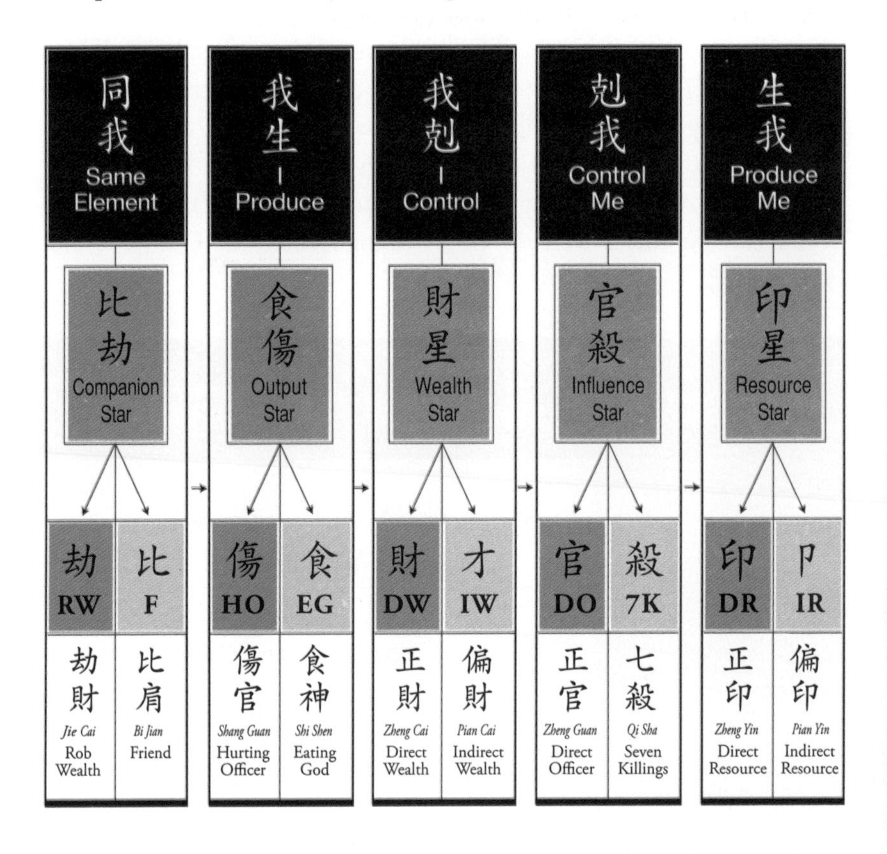

Thus, the Companion Element manifests into the Rob Wealth Star and the Friend Star. The Wealth Element manifests into the Direct Wealth and Indirect Wealth Star, and so on with the other Five Factors. These Yin and Yang variants of the Five Factors result in the 10 Gods (or 10 Stars).

The 10 Gods accordingly are:

Ten Gods 十神	Abbreviations	
正財星 Direct Wealth Star	DW	財
偏財星 Indirect Wealth Star	IW	才
正官星 Direct Officer Star	DO	官
七殺星 7 Killings Star	7K	殺
正印星 Direct Resource Star	DR	印
偏印星 Indirect Resource Star	IR	卩
食神星 Eating God Star	EG	食
傷官星 Hurting Officer Star	HO	傷
比肩星 Friend Star	F	比
劫財星 Rob Wealth Star	RW	劫

Before you proceed further, it is ideal to commit to memory again the Five Factors, and the 10 Gods associated with each of the Five Factors. Accordingly, you should know that the Output Element comprises the Eating God and Hurting Officer Stars, the Wealth Element comprises the Direct Wealth and Indirect Wealth Stars, and so on. This is important because it will prevent confusion as you start to delve into the 10 Gods of each of the individual 10 Day Masters.

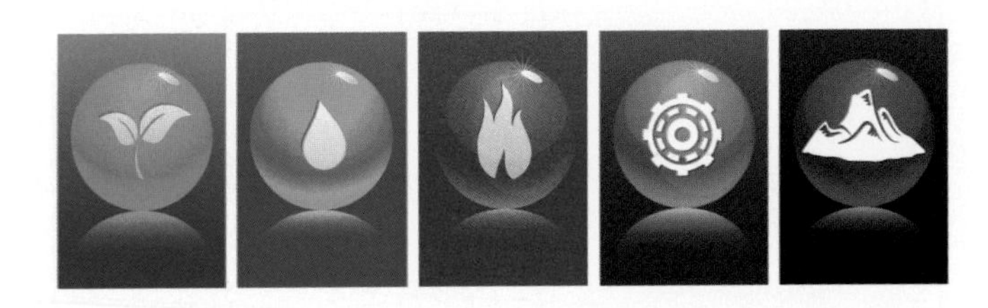

Day Master Polarity and the 10 Gods

By now you know that each Day Master has a unique set of elements that represents its Five Factors and the Five Factors in turn comprise of Yin and Yang variants that result in the 10 Gods. The question then is how do you know which Stem (Yin and Yang) represents which 10 Gods? For example, the Output Element of Water is Wood. Wood comprises of a Yin and Yang variant, namely, Yi Wood and Jia Wood. The Output Element in turn comprises of two Stars, namely, Hurting Officer and Eating God. How do you know which Wood corresponds with the Hurting Officer Star and which one corresponds with the Eating God Star?

This is dictated by the **polarity** (Yin or Yang) of the Day Master. The table below summarises how each 10 God is derived, utilising polarity.

Five Factors	Same Polarity as Day Master	Opposite Polarity as Day Master
食傷 Output Element	食神星 Eating God	傷官星 Hurting Officer
財星 Wealth Element	偏財星 Indirect Wealth	正財星 Direct Wealth
官殺 Influence Element	七殺星 7 Killings	正官星 Direct Officer
印星 Resource Element	偏印星 Indirect Resource	正印星 Direct Resource
比劫 Companion Element	比肩星 Friend	劫財星 Rob Wealth

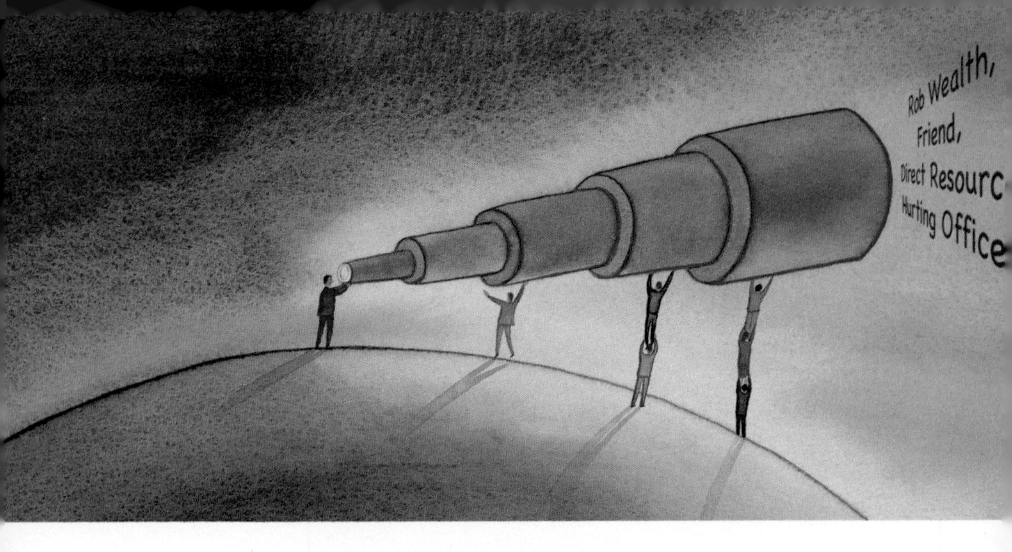

The individual 10 Gods do not have a specific fixed polarity assigned to them. It is NOT the case that the Eating God Star is always a Yang Stem, or that the Direct Wealth Star is always a Yin Stem. In the same vein, none of the 10 Gods have a specific Stem assigned to them. Each of the 10 Stems (Jia 甲, Yi 乙, Bing 丙, Ding 丁, Wu 戊, Ji 己, Geng 庚, Xin 辛, Ren 壬, Gui 癸) can represent ANY of the 10 Gods. Thus, the 10 Gods can be of either Yin or Yang polarity and can be any of the 10 Stems. Which Stem (Jia 甲, Yi 乙, Bing 丙, Ding 丁, Wu 戊, Ji 己, Geng 庚, Xin 辛, Ren 壬, Gui 癸) and which Polarity (Yin or Yang) a 10 God will take on is defined by the Day Master.

Accordingly Jia Wood can be the Direct Wealth Star or Indirect Wealth Star, it can be the 7 Killings or Direct Officer Star, it can be the Indirect Resource or Direct Resource Star, it can be the Hurting Officer or Eating God Star, or it can be the Friend or Rob Wealth Star, depending on which of the Five Factors the element of Wood represents, and the polarity of the Day Master in question.

This series of ten diagrams illustrates which Stems represents which 10 Gods for each of the individual 10 Day Masters. To help you better understand the diagram, I have provided a lengthy but detailed explanation.

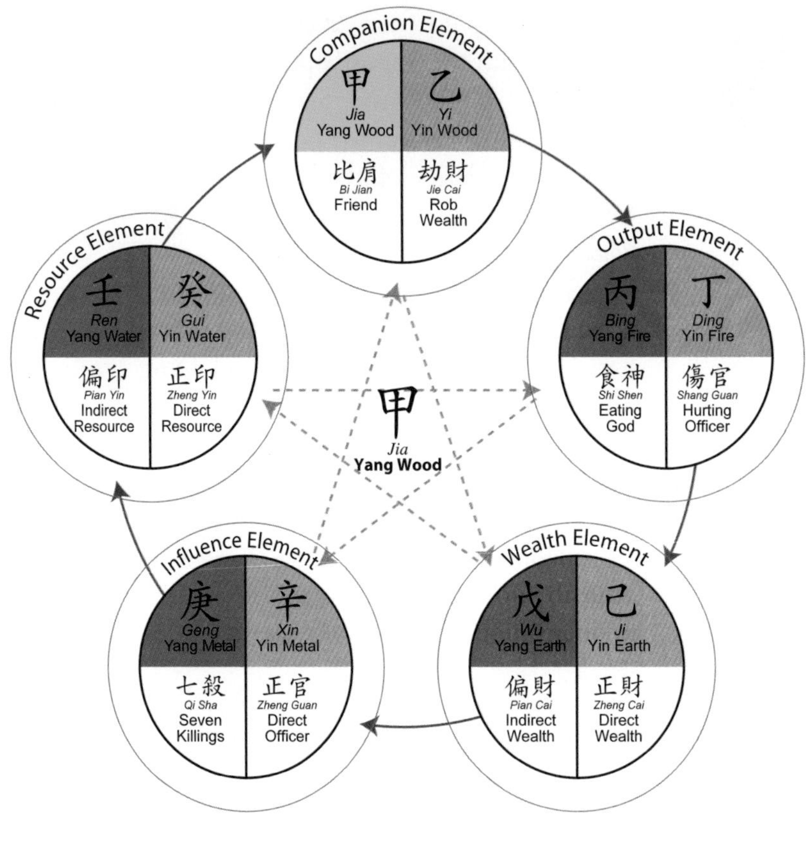

Jia Wood (Yang Wood) produces Fire. This makes Fire the Output Element of Jia Wood. Fire comprises of Bing Fire (Yang Fire) and Ding Fire (Yin Fire). The Output Element comprises the Hurting Officer and Eating God Stars.

Wood (Mu)

The Hurting Officer Star is always the Output Element with the opposite polarity of the Day Master whilst the Eating God Star is always the Output Element which shares the polarity of the Day Master. Here, the polarity of the Day Master is Yang. The Output Element that shares the polarity of the Day Master is Bing Fire (Yang Fire) and the Output Element that has the opposite polarity of the Day Master is Ding Fire (Yin Fire). Thus, Bing Fire is the Eating God Star of Jia Wood, and Ding Fire is the Hurting Officer Star of Jia Wood.

Jia Wood (Yang Wood) is produced by Water. This makes Water the Resource Element of Jia Wood. Water comprises of Ren Water (Yang Water) and Gui Water (Yin Water). The Resource Element comprises the Direct Resource and Indirect Resource Stars.

The Direct Resource Star is always the Resource Element with the opposite polarity of the Day Master whilst the Indirect Resource Star is always the Resource Element which shares the polarity of the Day Master. Here, the polarity of the Day Master is Yang. The Resource Element that shares the polarity of the Day Master is Ren Water (Yang Water) and the Resource Element that has the opposite polarity of the Day Master is Gui Water (Yin Water). Thus, Gui Water is the Indirect Resource Star of Jia Wood, and Ren Water is the Direct Resource Star of Jia Wood.

Jia Wood (Yang Wood) controls Earth. This makes Earth the Wealth Element of Jia Wood. Earth comprises of Wu Earth (Yang Earth) and Ji Earth (Yin Earth). The Wealth Element comprises the Direct Wealth and Indirect Wealth Stars.

The Direct Wealth Star is always the Wealth Element with the opposite polarity of the Day Master whilst the Indirect Wealth Star is always the Wealth Element which shares the polarity of the Day Master. Here, the polarity of the Day Master is Yang. The Wealth Element that shares the polarity of the Day Master is Wu Earth (Yang Earth) and the Wealth Element that has the opposite polarity of the Day Master is Ji Earth (Yin Earth). Thus, Wu Earth is the Indirect Wealth Star of Jia Wood, and Ji Earth is the Direct Wealth Star of Jia Wood.

Jia Wood (Yang Wood) is controlled by Metal. This makes Metal the Influence Element of Jia Wood. Metal comprises of Geng Metal (Yang Metal) and Xin Metal (Yin Metal). The Influence Element comprises the Direct Officer and 7 Killings Stars.

The Direct Officer Star is always the Influence Element with the opposite polarity of the Day Master whilst the 7 Killings Star is always the Influence Element which shares the polarity of the Day Master. Here, the polarity of the Day Master is Yang. The Influence Element that shares the polarity of the Day Master is Geng Metal (Yang Metal) and the Influence Element that has the opposite polarity of the Day Master is Xin Metal (Yin Metal). Thus, Geng Metal is the 7 Killings Star of Jia Wood, and Xin Metal is the Direct Officer Star of Jia Wood.

Jia Wood (Yang Wood) has Wood as its Companion Element. Wood comprises of Jia Wood (Yang Wood) and Yi Wood (Yin Wood).The Companion Element comprises the Friend and Rob Wealth Stars.

The Rob Wealth Star is always the Companion Element with the opposite polarity of the Day Master whilst the Friend Star is always the Companion Element which shares the polarity of the Day Master. Here, the polarity of the Day Master is Yang. The Companion Element that shares the polarity of the Day Master is Jia Wood (Yang Wood) and the Companion Element that has the opposite polarity of the Day Master is Yi Wood (Yin Wood). Thus, Jia Wood is the Friend Star of Gui Water, and Yi Wood is the Rob Wealth Star of Jia Wood.

Jia Wood (Yang Wood) produces Fire. This makes Fire the Output Element of Jia Wood. Fire comprises of Bing Fire (Yang Fire) and Ding Fire (Yin Fire). The Output Element comprises the Hurting Officer and Eating God Stars.

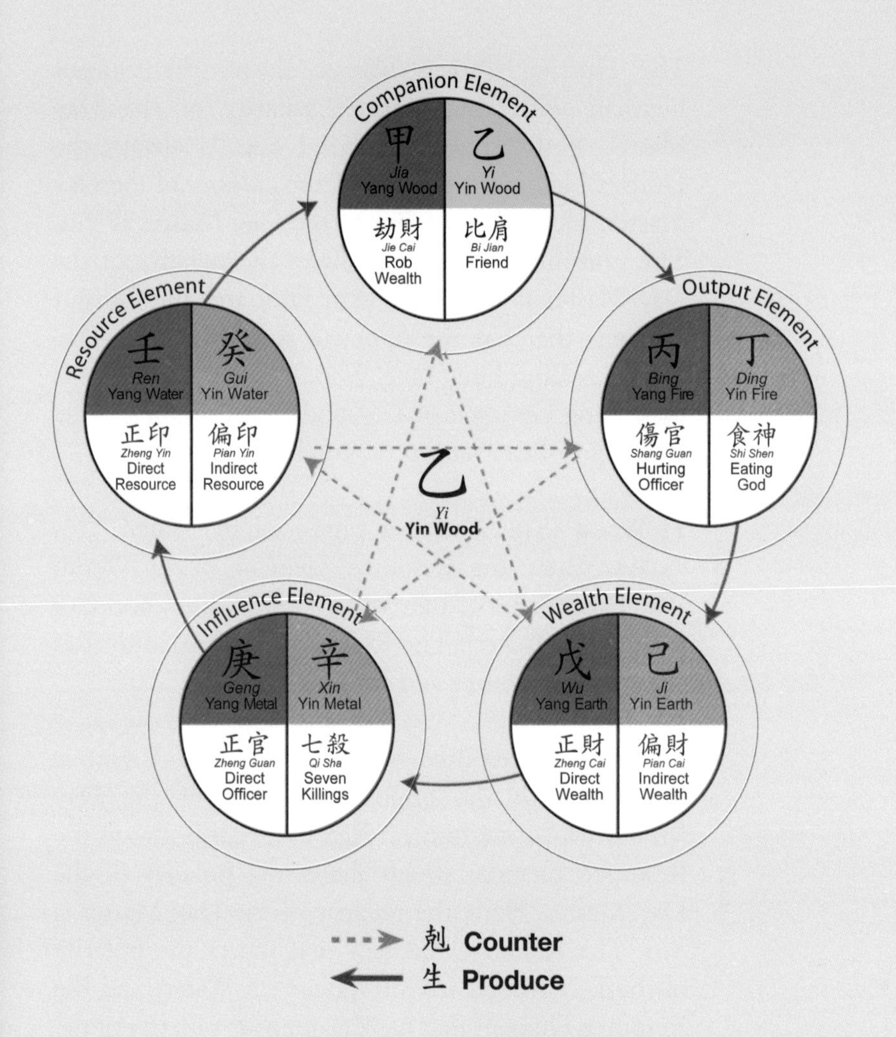

Yi Wood (Yin Wood) produces Fire. This makes Fire the Output Element of Yi Wood. Fire comprises of Bing Fire (Yang Fire) and Ding Fire (Yin Fire). The Output Element comprises the Hurting Officer and Eating God Stars.

The Hurting Officer Star is always the Output Element with the opposite polarity of the Day Master whilst the Eating God Star is always the Output Element which shares the polarity of the Day Master. Here, the polarity of the Day Master is Yin. The Output Element that shares the polarity of the Day Master is Ding Fire (Yin Fire) and the Output Element that has the opposite polarity of the Day Master is Bing Fire (Yang Wood). Thus, Ding Fire is the Eating God Star of Yi Wood, and Bing Fire is the Hurting Officer Star of Yi Wood.

Yi Wood (Yin Wood) is produced by Water. This makes Water the Resource Element of Yi Wood. Water comprises of Ren Water (Yang Water) and Gui Water (Yin Water). The Resource Element comprises the Direct Resource and Indirect Resource Stars.

The Direct Resource Star is always the Resource Element with the opposite polarity of the Day Master whilst the Indirect Resource Star is always the Resource Element which shares the polarity of the Day Master. Here, the polarity of the Day Master is Yin. The Resource Element that shares the polarity of the Day Master is Gui Water (Yin Water) and the Resource Element that has the opposite polarity of the Day Master is Ren Water (Yang Water). Thus, Gui Water is the Indirect Resource Star of Yi Wood, and Ren Water is the Direct Resource Star of Yi Wood.

Yi Wood (Yin Wood) controls Earth. This makes Earth the Wealth Element of Yi Wood. Fire comprises of Wu Earth (Yang Earth) and Ji Earth (Yin Earth). The Wealth Element comprises the Direct Wealth and Indirect Wealth Stars.

Yi Wood

The Direct Wealth Star is always the Wealth Element with the opposite polarity of the Day Master whilst the Indirect Wealth Star is always the Wealth Element which shares the polarity of the Day Master. Here, the polarity of the Day Master is Yin. The Wealth Element that shares the polarity of the Day Master is Ji Earth (Yin Earth) and the Wealth Element that has the opposite polarity of the Day Master is Wu Earth (Yang Earth). Thus, Ji Earth is the Indirect Wealth Star of Yi Wood, and Wu Earth is the Direct Wealth Star of Yi Wood.

Yi Wood (Yin Wood) is controlled by Metal. This makes Metal the Influence Element of Yi Wood. Metal comprises of Geng Metal (Yang Metal) and Xin Metal (Yin Metal). The Influence Element comprises the Direct Officer and 7 Killings Stars.

The Direct Officer Star is always the Influence Element with the opposite polarity of the Day Master whilst the 7 Killings Star is always the Influence Element which shares the polarity of the Day Master. Here, the polarity of the Day Master is Yin. The Influence Element that shares the polarity of the Day Master is Xin Metal (Yin Metal) and the Influence Element that has the opposite polarity of the Day Master is Geng Metal (Yang Metal). Thus, Xin Metal is the 7 Killings Star of Yi Wood, and Geng Metal is the Direct Officer Star of Yi Wood.

Yi Wood (Yin Wood) has Wood as its Companion Element. Wood comprises of Ren Wood (Yang Wood) and Gui Wood (Yin Wood).The Companion Element comprises the Friend and Rob Wealth Stars.

The Rob Wealth Star is always the Companion Element with the opposite polarity of the Day Master whilst the Friend Star is always the Companion Element which shares the polarity of the Day Master. Here, the polarity of the Day Master is Yin. The Companion Element that shares the polarity of the Day Master is Yi Wood (Yin Wood) and the Companion Element that has the opposite polarity of the Day Master is Jia Wood (Yang Wood). Thus, Yi Wood is the Friend Star of Yi Wood, and Jia Wood is the Rob Wealth Star of Yi Wood.

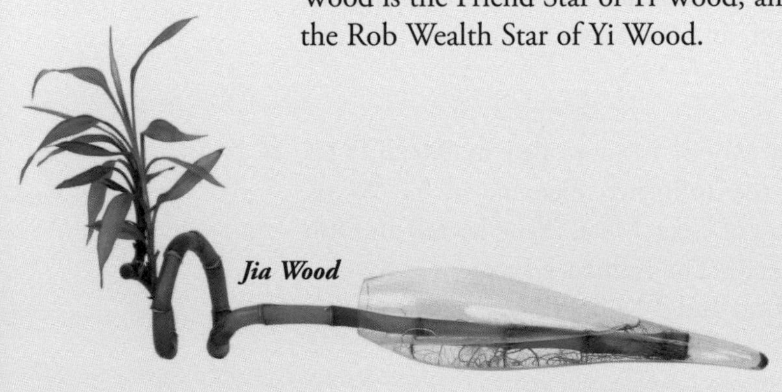
Jia Wood

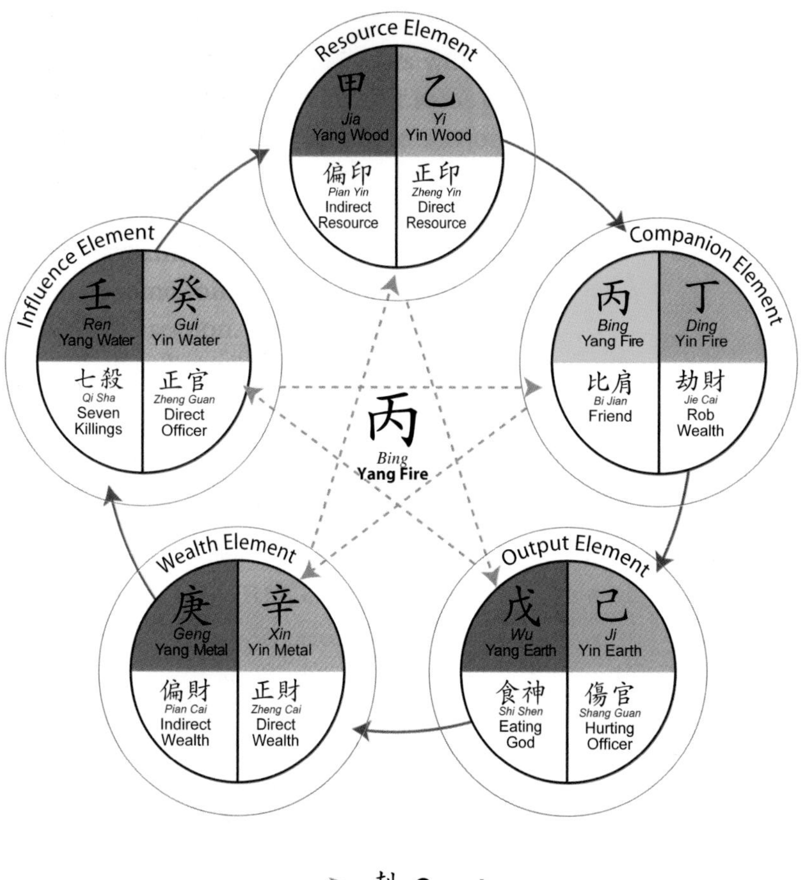

Bing Fire (Yang Fire) produces Earth. This makes Earth the Output Element of Bing Fire. Fire comprises of Wu Earth (Yang Earth) and Ji Earth (Yin Earth). The Output Element comprises the Hurting Officer and Eating God Stars.

The Hurting Officer Star is always the Output Element with the opposite polarity of the Day Master whilst the Eating God Star is always the Output Element which shares the polarity of the Day Master. Here, the polarity of the Day Master is Yang. The Output Element that shares the polarity of the Day Master is Wu Earth (Yang Earth) and the Output Element that has the opposite polarity of the Day Master is Ji Earth (Yin Earth). Thus, Wu Earth is the Eating God Star of Bing Fire, and Ji Earth is the Hurting Officer Star of Bing Fire.

Bing Fire (Yang Fire) is produced by Wood. This makes Wood the Resource Element of Bing Fire. Water comprises of Jia Wood (Yang Wood) and Yi Wood (Yin Wood). The Resource Element comprises the Direct Resource and Indirect Resource Stars.

Bing Fire

Fire (Huo)

The Direct Resource Star is always the Resource Element with the opposite polarity of the Day Master whilst the Indirect Resource Star is always the Resource Element which shares the polarity of the Day Master. Here, the polarity of the Day Master is Yang. The Resource Element that shares the polarity of the Day Master is Jia Wood (Yang Wood) and the Resource Element that has the opposite polarity of the Day Master is Yi Wood (Yin Wood). Thus, Jia Wood is the Indirect Resource Star of Bing Fire, and Yi Wood is the Direct Resource Star of Bing Fire.

Bing Fire (Yang Fire) controls Metal. This makes Metal the Wealth Element of Bing Fire. Earth comprises of Geng Metal (Yang Metal) and Xin Metal (Yin Metal). The Wealth Element comprises the Direct Wealth and Indirect Wealth Stars.

The Direct Wealth Star is always the Wealth Element with the opposite polarity of the Day Master whilst the Indirect Wealth Star is always the Wealth Element which shares the polarity of the Day Master. Here, the polarity of the Day Master is Yang. The Wealth Element that shares the polarity of the Day Master is Geng Metal (Yang Metal) and the Wealth Element that has the opposite polarity of the Day Master is Xin Metal (Yin Metal). Thus, Geng Metal is the Indirect Wealth Star of Bing Fire, and Xin Metal is the Direct Wealth Star of Bing Fire.

Bing Fire (Yang Fire) is controlled by Water. This makes Water the Influence Element of Bing Fire. Water comprises of Ren Water (Yang Water) and Gui Water (Yin Water). The Influence Element comprises the Direct Officer and 7 Killings Stars.

Bing Fire (Yang Fire) produces Earth. This makes Earth the Output Element of Bing Fire.

The Direct Officer Star is always the Influence Element with the opposite polarity of the Day Master whilst the 7 Killings Star is always the Influence Element which shares the polarity of the Day Master. Here, the polarity of the Day Master is Yang. The Influence Element that shares the polarity of the Day Master is Ren Water (Yang Water) and the Influence Element that has the opposite polarity of the Day Master is Gui Water (Yin Water). Thus, Ren Water is the 7 Killings Star of Bing Fire, and Gui Water is the Direct Officer Star of Bing Fire.

Bing Fire (Yang Fire) has Fire as its Companion Element. Fire comprises of Bing Fire (Yang Fire) and Ding Fire (Yin Fire).The Companion Element comprises the Friend and Rob Wealth Stars.

The Rob Wealth Star is always the Companion Element with the opposite polarity of the Day Master whilst the Friend Star is always the Companion Element which shares the polarity of the Day Master. Here, the polarity of the Day Master is Yang. The Companion Element that shares the polarity of the Day Master is Bing Fire (Yang Fire) and the Companion Element that has the opposite polarity of the Day Master is Ding Fire (Yin Fire). Thus, Bing Fire is the Friend Star of Bing Fire, and Ding Fire is the Rob Wealth Star of Bing Fire.

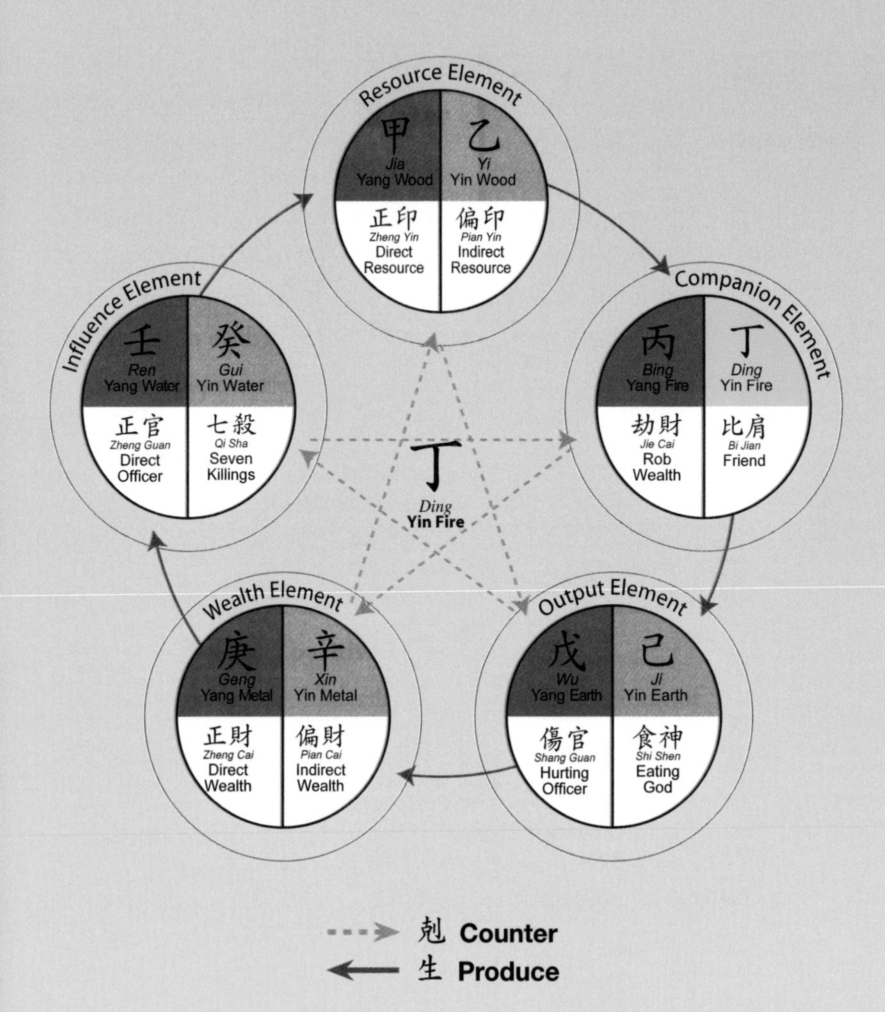

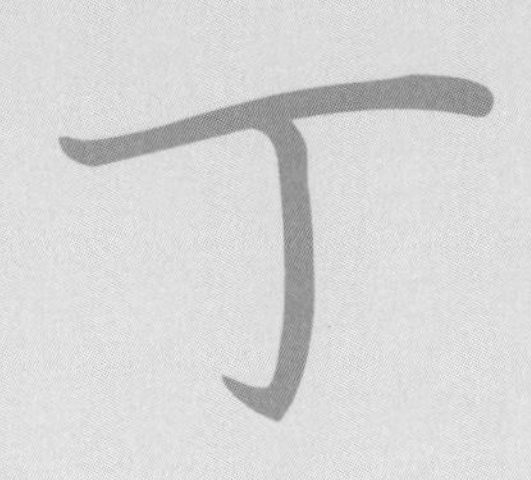

Ding Fire (Yin Fire) produces Earth. This makes Earth the Output Element of Ding Fire. Wood comprises of Jia Earth (Yang Earth) and Yi Earth (Yin Earth). The Output Element comprises the Hurting Officer and Eating God Stars.

Ding Fire (Yin Fire) produces Earth. This makes Earth the Output Element of Ding Fire.

The Hurting Officer Star is always the Output Element with the opposite polarity of the Day Master whilst the Eating God Star is always the Output Element which shares the polarity of the Day Master. Here, the polarity of the Day Master is Yin. The Output Element that shares the polarity of the Day Master is Ji Earth (Yin Earth) and the Output Element that has the opposite polarity of the Day Master is Wu Earth (Yang Earth). Thus, Ji Earth is the Eating God Star of Ding Fire, and Wu Earth is the Hurting Officer Star of Ding Fire.

Ding Fire (Yin Fire) is produced by Wood. This makes Wood the Resource Element of Ding Fire. Wood comprises of Jia Wood (Yang Wood) and Yi Wood (Yin Wood). The Resource Element comprises the Direct Resource and Indirect Resource Stars.

The Direct Resource Star is always the Resource Element with the opposite polarity of the Day Master whilst the Indirect Resource Star is always the Resource Element which shares the polarity of the Day Master. Here, the polarity of the Day Master is Yin. The Resource Element that shares the polarity of the Day Master is Yi Wood (Yin Wood) and the Resource Element that has the opposite polarity of the Day Master is Jia Wood (Yang Wood). Thus, Yi Wood is the Indirect Resource Star of Ding Fire, and Jia Wood is the Direct Resource Star of Ding Fire.

Ding Fire (Yin Fire) controls Metal. This makes Metal the Wealth Element of Ding Fire. Metal comprises of Bing Metal (Yang Metal) and Ding Metal (Yin Metal). The Wealth Element comprises the Direct Wealth and Indirect Wealth Stars.

The Direct Wealth Star is always the Wealth Element with the opposite polarity of the Day Master whilst the Indirect Wealth Star is always the Wealth Element which shares the polarity of the Day Master. Here, the polarity of the Day Master is Yin. The Wealth Element that shares the polarity of the Day Master is Xin Metal (Yin Metal) and the Wealth Element that has the opposite polarity of the Day Master is Geng Metal (Yang Metal). Thus, Xin Metal is the Indirect Wealth Star of Ding Fire, and Geng Metal is the Direct Wealth Star of Ding Fire.

Ding Fire (Yin Fire) is controlled by Water. This makes Water the Influence Element of Ding Fire. Earth comprises of Ren Water (Yang Water) and Gui Water (Yin Water). The Influence Element comprises the Direct Officer and 7 Killings Stars.

The Direct Officer Star is always the Influence Element with the opposite polarity of the Day Master whilst the 7 Killings Star is always the Influence Element which shares the polarity of the Day Master. Here, the polarity of the Day Master is Yin. The Influence Element that shares the polarity of the Day Master is Gui Water (Yin Water) and the Influence Element that has the opposite polarity of the Day Master is Ren Water (Yang Water). Thus, Gui Water is the 7 Killings Star of Ding Fire, and Ren Water is the Direct Officer Star of Ding Fire.

Ding Fire (Yin Fire) has Fire as its Companion Element. Fire comprises of Bing Fire (Yang Fire) and Ding Fire (Yin Fire). The Companion Element comprises the Friend and Rob Wealth Stars.

Ding Fire

The Rob Wealth Star is always the Companion Element with the opposite polarity of the Day Master whilst the Friend Star is always the Companion Element which shares the polarity of the Day Master. Here, the polarity of the Day Master is Yin. The Companion Element that shares the polarity of the Day Master is Ding Fire (Yin Fire) and the Companion Element that has the opposite polarity of the Day Master is Bing Fire (Yang Fire). Thus, Ding Fire is the Friend Star of Ding Fire, and Bing Fire is the Rob Wealth Star of Ding Fire.

Ding Fire

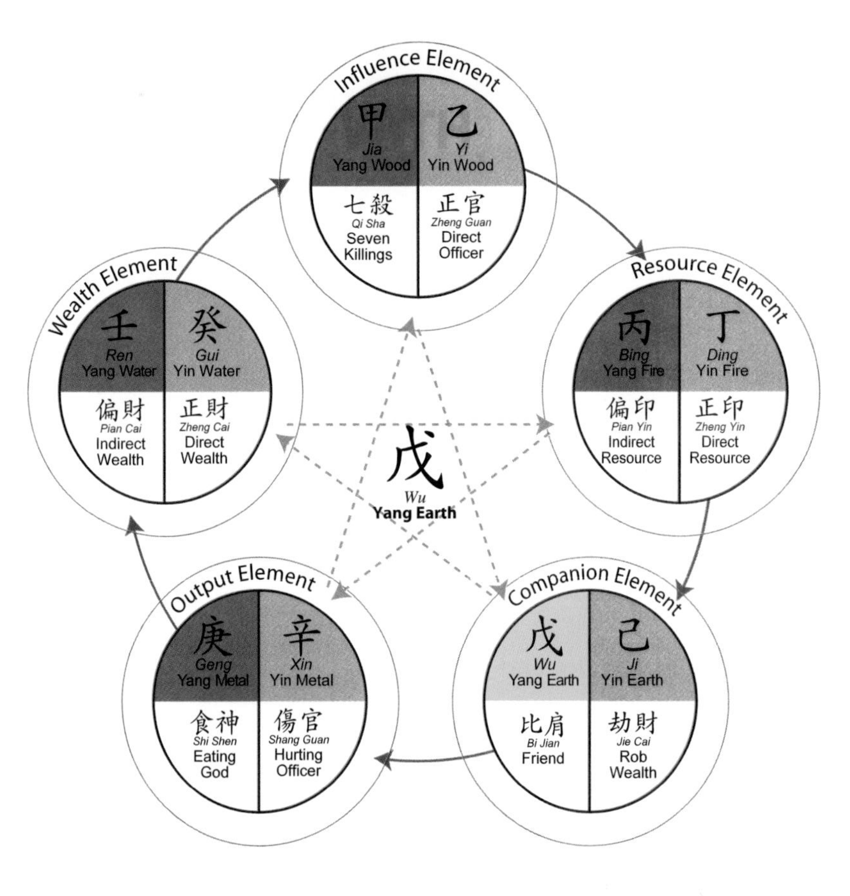

Wu Earth (Yang Earth) produces Metal. This makes Metal the Output Element of Wu Earth. Metal comprises of Geng Metal (Yang Metal) and Xin Metal (Yin Metal). The Output Element comprises the Hurting Officer and Eating God Stars.

The Hurting Officer Star is always the Output Element with the opposite polarity of the Day Master whilst the Eating God Star is always the Output Element which shares the polarity of the Day Master. Here, the polarity of the Day Master is Yang. The Output Element that shares the polarity of the Day Master is Geng Metal (Yang Metal) and the Output Element that has the opposite polarity of the Day Master is Xin Metal (Yin Metal). Thus, Geng Metal is the Eating God Star of Wu Earth, and Xin Metal is the Hurting Officer Star of Wu Earth.

Wu Earth (Yang Earth) is produced by Fire. This makes Fire the Resource Element of Wu Earth. Fire comprises of Bing Fire (Yang Fire) and Ding Fire (Yin Fire). The Resource Element comprises the Direct Resource and Indirect Resource Stars.

The Direct Resource Star is always the Resource Element with the opposite polarity of the Day Master whilst the Indirect Resource Star is always the Resource Element which shares the polarity of the Day Master. Here, the polarity of the Day Master is Yang. The Resource Element that shares the polarity of the Day Master is Bing Fire (Yang Fire) and the Resource Element that has the opposite polarity of the Day Master is Ding Fire (Yin Fire). Thus, Bing Fire is the Indirect Resource Star of Wu Earth, and Ding Fire is the Direct Resource Star of Wu Earth.

Wu Earth (Yang Earth) controls Water. This makes Water the Wealth Element of Wu Earth. Water comprises of Ren Water (Yang Water) and Gui Water (Yin Water). The Wealth Element comprises the Direct Wealth and Indirect Wealth Stars.

Earth (Tu)

The Direct Wealth Star is always the Wealth Element with the opposite polarity of the Day Master whilst the Indirect Wealth Star is always the Wealth Element which shares the polarity of the Day Master. Here, the polarity of the Day Master is Yang. The Wealth Element that shares the polarity of the Day Master is Ren Water (Yang Water) and the Wealth Element that has the opposite polarity of the Day Master is Gui Water (Yin Water). Thus, Ren Water is the Indirect Wealth Star of Wu Earth, and Gui Water is the Direct Wealth Star of Wu Earth.

Wu Earth (Yang Earth) is controlled by Wood. This makes Wood the Influence Element of Wu Earth. Wood comprises of Jia Wood (Yang Wood) and Yi Wood (Yin Wood). The Influence Element comprises the Direct Officer and 7 Killings Stars.

Wu Earth

The Direct Officer Star is always the Influence Element with the opposite polarity of the Day Master whilst the 7 Killings Star is always the Influence Element which shares the polarity of the Day Master. Here, the polarity of the Day Master is Yang. The Influence Element that shares the polarity of the Day Master is Jia Wood (Yang Wood) and the Influence Element that has the opposite polarity of the Day Master is Yi Wood (Yin Wood). Thus, Jia Wood is the 7 Killings Star of Wu Earth, and Yi Wood is the Direct Officer Star of Wu Earth.

Wu Earth (Yang Earth) has Earth as its Companion Element. Earth comprises of Wu Earth (Yang Earth) and Ji Earth (Yin Earth).The Companion Element comprises the Friend and Rob Wealth Stars.

The Rob Wealth Star is always the Companion Element with the opposite polarity of the Day Master whilst the Friend Star is always the Companion Element which shares the polarity of the Day Master. Here, the polarity of the Day Master is Yang. The Companion Element that shares the polarity of the Day Master is Wu Earth (Yang Earth) and the Companion Element that has the opposite polarity of the Day Master is Ji Earth (Yin Earth). Thus, Wu Earth is the Friend Star of Gui Water, and Ji Earth is the Rob Wealth Star of Wu Earth.

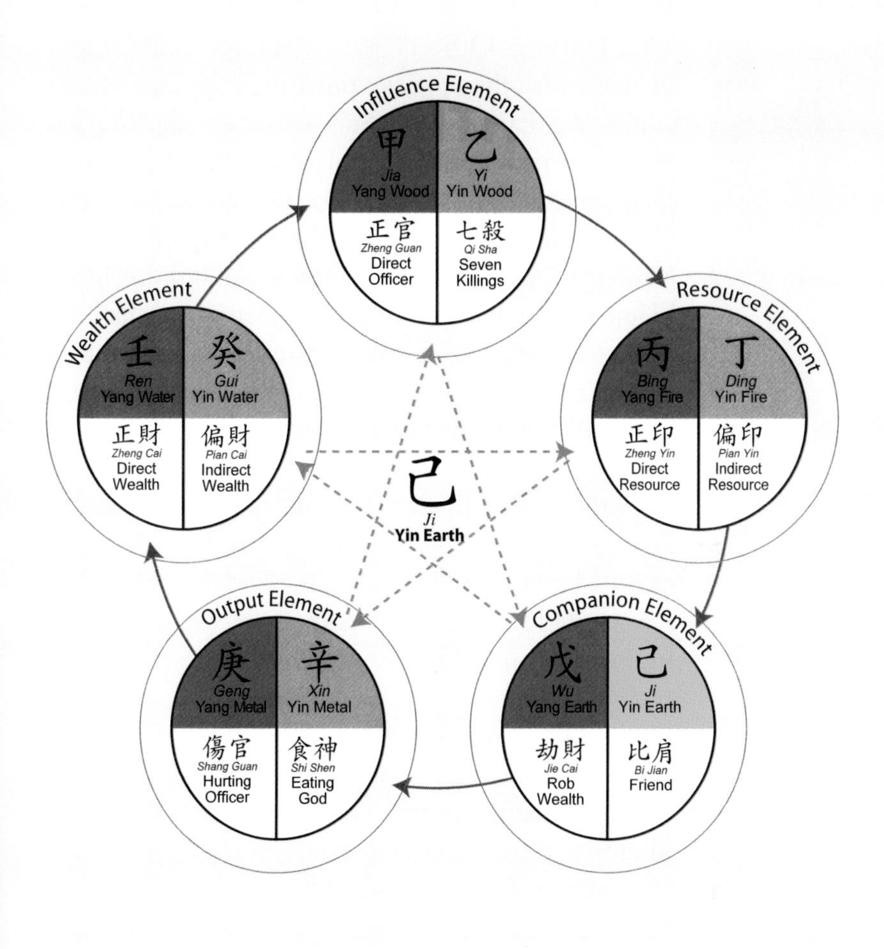

Ji Earth (Yin Earth) produces Metal. This makes Wood the Output Element of Ji Earth. Wood comprises of Geng Metal (Yang Metal) and Xin Metal (Yin Metal). The Output Element comprises the Hurting Officer and Eating God Stars.

Ji Earth (Yin Earth) produces Metal. This makes Wood the Output Element of Ji Earth.

The Hurting Officer Star is always the Output Element with the opposite polarity of the Day Master whilst the Eating God Star is always the Output Element which shares the polarity of the Day Master. Here, the polarity of the Day Master is Yin. The Output Element that shares the polarity of the Day Master is Xin Metal (Yin Metal) and the Output Element that has the opposite polarity of the Day Master is Geng Metal (Yang Metal). Thus, Xin Metal is the Eating God Star of Ji Earth, and Geng Metal is the Hurting Officer Star of Ji Earth.

Ji Earth (Yin Earth) is produced by Fire. This makes Fire the Resource Element of Ji Earth. Fire comprises of Bing Fire (Yang Fire) and Ding Fire (Yin Fire). The Resource Element comprises the Direct Resource and Indirect Resource Stars.

The Direct Resource Star is always the Resource Element with the opposite polarity of the Day Master whilst the Indirect Resource Star is always the Resource Element which shares the polarity of the Day Master. Here, the polarity of the Day Master is Yin. The Resource Element that shares the polarity of the Day Master is Ding Fire (Yin Fire) and the Resource Element that has the opposite polarity of the Day Master is Bing Fire (Yang Fire). Thus, Ding Fire is the Indirect Resource Star of Ji Earth and Bing Fire is the Direct Resource Star of Ji Earth.

Ji Earth (Yin Earth) controls Water. This makes Water the Wealth Element of Ji Earth. Water comprises of Ren Water (Yang Water) and Gui Water (Yin Water). The Wealth Element comprises the Direct Wealth and Indirect Wealth Stars.

The Direct Wealth Star is always the Wealth Element with the opposite polarity of the Day Master whilst the Indirect Wealth Star is always the Wealth Element which shares the polarity of the Day Master. Here, the polarity of the Day Master is Yin. The Wealth Element that shares the polarity of the Day Master is Gui Water (Yin Water) and the Wealth Element that has the opposite polarity of the Day Master is Ren Water (Yang Water). Thus, Gui Water is the Indirect Wealth Star of Ji Earth, and Ren Water is the Direct Wealth Star of Ji Earth.

Ji Earth (Yin Earth) is controlled by Wood. This makes Wood the Influence Element of Ji Earth. Wood comprises of Jia Wood (Yang Wood) and Yi Wood (Yin Wood). The Influence Element comprises the Direct Officer and 7 Killings Stars.

The Direct Officer Star is always the Influence Element with the opposite polarity of the Day Master whilst the 7 Killings Star is always the Influence Element which shares the polarity of the Day Master. Here, the polarity of the Day Master is Yin. The Influence Element that shares the polarity of the Day Master is Jia Wood (Yin Wood) and the Influence Element that has the opposite polarity of the Day Master is Yi Wood (Yang Wood). Thus, Yi Wood is the 7 Killings Star of Ji Earth, and Jia Wood is the Direct Officer Star of Ji Earth.

Ji Earth (Yin Earth) has Earth as its Companion Element. Earth comprises of Ren Earth (Yang Earth) and Gui Earth (Yin Earth).The Companion Element comprises the Friend and Rob Wealth Stars.

The Rob Wealth Star is always the Companion Element with the opposite polarity of the Day Master whilst the Friend Star is always the Companion Element which shares the polarity of the Day Master. Here, the polarity of the Day Master is Yin. The Companion Element that shares the polarity of the Day Master is Ji Earth (Yin Earth) and the Companion Element that has the opposite polarity of the Day Master is Wu Earth (Yang Earth). Thus, Ji Earth is the Friend Star of Ji Earth, and Wu Earth is the Rob Wealth Star of Ji Earth.

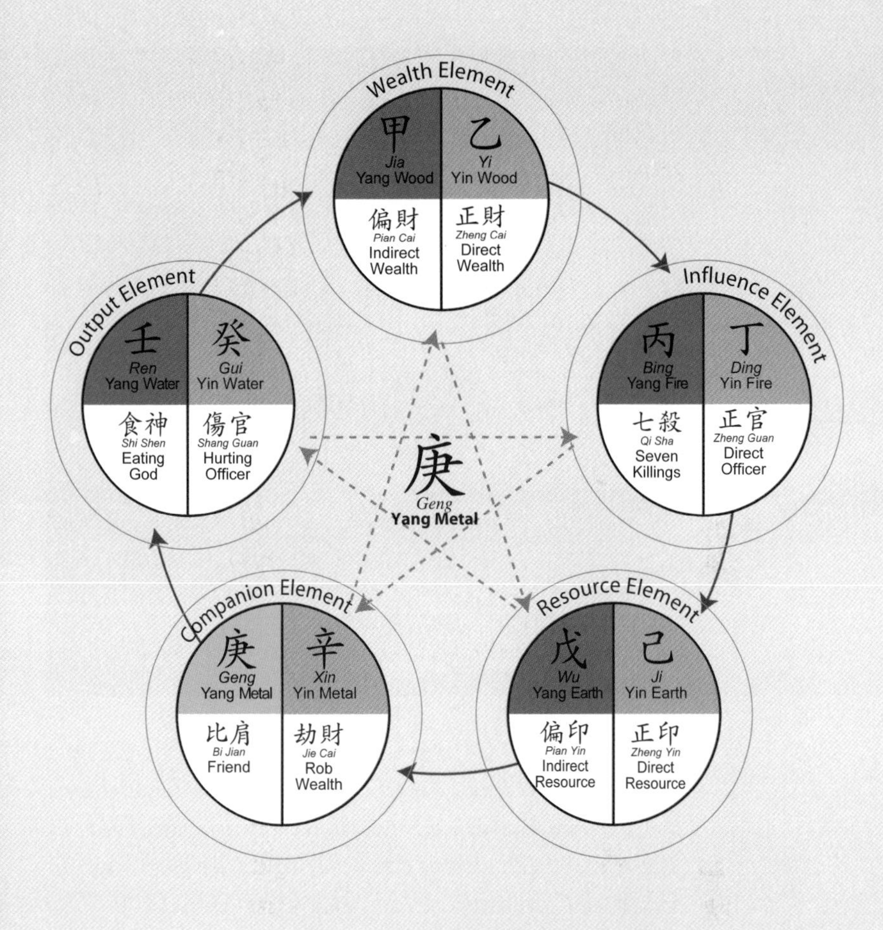

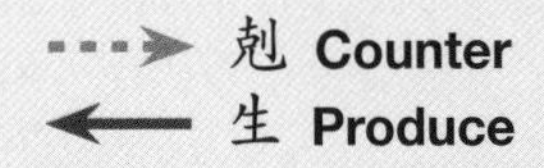

Geng Metal (Yang Metal) produces Water. This makes Water the Output Element of Geng Metal. Water comprises of Ren Water (Yang Water) and Gui Water (Yin Water). The Output Element comprises the Hurting Officer and Eating God Stars.

Geng Metal

The Hurting Officer Star is always the Output Element with the opposite polarity of the Day Master whilst the Eating God Star is always the Output Element which shares the polarity of the Day Master. Here, the polarity of the Day Master is Yang. The Output Element that shares the polarity of the Day Master is Ren Water (Yang Water) and the Output Element that has the opposite polarity of the Day Master is Gui Water (Yin Water). Thus, Ren Water is the Eating God Star of Geng Metal, and Gui Water is the Hurting Officer Star of Geng Metal.

Geng Metal (Yang Metal) is produced by Earth. This makes Earth the Resource Element of Geng Metal. Earth comprises of Wu Earth (Yang Earth) and Ji Earth (Yin Earth). The Resource Element comprises the Direct Resource and Indirect Resource Stars.

The Direct Resource Star is always the Resource Element with the opposite polarity of the Day Master whilst the Indirect Resource Star is always the Resource Element which shares the polarity of the Day Master. Here, the polarity of the Day Master is Yang. The Resource Element that shares the polarity of the Day Master is Wu Earth (Yang Earth) and the Resource Element that has the opposite polarity of the Day Master is Ji Earth (Yin Earth). Thus, Wu Earth is the Indirect Resource Star of Geng Metal, and Ji Earth is the Direct Resource Star of Geng Metal.

Metal (Jin)

Geng Metal (Yang Metal) controls Wood. This makes Wood the Wealth Element of Geng Metal. Earth comprises of Jia Wood (Yang Wood) and Yi Wood (Yin Wood). The Wealth Element comprises the Direct Wealth and Indirect Wealth Stars.

The Direct Wealth Star is always the Wealth Element with the opposite polarity of the Day Master whilst the Indirect Wealth Star is always the Wealth Element which shares the polarity of the Day Master. Here, the polarity of the Day Master is Yang. The Wealth Element that shares the polarity of the Day Master is Jia Wood (Yang Wood) and the Wealth Element that has the opposite polarity of the Day Master is Yi Wood (Yin Wood). Thus, Jia Wood is the Indirect Wealth Star of Geng Metal, and Yi Wood is the Direct Wealth Star of Geng Metal.

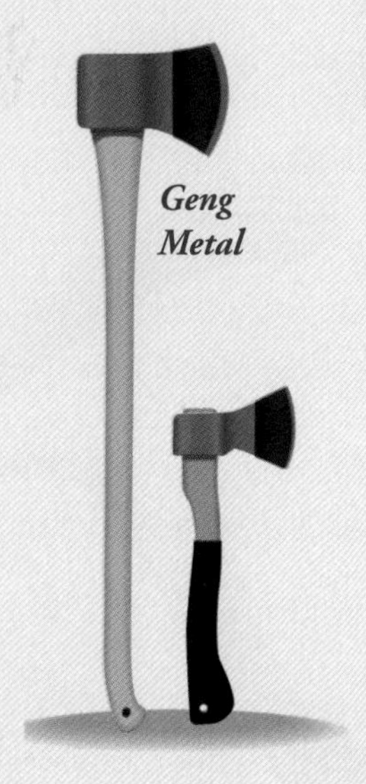
Geng Metal

Geng Metal (Yang Metal) is controlled by Fire. This makes Fire the Influence Element of Geng Metal. Fire comprises of Bing Fire (Yang Fire) and Ding Fire (Yin Fire). The Influence Element comprises the Direct Officer and 7 Killings Stars.

The Direct Officer Star is always the Influence Element with the opposite polarity of the Day Master whilst the 7 Killings Star is always the Influence Element which shares the polarity of the Day Master. Here, the polarity of the Day Master is Yang. The Influence Element that shares the polarity of the Day Master is Bing Fire (Yang Fire) and the Influence Element that has the opposite polarity of the Day Master is Ding Fire (Yin Fire). Thus, Bing Fire is the 7 Killings Star of Geng Metal, and Ding Fire is the Direct Officer Star of Geng Metal.

Geng Metal (Yang Metal) has Metal as its Companion Element. Metal comprises of Geng Metal (Yang Metal) and Xin Metal (Yin Metal).The Companion Element comprises the Friend and Rob Wealth Stars.

The Rob Wealth Star is always the Companion Element with the opposite polarity of the Day Master whilst the Friend Star is always the Companion Element which shares the polarity of the Day Master. Here, the polarity of the Day Master is Yang. The Companion Element that shares the polarity of the Day Master is Geng Metal (Yang Metal) and the Companion Element that has the opposite polarity of the Day Master is Xin Metal (Yin Metal). Thus, Geng Metal is the Friend Star of Geng Metal, and Xin Metal is the Rob Wealth Star of Geng Metal.

Geng Metal

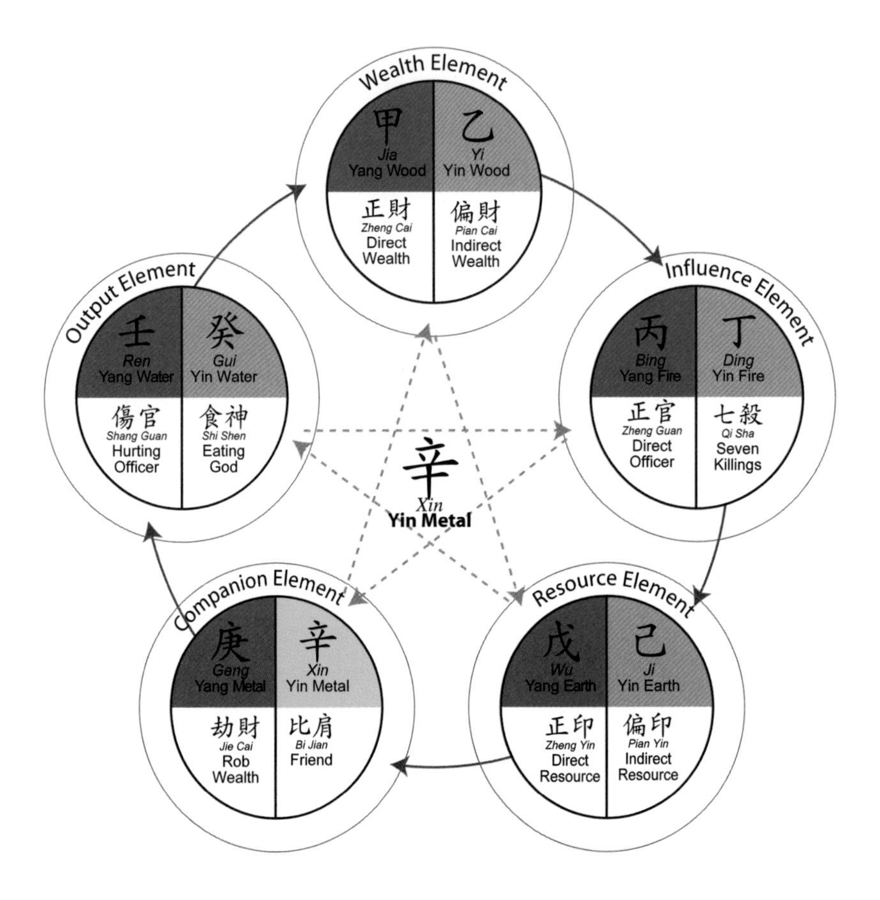

Xin Metal (Yin Metal) produces Water. This makes Water the Output Element of Xin Metal. Water comprises of Ren Water (Yang Water) and Gui Water (Yin Water). The Output Element comprises the Hurting Officer and Eating God Stars.

The Hurting Officer Star is always the Output Element with the opposite polarity of the Day Master whilst the Eating God Star is always the Output Element which shares the polarity of the Day Master. Here, the polarity of the Day Master is Yin. The Output Element that shares the polarity of the Day Master is Gui Water (Yin Water) and the Output Element that has the opposite polarity of the Day Master is Ren Water (Yang Water). Thus, Gui Water is the Eating God Star of Xin Metal, and Ren Water is the Hurting Officer Star of Xin Metal.

Xin Metal (Yin Metal) is produced by Earth. This makes Earth the Resource Element of Xin Metal. Earth comprises of Wu Earth (Yang Earth) and Ji Earth (Yin Earth). The Resource Element comprises the Direct Resource and Indirect Resource Stars.

The Direct Resource Star is always the Resource Element with the opposite polarity of the Day Master whilst the Indirect Resource Star is always the Resource Element which shares the polarity of the Day Master. Here, the polarity of the Day Master is Yin. The Resource Element that shares the polarity of the Day Master is Ji Earth (Yin Earth) and the Resource Element that has the opposite polarity of the Day Master is Wu Earth (Yang Earth). Thus, Ji Earth is the Indirect Resource Star of Xin Earth, and Wu Earth is the Direct Resource Star of Xin Metal.

Xin Metal

Xin Metal

Xin Metal (Yin Metal) controls Wood. This makes Wood the Wealth Element of Xin Metal. Wood comprises of Jia Wood (Yang Wood) and Yi Wood (Yin Wood). The Wealth Element comprises the Direct Wealth and Indirect Wealth Stars.

The Direct Wealth Star is always the Wealth Element with the opposite polarity of the Day Master whilst the Indirect Wealth Star is always the Wealth Element which shares the polarity of the Day Master. Here, the polarity of the Day Master is Yin. The Wealth Element that shares the polarity of the Day Master is Yi Wood (Yin Wood) and the Wealth Element that has the opposite polarity of the Day Master is Jia Wood (Yang Wood). Thus, Yi Wood is the Indirect Wealth Star of Xin Metal, and Jia Wood is the Direct Wealth Star of Xin Metal.

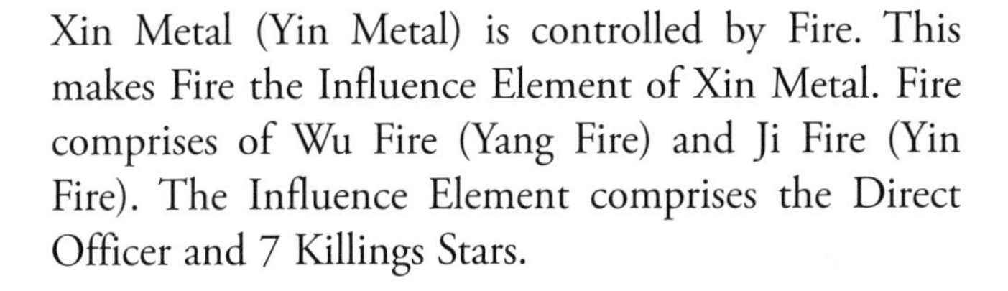

Xin Metal (Yin Metal) is controlled by Fire. This makes Fire the Influence Element of Xin Metal. Fire comprises of Wu Fire (Yang Fire) and Ji Fire (Yin Fire). The Influence Element comprises the Direct Officer and 7 Killings Stars.

The Direct Officer Star is always the Influence Element with the opposite polarity of the Day Master whilst the 7 Killings Star is always the Influence Element which shares the polarity of the Day Master. Here, the polarity of the Day Master is Yin. The Influence Element that shares the polarity of the Day Master is Ding Fire (Yin Fire) and the Influence Element that has the opposite polarity of the Day Master is Bing Fire (Yang Fire). Thus, Ding Fire is the 7 Killings Star of Xin Metal, and Bing Fire is the Direct Officer Star of Xin Metal.

Xin Metal (Yin Metal) has Metal as its Companion Element. Metal comprises of Geng Metal (Yang Metal) and Xin Metal (Yin Metal).The Companion Element comprises the Friend and Rob Wealth Stars.

The Rob Wealth Star is always the Companion Element with the opposite polarity of the Day Master whilst the Friend Star is always the Companion Element which shares the polarity of the Day Master. Here, the polarity of the Day Master is Yin. The Companion Element that shares the polarity of the Day Master is Xin Metal (Yin Metal) and the Companion Element that has the opposite polarity of the Day Master is Geng Water (Yang Metal). Thus, Xin Metal is the Friend Star of Xin Metal, and Geng Metal is the Rob Wealth Star of Xin Metal.

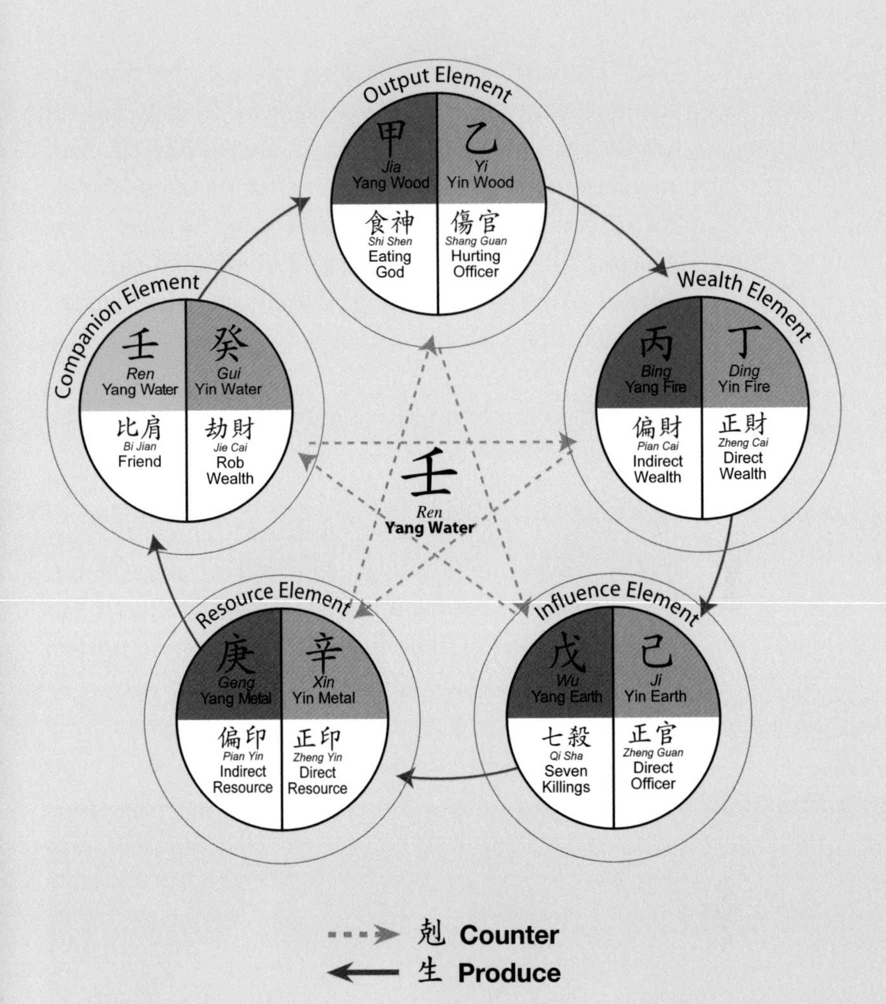

Ren Water (Yang Water) produces Wood. This makes Wood the Output Element of Ren Water. Wood comprises of Jia Wood (Yang Wood) and Yi Wood (Yin Wood). The Output Element comprises the Hurting Officer and Eating God Stars.

The Hurting Officer Star is always the Output Element with the opposite polarity of the Day Master whilst the Eating God Star is always the Output Element which shares the polarity of the Day Master. Here, the polarity of the Day Master is Yang. The Output Element that shares the polarity of the Day Master is Jia Wood (Yang Wood) and the Output Element that has the opposite polarity of the Day Master is Yi Wood (Yin Wood). Thus, Jia Wood is the Eating God Star of Ren Water, and Yi Wood is the Hurting Officer Star of Ren Water.

Ren Water (Yang Water) is produced by Metal. This makes Metal the Resource Element of Ren Water. Water comprises of Geng Metal (Yang Metal) and Xin Metal (Yin Metal). The Resource Element comprises the Direct Resource and Indirect Resource Stars.

Ren Water

The Direct Resource Star is always the Resource Element with the opposite polarity of the Day Master whilst the Indirect Resource Star is always the Resource Element which shares the polarity of the Day Master. Here, the polarity of the Day Master is Yang. The Resource Element that shares the polarity of the Day Master is Geng Metal (Yang Metal) and the Resource Element that has the opposite polarity of the Day Master is Xin Metal (Yin Metal). Thus, Xin Metal is the Indirect Resource Star of Ren Water (Yang Water), and Geng Metal is the Direct Resource Star of Ren Water (Yang Water)

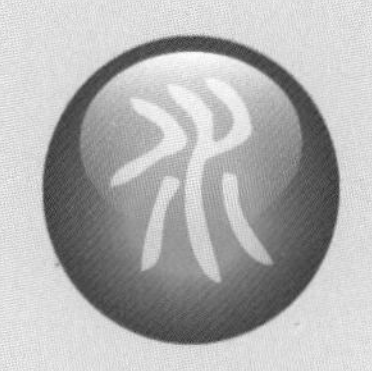
Water (Shui)

Ren Water (Yang Water) controls Fire. This makes Fire the Wealth Element of Ren Water. Fire comprises of Bing Fire (Yang Fire) and Ding Earth (Yin Fire). The Wealth Element comprises the Direct Wealth and Indirect Wealth Stars.

The Direct Wealth Star is always the Wealth Element with the opposite polarity of the Day Master whilst the Indirect Wealth Star is always the Wealth Element which shares the polarity of the Day Master. Here, the polarity of the Day Master is Yang. The Wealth Element that shares the polarity of the Day Master is Bing Fire (Yang Fire) and the Wealth Element that has the opposite polarity of the Day Master is Ding Fire (Yin Fire). Thus, Bing Fire is the Indirect Wealth Star of Ren Water, and Ding Fire is the Direct Wealth Star of Ren Water.

Ren Water (Yang Water) is controlled by Earth. This makes Earth the Influence Element of Ren Water. Earth comprises of Wu Earth (Yang Earth) and Ji Earth (Yin Earth). The Influence Element comprises the Direct Officer and 7 Killings Stars.

The Direct Officer Star is always the Influence Element with the opposite polarity of the Day Master whilst the 7 Killings Star is always the Influence Element which shares the polarity of the Day Master. Here, the polarity of the Day Master is Yang. The Influence Element that shares the polarity of the Day Master is Wu Earth (Yang Earth) and the Influence Element that has the opposite polarity of the Day Master is Ji Earth (Yin Earth). Thus, Wu Earth is the 7 Killings Star of Ren Water, and Ji Earth is the Direct Officer Star of Ren Water.

Ren Water (Yang Water) has Water as its Companion Element. Water comprises of Ren Water (Yang Water) and Gui Water (Yin Water). The Companion Element comprises the Friend and Rob Wealth Stars.

The Rob Wealth Star is always the Companion Element with the opposite polarity of the Day Master whilst the Friend Star is always the Companion Element which shares the polarity of the Day Master. Here, the polarity of the Day Master is Yang. The Companion Element that shares the polarity of the Day Master is Ren Water (Yang Water) and the Companion Element that has the opposite polarity of the Day Master is Gui Water (Yin Water). Thus, Ren Water is the Friend Star of Ren Water, and Gui Water is the Rob Wealth Star of Ren Water.

Ren Water

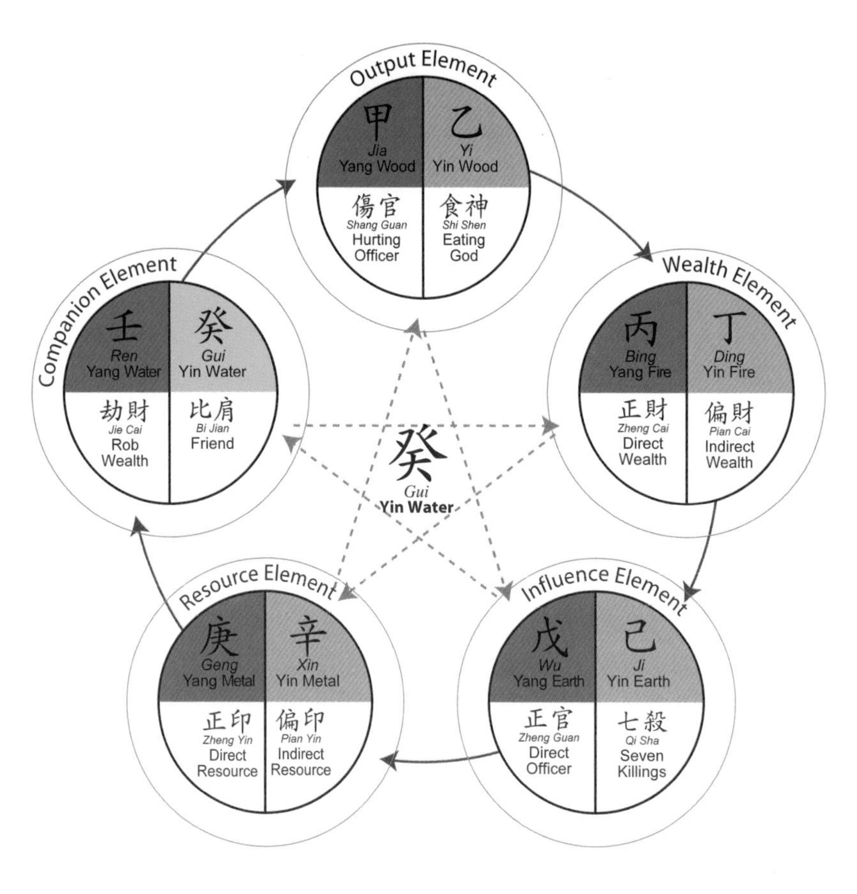

Gui Water (Yin Water) produces Wood. This makes Wood the Output Element of Gui Water. Wood comprises of Jia Wood (Yang Wood) and Yi Wood (Yin Wood). The Output Element comprises the Hurting Officer and Eating God Stars.

The Hurting Officer Star is always the Output Element with the opposite polarity of the Day Master whilst the Eating God Star is always the Output Element which shares the polarity of the Day Master. Here, the polarity of the Day Master is Yin. The Output Element that shares the polarity of the Day Master is Yi Wood (Yin Wood) and the Output Element that has the opposite polarity of the Day Master is Jia Wood (Yang Wood). Thus, Yi Wood is the Eating God Star of Gui Water, and Jia Wood is the Hurting Officer Star of Gui Water.

Gui Water (Yin Water) is produced by Metal. This makes Metal the Resource Element of Gui Water. Metal comprises of Geng Metal (Yang Metal) and Xin Metal (Yin Metal). The Resource Element comprises the Direct Resource and Indirect Resource Stars.

The Direct Resource Star is always the Resource Element with the opposite polarity of the Day Master whilst the Indirect Resource Star is always the Resource Element which shares the polarity of the Day Master. Here, the polarity of the Day Master is Yin. The Resource Element that shares the polarity of the Day Master is Xin Metal (Yin Metal) and the Resource Element that has the opposite polarity of the Day Master is Geng Metal (Yang Metal). Thus, Xin Metal is the Indirect Resource Star of Gui Water, and Geng Metal is the Direct Resource Star of Gui Water.

Gui Water (Yin Water) produces Wood. This makes Wood the Output Element of Gui Water.

Gui Water (Yin Water) controls Fire. This makes Fire the Wealth Element of Gui Water. Fire comprises of Bing Fire (Yang Fire) and Ding Fire (Yin Fire). The Wealth Element comprises the Direct Wealth and Indirect Wealth Stars.

Gui Water

The Direct Wealth Star is always the Wealth Element with the opposite polarity of the Day Master whilst the Indirect Wealth Star is always the Wealth Element which shares the polarity of the Day Master. Here, the polarity of the Day Master is Yin. The Wealth Element that shares the polarity of the Day Master is Ding Fire (Yin Fire) and the Wealth Element that has the opposite polarity of the Day Master is Bing Fire (Yang Fire). Thus, Ding Fire is the Indirect Wealth Star of Gui Water, and Bing Fire is the Direct Wealth Star of Gui Water.

Gui Water (Yin Water) is controlled by Earth. This makes Earth the Influence Element of Gui Water. Earth comprises of Wu Earth (Yang Earth) and Ji Earth (Yin Earth). The Influence Element comprises the Direct Officer and 7 Killings Stars.

The Direct Officer Star is always the Influence Element with the opposite polarity of the Day Master whilst the 7 Killings Star is always the Influence Element which shares the polarity of the Day Master. Here, the polarity of the Day Master is Yin. The Influence Element that shares the polarity of the Day Master is Ji Earth (Yin Earth) and the Influence Element that has the opposite polarity of the Day Master is Wu Earth (Yang Earth). Thus, Ji Earth is the 7 Killings Star of Gui Water, and Wu Earth is the Direct Officer Star of Gui Water.

Gui Water (Yin Water) has Water as its Companion Element. Water comprises of Ren Water (Yang Water) and Gui Water (Yin Water).The Companion Element comprises the Friend and Rob Wealth Stars.

The Rob Wealth Star is always the Companion Element with the opposite polarity of the Day Master whilst the Friend Star is always the Companion Element which shares the polarity of the Day Master. Here, the polarity of the Day Master is Yin. The Companion Element that shares the polarity of the Day Master is Gui Water (Yin Water) and the Companion Element that has the opposite polarity of the Day Master is Ren Water (Yang Water). Thus, Gui Water is the Friend Star of Gui Water, and Ren Water is the Rob Wealth Star of Gui Water.

The 10 Gods Cheat Sheet

This Cheat Sheet will help you not just quickly determine which Stem represents which 10 God for each of the 10 Day Masters, but will also illustrate to you the concept of how each of the 10 Stems can be any of the 10 Gods, depending on the Day Master being referenced.

天干 十神 Heavenly Stems / 日主 Day Master	甲 Jia Yang Wood	乙 Yi Yin Wood	丙 Bing Yang Fire	丁 Ding Yin Fire	戊 Wu Yang Earth	己 Ji Yin Earth	庚 Geng Yang Metal	辛 Xin Yin Metal	壬 Ren Yang Water	癸 Gui Yin Water
甲 Jia Yang Wood	比肩 Bi Jian Friend	劫財 Jie Cai Rob Wealth	食神 Shi Shen Eating God	傷官 Shang Guan Hurting Officer	偏財 Pian Cai Indirect Wealth	正財 Zheng Cai Direct Wealth	七殺 Qi Sha Seven Killing	正官 Zheng Guan Direct Officer	偏印 Pian Yin Indirect Resource	正印 Zheng Yin Direct Resource
乙 Yi Yin Wood	劫財 Jie Cai Rob Wealth	比肩 Bi Jian Friend	傷官 Shang Guan Hurting Officer	食神 Shi Shen Eating God	正財 Zheng Cai Direct Wealth	偏財 Pian Cai Indirect Wealth	正官 Zheng Guan Direct Officer	七殺 Qi Sha Seven Killing	正印 Zheng Yin Direct Resource	偏印 Pian Yin Indirect Resource
丙 Bing Yang Fire	偏印 Pian Yin Indirect Resource	正印 Zheng Yin Direct Resource	比肩 Bi Jian Friend	劫財 Jie Cai Rob Wealth	食神 Shi Shen Eating God	傷官 Shang Guan Hurting Officer	偏財 Pian Cai Indirect Wealth	正財 Zheng Cai Direct Wealth	七殺 Qi Sha Seven Killing	正官 Zheng Guan Direct Officer
丁 Ding Yin Fire	正印 Zheng Yin Direct Resource	偏印 Pian Yin Indirect Resource	劫財 Jie Cai Rob Wealth	比肩 Bi Jian Friend	傷官 Shang Guan Hurting Officer	食神 Shi Shen Eating God	正財 Zheng Cai Direct Wealth	偏財 Pian Cai Indirect Wealth	正官 Zheng Guan Direct Officer	七殺 Qi Sha Seven Killing
戊 Wu Yang Earth	七殺 Qi Sha Seven Killing	正官 Zheng Guan Direct Officer	偏印 Pian Yin Indirect Resource	正印 Zheng Yin Direct Resource	比肩 Bi Jian Friend	劫財 Jie Cai Rob Wealth	食神 Shi Shen Eating God	傷官 Shang Guan Hurting Officer	偏財 Pian Cai Indirect Wealth	正財 Zheng Cai Direct Wealth
己 Ji Yin Earth	正官 Zheng Guan Direct Officer	七殺 Qi Sha Seven Killing	正印 Zheng Yin Direct Resource	偏印 Pian Yin Indirect Resource	劫財 Jie Cai Rob Wealth	比肩 Bi Jian Friend	傷官 Shang Guan Hurting Officer	食神 Shi Shen Eating God	正財 Zheng Cai Direct Wealth	偏財 Pian Cai Indirect Wealth
庚 Geng Yang Metal	偏財 Pian Cai Indirect Wealth	正財 Zheng Cai Direct Wealth	七殺 Qi Sha Seven Killing	正官 Zheng Guan Direct Officer	偏印 Pian Yin Indirect Resource	正印 Zheng Yin Direct Resource	比肩 Bi Jian Friend	劫財 Jie Cai Rob Wealth	食神 Shi Shen Eating God	傷官 Shang Guan Hurting Officer
辛 Xin Yin Metal	正財 Zheng Cai Direct Wealth	偏財 Pian Cai Indirect Wealth	正官 Zheng Guan Direct Officer	七殺 Qi Sha Seven Killing	正印 Zheng Yin Direct Resource	偏印 Pian Yin Indirect Resource	劫財 Jie Cai Rob Wealth	比肩 Bi Jian Friend	傷官 Shang Guan Hurting Officer	食神 Shi Shen Eating God
壬 Ren Yang Water	食神 Shi Shen Eating God	傷官 Shang Guan Hurting Officer	偏財 Pian Cai Indirect Wealth	正財 Zheng Cai Direct Wealth	七殺 Qi Sha Seven Killing	正官 Zheng Guan Direct Officer	偏印 Pian Yin Indirect Resource	正印 Zheng Yin Direct Resource	比肩 Bi Jian Friend	劫財 Jie Cai Rob Wealth
癸 Gui Yin Water	傷官 Shang Guan Hurting Officer	食神 Shi Shen Eating God	正財 Zheng Cai Direct Wealth	偏財 Pian Cai Indirect Wealth	正官 Zheng Guan Direct Officer	七殺 Qi Sha Seven Killing	正印 Zheng Yin Direct Resource	偏印 Pian Yin Indirect Resource	劫財 Jie Cai Rob Wealth	比肩 Bi Jian Friend

Learning to identify the 10 Gods in a BaZi chart

You might be wondering: what is the point in learning to identify the 10 Gods in a BaZi chart? After all, the BaZi MingPan calculator already does this for you and even helpfully labels the 10 Gods in the chart, including those in the Hidden Stems of the Earthly Branches. Worse comes to worse, there's always the 10 Gods Cheat Sheet that you can use (see p71) right?

The problem with the MingPan calculator or the Cheat Sheet is that many students end up never graduating from that Cheat Sheet. In other words, they become dependant on the Cheat Sheet or the labels from the calculator. Thus, in the absence of the Cheat Sheet or if they are forced to look at a hand-written chart or if they are discussing a chart with someone, they are simply not able to determine which element connects with which of the 10 Gods. Also, many students frequently do not bother to learn the 10 Gods of the other 9 Day Masters, aside from their own. They tend to navel-gaze and focus only on their own charts.

However, true mastery of BaZi and the 10 Gods requires a familiarity with not just the 10 Gods that are relevant to your Day Master, but those of the other 9 Day Masters. This is because the 10 Gods manifest in subtly different ways, depending on which Day Master is used to derive the 10 Gods. The Eating God Star of a Jia Wood Day Master will have subtle differences in the way it works and affects the Day Master compared to the Eating God

Star of a Wu Earth Day Master. Equally, each of the 10 Gods has a slightly unique relationship with its corresponding Day Master, depending on the Five Elements cycles.

For example, Bing Fire's Resource Stars are Jia and Yi. Although conventionally Resource produces the Day Master in the Five Element Production Cycle, the reality is that it is Bing Fire that grows the Jia and Yi Wood, in the way sunshine is required by every living thing on the planet in order to stay alive. Ding, on the other hand, needs source material, namely Wood, to keep burning. Thus, Ding does get produced by its Resource, Wood, but Bing does not rely on its Resource to be produced.

The two Fire Day Master's relationship with its respective Resource Stars will not be the same as say, Xin or Ren's relationship with its respective Resource Stars.

Accordingly, the sooner a student can master identifying the 10 Gods in a given BaZi chart without the use of the Cheat Sheet or relying on the aid of the BaZi MingPan program, the quicker they can move onto developing a more sophisticated outlook on each of the individual 10 Gods. In turn, the better their overall understanding of the 10 Gods and BaZi will be as a result. Many students who don't bother to go through the rigours of this process rarely end up with a real mastery of the 10 Gods, and thus, struggle when they progress to the analysis stage because they don't have the information at their fingertips.

Further, whilst an important purpose of learning BaZi is to enable you to better understand yourself, I am quite sure that many of my readers are interested in utilising it for the purposes of better understanding the people around them, be it in the context of their personal lives or professional lives. Whilst it is true that birds of a feather flock together (hence, you will find quite a number of your friends tend to share your Day Master or be of the same Element), the reality is that you will most likely find yourself looking at charts that comprise of Day Masters other than your own. As such, it is important to go beyond just the 10 Gods that are relevant to your own chart, but to make an effort to be familiar with those relating to Day Masters other than that of your own.

IDENTIFYING THE 10 GODS: WALKTHROUGH

Here is a walk-through to familiarise you with the process of identifying the 10 Gods in a given BaZi chart. A series of worksheets have been provided at the back of this book to help you practice this process.

時 Hour	日 Day	月 Month	年 Year	
乙 Yi Yin Wood	己 Ji Yin Earth	戊 Wu Yang Earth	乙 Yi Yin Wood	天干 Heavenly Stems
亥 Hai **Pig** Yin Water	酉 You **Rooster** Yin Metal	寅 Yin **Tiger** Yang Wood	卯 Mao **Rabbit** Yin Wood	地支 Earthly Branches
壬 Ren + Water 甲 Jia + Wood	辛 Xin - Metal	戊 Wu + Earth 甲 Jia + Wood 丙 Bing + Fire	乙 Yi - Wood	藏干 Hidden Stems

Step #1: What is the Day Master and what is the Day Master's polarity.

The Day Master is Ji 己 Earth – it is a Yin Stem.

To derive the 10 Gods, we begin with the 5 Element Production and Control Cycles, using the Earth element as the kick-off point.

Step #2: Determine the elements that represent the Output, Influence, Wealth, Resource and Companion Elements for a Ji Earth Day Master.

For a Ji Earth Day Master, Metal represents the Output Element, Water represents the Wealth Element, Wood represents the Influence Element, Fire represents the Resource Element and finally, Earth represents the Companion Element.

Five Factors	Element	Yin 陰	Yang 陽
Output (EG 食, HO 傷)	金 Metal		
Wealth (IW 才, DW 財)	水 Water		
Influence (7K 殺, DO 官)	木 Wood		
Resource (IR 卩, DR 印)	火 Fire		
Companion (F 比, RW 劫)	土 Earth		

Step #3: Which elements share the polarity of the Day Master and which elements have the opposite polarity of the Day Master?

Ji Earth is Yin Earth. Accordingly, all the Yin elements (Yi Wood, Ding Fire, Xin Metal, Gui Water, and Ji Earth) share the polarity of the Day Master. All the Yang elements (Jia Wood, Bing Fire, Geng Metal, Ren Water and Wu Earth) have the opposite polarity of the Day Master.

Five Factors	Element	Yin 陰	Yang 陽
Output (EG 食, HO 傷)	金 Metal	辛 Xin Yin Metal	庚 Geng Yang Metal
Wealth (IW 才, DW 財)	水 Water	癸 Gui Yin Water	壬 Ren Yang Water
Influence (7K 殺, DO 官)	木 Wood	乙 Yi Yin Wood	甲 Jia Yang Wood
Resource (IR 卩, DR 印)	火 Fire	丁 Ding Yin Fire	丙 Bing Yang Fire
Companion (F 比, RW 劫)	土 Earth	己 Ji Yin Earth	戊 Wu Yang Earth

Step #4: Which 10 Gods share the Day Master's polarity?

The Eating God, Indirect Wealth, 7 Killings, Indirect Resource and Friend Star share the Day Master's polarity. Now fill in the information accordingly.

Five Factors	Element	Yin 陰	Yang 陽
Output (EG 食, HO 傷)	金 Metal	辛 *Xin* Yin Metal 食 EG	庚 *Geng* Yang Metal
Wealth (IW 才, DW 財)	水 Water	癸 *Gui* Yin Water 才 IW	壬 *Ren* Yang Water
Influence (7K 殺, DO 官)	木 Wood	乙 *Yi* Yin Wood 殺 7K	甲 *Jia* Yang Wood
Resource (IR 卩, DR 印)	火 Fire	丁 *Ding* Yin Fire 卩 IR	丙 *Bing* Yang Fire
Companion (F 比, RW 劫)	土 Earth	己 *Ji* Yin Earth 比 F	戊 *Wu* Yang Earth

Step #5: Which 10 Gods have the opposite polarity to the Day Master?

The Hurting Officer, Direct Wealth, Direct Officer, Direct Resource and Rob Wealth Star have the opposite polarity to the Day Master.

Five Factors	Element	Yin 陰	Yang 陽
Output (EG 食, HO 傷)	金 Metal	辛 *Xin* Yin Metal 食 EG	庚 *Geng* Yang Metal 傷 HO
Wealth (IW 才, DW 財)	水 Water	癸 *Gui* Yin Water 才 IW	壬 *Ren* Yang Water 財 DW
Influence (7K 殺, DO 官)	木 Wood	乙 *Yi* Yin Wood 殺 7K	甲 *Jia* Yang Wood 官 DO
Resource (IR 卩, DR 印)	火 Fire	丁 *Ding* Yin Fire 卩 IR	丙 *Bing* Yang Fire 印 DR
Companion (F 比, RW 劫)	土 Earth	己 *Ji* Yin Earth 比 F	戊 *Wu* Yang Earth 劫 RW

When we put together all the information, we derive the following 10 Gods for this Ji Earth Day Master:

十神 Ten Gods	十天干 10 Heavenly Stems
正財星 Direct Wealth Star	壬 Ren Water
偏財星 Indirect Wealth Star	癸 Gui Water
正官星 Direct Officer Star	甲 Jia Wood
七殺星 7 Killings Star	乙 Yi Wood
傷官星 Hurting Officer Star	庚 Geng Metal
食神星 Eating God Star	辛 Xin Metal
正印星 Direct Resource Star	丙 Bing Fire
偏印星 Indirect Resource Star	丁 Ding Fire
比肩星 Friend Star	己 Ji Earth
劫財星 Rob Wealth Star	戊 Wu Earth

Now label each 10 God in the chart.

時 Hour	日 Day	月 Month	年 Year	
七殺 7K 乙 *Yi* Yin Wood	日元 DM 己 *Ji* Yin Earth	劫財 RW 戊 *Wu* Yang Earth	七殺 7K 乙 *Yi* Yin Wood	天干 Heavenly Stems
亥 *Hai* **Pig** Yin Water	酉 *You* **Rooster** Yin Metal	寅 *Yin* **Tiger** Yang Wood	卯 *Mao* **Rabbit** Yin Wood	地支 Earthly Branches
壬 *Ren* + Water 財 DW; 甲 *Jia* + Wood 官 DO	辛 *Xin* - Metal 食 EG	戊 *Wu* + Earth 劫 RW; 甲 *Jia* + Wood 官 DO; 丙 *Bing* + Fire 印 DR	乙 *Yi* - Wood 殺 7K	藏干 Hidden Stems

I advocate doing a couple of charts by hand and engaging in the process of labelling the 10 Gods because it is very useful towards helping you mentally connect the elements in a given chart to the 10 Gods. Ideally, try to do about 20-30 charts, all with different Day Masters, to really master the connection between the elements and the 10 Gods.

Labelling also serves the purpose of forcing students to really examine a chart carefully. I have lost count of the number of times a student has declared that they do not have a particular 10 God in their chart, only to discover that the particular 10 God is definitively clear and present, in the Hidden Stems, upon closer inspection.

The Significance of the 10

Without the 10 Gods, it is virtually impossible to accurately draw out information from a BaZi chart about a person, be it their character, or their destiny. The 10 Gods represent every conceivable aspect, object and item in life; both the tangible and the intangible. As such, a person's life, in every sense of the word, is ultimately defined by the 10 Gods present (and absent) in a BaZi chart.

The interactions between these 10 Gods, within a person's natal BaZi chart, and externally with the 10 Year Luck Pillar and Annual Pillar in turn detail a person's path through life, at a given point of time. Again, by understanding the 10 Gods thoroughly, and understanding how the interactions between the 10 Gods, 10 Year Luck Pillar and Annual Pillar impact on the Day Master, the predictive power of BaZi can be harnessed.

The Ten Gods represent every conceivable aspect, object and item in life

Without knowledge of the 10 Gods, the interpretation of a person's BaZi is highly limited to an extremely rudimentary interpretation of the person's character utilising the Day Master. It is essentially impossible to read the BaZi and derive answers to any questions about the chart without knowing what 10 Gods are present in a BaZi chart and how they behave with each other within the chart. I would go so far as to say that without the 10 Gods, reading a BaZi chart is essentially a fruitless exercise. Without the 10 Gods, only the technical component of the Chart (ie: the Day Master, the Strength/Weakness of the Day Master, Strength of the Elements, interactions with the chart) is discerning.

But merely knowing the technical components of the chart is of no practical use. What is the point in knowing that a Day Master is strong, and thus favours Output, Wealth and Influence if one does not know what these Elements relate to and how they relate back to the individual? Similarly, knowing that a chart has weak Water will not actually result in the individual knowing what actual form of action that can be taken, beyond possibly an absurd suggestion that they drink more water or paint their home blue. And even then, that is to assume that Water being weak in person's chart is necessarily something that has to be rectified.

The purpose of understanding one's BaZi is so that one may take the right action, at the right time. It is only with a knowledge of the 10 Gods that the individual can ascertain what is the right action in a given situation because each 10 God is associated with a matter, a relationship, a person or a particular trait, characteristic or attitude. For example, if Fire is a favourable element in a person's chart, the 10 Gods will reveal what Fire means to that person, by way of a relationship, an individual, an object, a matter or perhaps a way of behaving, thinking, acting or an attitude. Once the individual has this knowledge, he or she is then able to take appropriate action to utilise and tap into their Favourable Element for advantageous purposes.

Thus, knowing how to identify the Ten Gods of each of the 10 Day Masters and understanding the basic fundamentals of each of the Ten Gods is a critical breakthrough step towards developing the ability to analyse and accurately derive information about an individual from their BaZi chart.

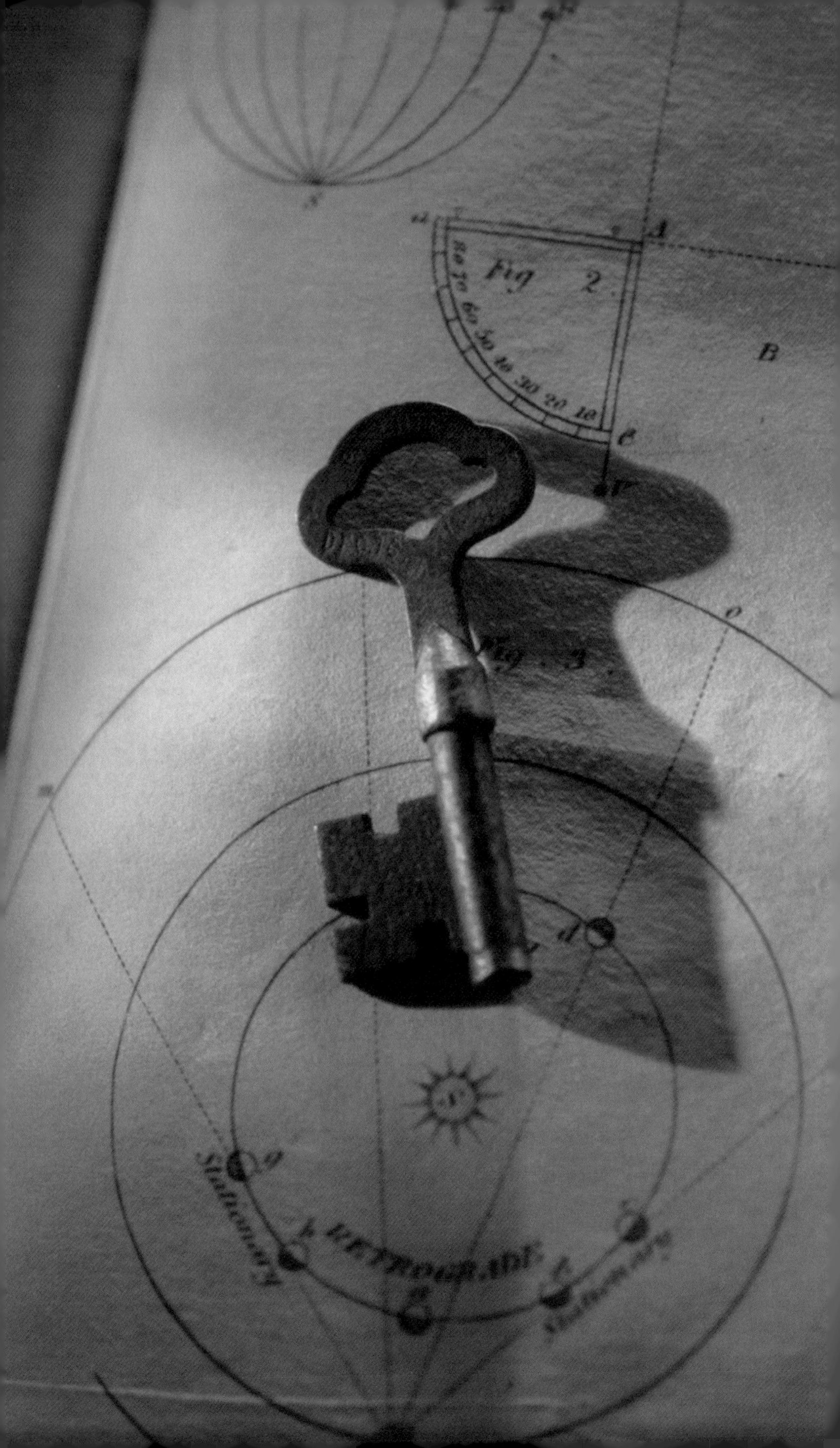

Fig 2
80 70 60 50 40 30 20 10
A
B
RETROGRADE
Stationary
Stationary

Chapter 3: The 10 Gods Essentials

By this stage, you should have a reasonably good grasp of how the 10 Gods are derived, and you should at the very minimum be able to tell which of the 10 Stems represents the 10 Gods for your own personal Day Master. Obviously the more you know the better, but at the very least, you should know the 10 Gods for your own Day Master, preferably without referencing the Cheat Sheet!

However, you are probably aware that knowing which Stem represents the 10 Gods for your Day Master isn't making the earth move in so far as helping you better understand yourself. Knowing that Yi Wood represents your Hurting Officer Star is not of much use if you don't know what a Hurting Officer Star does or what it means. As such, up to this point, the information you possess about the 10 Gods is purely technical in nature. It is not information that can actually tell you anything meaningful about yourself. That's where the information in this chapter comes in – we're going to explore the meaning behind each of the 10 Gods.

The Infinity of the 10

An important caveat has to first precede any discussion of the meaning of each of the 10 Gods. The 10 Gods is at the heart of decoding one's Destiny Code because the 10 Gods are essentially the shorthand used to cover everything in this universe, existing and not yet existing, that could impact on an individual's life path. The 10 Gods effectively represent **everything** in our lives - from characteristics, actions, thoughts and behaviour to specific people, items, objects and relationships.

As the 10 Gods span such a tremendous range of tangible and intangible matters, it is NOT POSSIBLE to entirely plumb the depths of the subject comprehensively. The meaning of the 10 Gods cannot be explained in just one book or even half a dozen tomes, for the simple reason that the definition of each of the 10 Gods, in terms of what it can represent, is continuously expanding as our world and universe expands.

Accordingly, the focus of this Chapter will be on the character traits and attributes that are associated with each of the 10 Gods. The reason for focusing on character is two-fold: firstly, it is the easiest manifestation of the 10 Gods to actually perceive – most people understand character traits and attributes as a concept and it is relatively easy to identify them in a person. Secondly, character is the starting block for any BaZi analysis. Indeed, BaZi, although it is defined by the Chinese as a study of Life (命) is in reality, a study of the interplay between the forces of Destiny and Character. Why does an individual have a certain character? Because of Destiny. Why does an individual's Destiny unfold in a particular manner? Because their Character drives them to make certain decisions a particular way.

Determining, understanding and unravelling character as such is an integral part of decoding anyone's Destiny Code. It is half the battle won when it comes to decoding a person's Destiny.

Each of the subsequent books in the *Destiny Code: Power of X* series will explore a different aspect of the 10 Gods, enabling you to expand and grow your understanding of the 10 Gods in a progressive and structured manner. But ultimately, every student of BaZi needs to progress to the realisation that there no dictionary or encyclopaedia of the 10 Gods that will explain what every possible object (tangible or intangible) that exists in this world and will soon exist in this world, is in the language of the 10 Gods. At the problem-solving and solution-development stage of BaZi, the ability to figure out which 10 God to deploy and how that 10 God translates into action or thought or a specific relationship, depends less on book knowledge as it does on the ability to reason it out, based on a comprehension of the core essence of each of the 10 Gods.

Character Attributes and the 10 Gods.

Each 10 God represents a specific set of character attributes, both negative and positive in nature. Accordingly the collective of 10 Gods present in a person's BaZi chart represent their overall personality, reflecting both the individual's virtues and vices. If a person possesses a particular 10 God in their chart, they will possess both the positive and negative character attributes associated with that 10 God. The term 'character attribute' here goes a little further than just a description of the person in simple terms (ie: hard-working, industrious, prudent, domineering, witty, stubborn). It is also in some ways markedly more sophisticated than the term 'personality' since it also looks at a person's outlook and perception. As such, the phrase 'character attributes' used here in reality encapsulates a person's outlook and perception of the world and those around them, thought processes, mindset, attitudes and actions.

The Hurting Officer Star 傷官星

Hurting Officer Star

The Hurting Officer Star is always the Output Element that is of the opposite polarity to the Day Master.

日元 Day Master	傷官星 Hurting Officer Star
甲 *Jia* Yang Wood	丁 *Ding* Yin Fire
乙 *Yi* Yin Wood	丙 *Bing* Yang Fire
丙 *Bing* Yang Fire	己 *Ji* Yin Earth
丁 *Ding* Yin Fire	戊 *Wu* Yang Earth
戊 *Wu* Yang Earth	辛 *Xin* Yin Metal
己 *Ji* Yin Earth	庚 *Geng* Yang Metal
庚 *Geng* Yang Metal	癸 *Gui* Yin Water
辛 *Xin* Yin Metal	壬 *Ren* Yang Water
壬 *Ren* Yang Water	乙 *Yi* Yin Wood
癸 *Gui* Yin Water	甲 *Jia* Yang Wood

Positive Character Attributes Associated with the Hurting Officer Star

- **Outgoing** and extroverted
- Quick-witted
- **Street smart**
- Vivid imagination
- **Talkative**
- Good communicators
- Never-say-die types
- Highly intelligent and **inventive**
- Sharp-tongued, and **sarcastic**
- Bulldog tenacity and perseverance
- Adores the limelight and loves being **the center of attention**
- Bends rules or looks for ways around the rules without overtly breaking them
- Charismatic speakers, who have an innate sense of drama and showmanship
- Love a good challenge, and enjoy rising to the occasion
- Sees the world in the context of winners and losers
- Influential and persuasive, through the power of speech or ideas or thoughts
- Fast learners and highly adaptive personalities
- Likes to **debate**, discuss and brainstorm

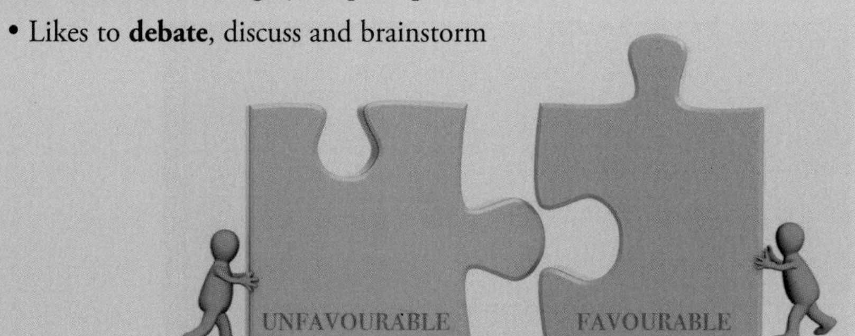

Negative Character Attributes Associated with the Hurting Officer Star

- Attention seeking and clingy
- Different for the sake of being different, **outrageous for the sake of being outrageous**
- Outrageous opinions that they force upon other people
- Break the rules (rather than just bend them)
- See themselves as **always right**, and everyone else is wrong
- Has no respect for boundaries or conventions
- Will use dirty tactics to win, victory at whatever cost
- Impulsive, hasty, pig-headed, extremely **stubborn**
- My way or the highway attitude
- **Lone rangers**
- **Temperamental**, prone to tantrums or diva-like behaviour
- Excessively argumentative – unable to let go or back-off from a situation or debate and argue for the sake of argument
- Self-centered and me-first mentality
- Suspicious-minded
- Ungracious in defeat
- Intolerant and impatient
- **Superiority complex**
- **Interfering**
- **Egotistical**
- **Tactless**
- **Rebellious**, highly individualistic, non-conformist
- **Opinionated**, sometimes to the point of obnoxious

Eating God Star

The Eating God Star 食神星

The Eating God Star is always the Output Element that is of the same polarity as the Day Master.

日元 Day Master	食神星 Eating God Star
甲 *Jia* Yang Wood	丙 *Bing* Yang Fire
乙 *Yi* Yin Wood	丁 *Ding* Yin Fire
丙 *Bing* Yang Fire	戊 *Wu* Yang Earth
丁 *Ding* Yin Fire	己 *Ji* Yin Earth
戊 *Wu* Yang Earth	庚 *Geng* Yang Metal
己 *Ji* Yin Earth	辛 *Xin* Yin Metal
庚 *Geng* Yang Metal	壬 *Ren* Yang Water
辛 *Xin* Yin Metal	癸 *Gui* Yin Water
壬 *Ren* Yang Water	甲 *Jia* Yang Wood
癸 *Gui* Yin Water	乙 *Yi* Yin Wood

Positive Character Attributes Associated with the Eating God Star

- Gentle and reserved
- **Introverted**
- Thoughtful, deep thinkers
- Internal and inward-looking – Eating Gods love to retreat to their own inner sanctum and do not see the need to live according to the rules of others
- **Great strategists** – the Eating God star enables the person to look at things from a 360 degree point of view
- Long-term outlook
- An eye for details, extremely **meticulous**, ultra-organised nature
- Classy and refined
- **Philosophical**
- **Perfectionists**
- Superior appreciation of aesthetics – Eating Gods love beautiful things, including beautiful people!
- Long tail types when it comes to business endeavours. They are interested in opportunities that last, not just the quick and immediate buck.
- Pleasure-centric and **hedonistic** – living the good life is high on their list of priorities in life
- Highly analytic and objective mind
- Wealth generation ability through original ideas, or creativity
- Enjoy the finer things in life but not necessarily on a materialistic level. The Eating God is less interested in the number of items owned, so much as the novelty, exoticism and uniqueness of their possessions
- Proud and snobbish on some levels, have an **air of superiority** about them
- Good listeners with a very understanding and patient nature
- Open-minded

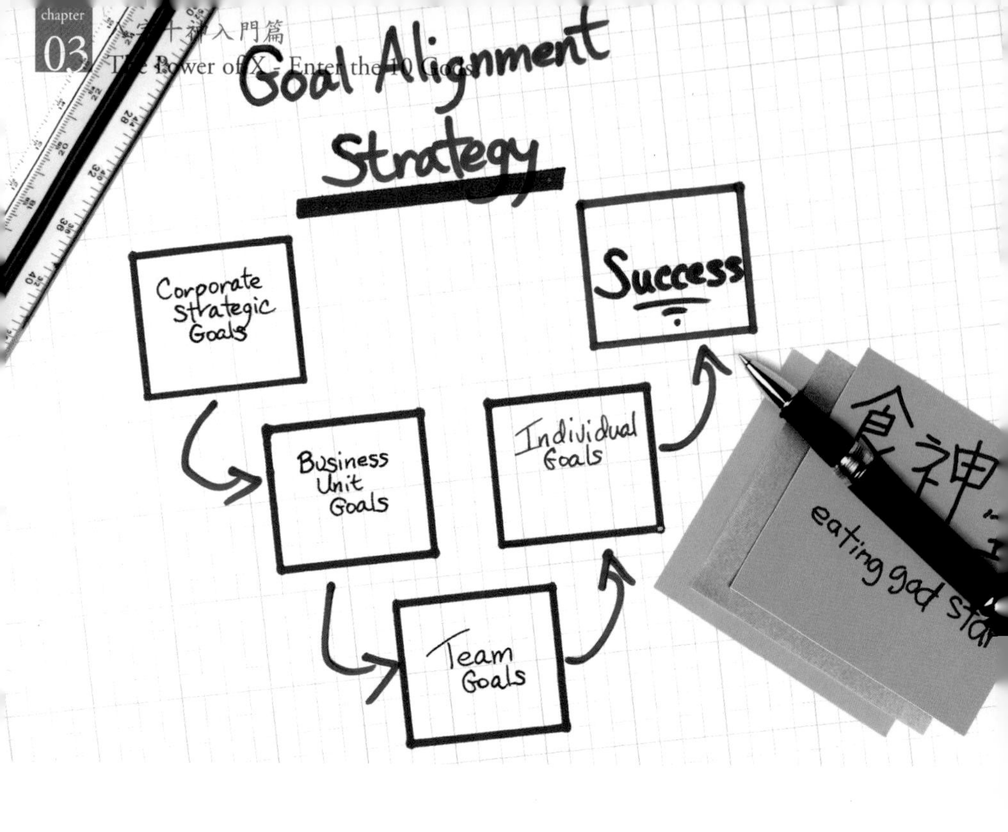

- Artistic and creative
- Quixotic and a little **eccentric**
- **Cultivated**, well-mannered and refined
- Altruistic and virtuous
- **Gourmands** and great appreciators of fine wines and foods
- Passion for knowledge, personal cultivation, and self-improvement Eating Gods are often well-read generally, but display a tremendous depth of knowledge in their field of speciality
- **Non-confrontational**, not the kind to pick fights or launch battles. Prefers psychological warfare to make their point
- Romantic, poetic, emotionally in-tune with their inner thoughts and feelings, and able to express these thoughts and feelings well in written and spoken words. But also capable of very bawdy thoughts – Eating God types are usually people who tell the best dirty jokes!

Negative Character Attributes Associated with the Eating God Star

- **Impractical** perfectionists – they spend too long tinkering and fiddling with their ideas and never take them to market/execute their plans
- Aimless **daydreamers**
- Divorced from reality
- Stubborn and **dogmatic**
- Isolated and anti-social
- Score-keepers who like to pick on small things
- **Weird**, extreme eccentricity and ultra-unorthodox
- **Peter Pan syndrome** – the person does not want to face reality or grow up and look at the real world, and lives in their own fantasy world
- Over-thinkers and prone to over-complicating a problem
- Inability to focus and a wandering mind
- Prone to gluttony and alcoholism
- Over-analytical
- **Pedantic** and prone to splitting hairs
- Excessive need for luxury in every facet of their life
- Keep their burdens and problems to themselves
- Churlish, spiteful and **mean-spirited**
- **Lecherous** and lustful

Direct Wealth Star

The Direct Wealth Star 正財星

The Direct Wealth Star is always the star that is of the opposite polarity with the Day Master.

Day Master 日元	Direct Wealth Star 正財星
甲 *Jia* Yang Wood	己 *Ji* Yin Earth
乙 *Yi* Yin Wood	戊 *Wu* Yang Earth
丙 *Bing* Yang Fire	辛 *Xin* Yin Metal
丁 *Ding* Yin Fire	庚 *Geng* Yang Metal
戊 *Wu* Yang Earth	癸 *Gui* Yin Water
己 *Ji* Yin Earth	壬 *Ren* Yang Water
庚 *Geng* Yang Metal	乙 *Yi* Yin Wood
辛 *Xin* Yin Metal	甲 *Jia* Yang Wood
壬 *Ren* Yang Water	丁 *Ding* Yin Fire
癸 *Gui* Yin Water	丙 *Bing* Yang Fire

Positive Character Attributes Associated with the Direct Wealth Star

- **Responsible**
- Reliable
- Sees the world as black and white
- Strong value system when it comes to right and wrongs
- Hard-working/Workaholic
- Not the type to upset the apple cart
- Reasonable
- **Practical**
- **Routine-driven**
- Steady
- Law-abiding
- Down to Earth
- **Modest**
- **Prudent** financially
- Fiscally responsible
- Family Man (if male)
- **Trustworthy**
- Sentimental
- Principled
- Sensible
- **Conservative**
- **Orthodox**

Negative Character Attributes Associated with the Direct Wealth Star

- Extremely controlling. For men, this can manifest in the form of an excessively possessive nature towards their wife. For women, they tend to keep their husbands on a short leash
- Fixated on money and seem to have no interests other than talking about money or counting money
- Determines the basis of a relationship based on tangible advantages obtained from the relationship
- Rigid minded, **ultra-conservative**
- Calculative and **Scrooge-like**
- Miserly
- Risk adverse
- **Greedy**
- Poor work-life balance
- **Small-minded**
- Hard taskmaster
- **Over-planners**

Indirect Wealth Star 偏財星

Indirect Wealth Star

The Indirect Wealth Star is always the star that is of the same polarity with the Day Master.

Day Master 日元	Indirect Wealth Star 偏財星
甲 *Jia* Yang Wood	戊 *Wu* Yang Earth
乙 *Yi* Yin Wood	己 *Ji* Yin Earth
丙 *Bing* Yang Fire	庚 *Geng* Yang Metal
丁 *Ding* Yin Fire	辛 *Xin* Yin Metal
戊 *Wu* Yang Earth	壬 *Ren* Yang Water
己 *Ji* Yin Earth	癸 *Gui* Yin Water
庚 *Geng* Yang Metal	甲 *Jia* Yang Wood
辛 *Xin* Yin Metal	乙 *Yi* Yin Wood
壬 *Ren* Yang Water	丙 *Bing* Yang Fire
癸 *Gui* Yin Water	丁 *Ding* Yin Fire

Positive Character Attributes Associated with the Indirect Wealth Star

- **Generosity**
- Flamboyance and extravagance
- Sharp **business acumen**
- **Big Picture** types
- Good sense of judgment
- **Adrenaline-driven** – they are all about the excitement, the thrill, the high of a deal or an opportunity
- All about efficiency and speed – fast cars, fast women, fast-paced lifestyle
- Naturally **entrepreneurial** - Able to see opportunities and sniff out great deals
- **Multi-taskers** – they like to run with more than one idea or goal at a time.
- **Wheeler-dealers** – see everything in the context of a negotiation, and a deal
- Get pleasure and thrill from making the money or the deal – the actual money itself is of little interest.
- **Fickle-minded** and cool quickly off something that isn't moving forward or showing progress

Negative Character Attributes Associated with the Indirect Wealth Star

- Financially imprudent and **not detail-orientated** when it comes to money-matters. They think in terms of revenue, not profit.
- **Poor sense of value** - these are people who have no idea how much a carton of milk costs and determine if something is expensive or cheat based on impulse and the experience they associate with it. If they love it, money is no object
- **Excessively generous** or spendthrift due to impulsiveness when it comes to money. Calculative over the wrong things
- **Easy come, easy go** attitude when it comes to money
- Problems with focusing on a single task at hand, and usually are poor finishers
- Lack the perseverance and persistence to make their dreams into reality because they are all about The Vision
- Prefers to **throw money at a problem** rather than find out why the problem exists in the first place
- Short-cut driven and short on ethics or principles.
- Impatient and no staying power
- Prone to taking short-cuts
- **Impulsive** decision-makers

Direct Officer Star

The Direct Officer Star 正官星

The Direct Officer Star is always the Influence Star that is of the opposite polarity from the Day Master.

日元 Day Master	正官星 Direct Officer Star
甲 *Jia* Yang Wood	辛 *Xin* Yin Metal
乙 *Yi* Yin Wood	庚 *Geng* Yang Metal
丙 *Bing* Yang Fire	癸 *Gui* Yin Water
丁 *Ding* Yin Fire	壬 *Ren* Yang Water
戊 *Wu* Yang Earth	乙 *Yi* Yin Wood
己 *Ji* Yin Earth	甲 *Jia* Yang Wood
庚 *Geng* Yang Metal	丁 *Ding* Yin Fire
辛 *Xin* Yin Metal	丙 *Bing* Yang Fire
壬 *Ren* Yang Water	己 *Ji* Yin Earth
癸 *Gui* Yin Water	戊 *Wu* Yang Earth

Positive Character Attributes Associated with the Direct Officer Star

- **Honourable**, righteous, principled
- Polite, courteous, well-mannered
- Law abiding and ethical
- Respectful of norms, conventions and traditions
- **Independent**
- Great personal **integrity**
- Even-tempered
- **Honest** and upright
- Like to manage situations, dislikes chaos and disorder
- Take-charge types
- Responsible and **reliable**
- **Reasonable** and level-headed
- Naturally **authoritative**
- Command respect from those around them
- Conservative and orthodox
- **Disciplined** and **organised**
- Like order in their lives – a place for everything, and everything in its place is their motto.
- Planners
- **Straight-shooters**
- See the world as black or white, right or wrong.
- Have an **impeccable reputation**

Negative Character Attributes Associated with the Direct Officer Star

- Rigid, **unyielding**, inflexible
- Set in their ways and thoughts, uncompromising manner
- Ultra-orthodox and **ultra-conservative**
- Fearful of change
- Unable to compromise or find a middle ground
- **Fastidious**
- Poor negotiators
- Unwilling to take risks, or stick their neck out for anything
- Fearful, **timid**, nervous
- **Indecisive**, hesitant
- Lack leadership skills or the ability to step up
- **Weak** and dependant on other people for guidance or direction
- Obedient to the point of **subservient**
- Lack initiative
- Shun responsibility or are **irresponsible**
- Poor reputation and don't command much respect from those around them

The 7 Killings Star 七殺星

7 Killings Star

The 7 Killings Star is always the Influence Star that is of the same polarity as the Day Master.

日元 Day Master	七殺星 Seven Killings Star
甲 *Jia* Yang Wood	庚 *Geng* Yang Metal
乙 *Yi* Yin Wood	辛 *Xin* Yin Metal
丙 *Bing* Yang Fire	壬 *Ren* Yang Water
丁 *Ding* Yin Fire	癸 *Gui* Yin Water
戊 *Wu* Yang Earth	甲 *Jia* Yang Wood
己 *Ji* Yin Earth	乙 *Yi* Yin Wood
庚 *Geng* Yang Metal	丙 *Bing* Yang Fire
辛 *Xin* Yin Metal	丁 *Ding* Yin Fire
壬 *Ren* Yang Water	戊 *Wu* Yang Earth
癸 *Gui* Yin Water	己 *Ji* Yin Earth

Positive Character Attributes Associated with the 7 Killings Star

- Authoritative and **commanding** presence
- Have an aura of **charisma**
- **Edgy**, possess a certain dangerousness that makes them highly attractive and appealing
- Draw people to them through their ability to lead and their **authoritative** manner
- Highly **ambitious** and will stop at nothing to get what they want
- Thrive on being powerful and influential
- Like to play hardball but can also be supremely manipulative
- **Machiavellian** – believe the ends justify the means
- **Never-say-die attitude**
- Are able to harness their aggressive streak and channel it
- **Over-achievers**
- Have a war-like mentality – there is no honour or valour or meaning in defeat
- Like to win and see the world as divided into people who are either winners, or losers
- **Hate to lose** and will scrap and fight to the bitter end.
- Sharp, quick-witted, fast reflexes, **swift thinkers**
- **Decisive** and unemotional in making decisions
- Ability to weigh up risks and opportunities well
- Thrive in pressure cooker situations
- **Courageous** and fearless
- **Dictatorial**
- Enjoy heroic grandeur – 7 Killings types see themselves as underdogs and thus like to side with underdogs.
- Driven by a need to save those around them from themselves
- People who believe you need to make your own rules in life

Negative Character Attributes Associated with the 7 Killings Star

- Extremely unreasonable, hasty and **impulsive** in their actions
- Prone to ballistic temper or explosive emotional behaviour
- Put people on the back foot with their **overly-aggressive** stance – have difficulty eliciting cooperation or assistance when they need it
- Warmongers and **troublemaker** types
- Lone rangers
- Crack under pressure
- **Reckless** behaviour
- **Abuse power** rather than wield it
- Take risks without understanding the implications or bothering to stop and think about the outcomes
- **Despotic**
- Out of control **mavericks**
- Lack true courage, cowards at heart
- Wield power without really knowing how to use it
- **Thoughtless**
- Seek to win at all costs, even if it means resorting to underhand methods.
- Practices double standards
- Suspicious-minded and **petty**
- **Spiteful**

Direct Resource Star

The Direct Resource Star 正印星

The Direct Resource Star is always the Resource Element that is of the opposite polarity to the Day Master.

日柱 Day Master	正印星 Direct Resource Star
甲 *Jia* Yang Wood	癸 *Gui* Yin Water
乙 *Yi* Yin Wood	壬 *Ren* Yang Water
丙 *Bing* Yang Fire	乙 *Yi* Yin Wood
丁 *Ding* Yin Fire	甲 *Jia* Yang Wood
戊 *Wu* Yang Earth	丁 *Ding* Yin Fire
己 *Ji* Yin Earth	丙 *Bing* Yang Fire
庚 *Geng* Yang Metal	己 *Ji* Yin Earth
辛 *Xin* Yin Metal	戊 *Wu* Yang Earth
壬 *Ren* Yang Water	辛 *Xin* Yin Metal
癸 *Gui* Yin Water	庚 *Geng* Yang Metal

Positive Character Attributes Associated with the Direct Resource Star

- **Knowledgeable** and **cultured**
- Respectable, upright, pleasant, refined
- Comfortable with themselves and who they are, contented
- Contemplative and **thoughtful**
- **Self-aware** and able to empathise with others
- **Curious**
- Focused on self-cultivation and **self-improvement**
- Respects boundaries and is always appropriate
- Honours their word and fulfils their promises
- Compassionate, benevolent and sentimental
- Thirsts for knowledge
- **Optimistic**
- Tolerant and non-judgmental
- Forgiving and **merciful**
- **Patient**
- Peace-loving
- Gentle and **kind**
- **Thoughtful** and considerate
- **Civilised**
- Good-natured, doesn't hold a grudge
- Good memory and good learning ability
- Prim and proper, with a strong emphasis on good manners and appropriate behaviour
- **Imaginative**
- **Resourceful** as a result of a wide pool of knowledge and/or a cultivated group of experts helpers that they can all on for guidance or wisdom

Negative Character Attributes Associated with the Direct Resource Star

- Uncomfortable with themselves and who they are, **feel inadequate** or uncomfortable in their own skin
- **Worriers**
- **Uncivilized**, ill-mannered, uncouth and lack proper manners
- Inability to be content with anything – can't count their blessings, or smell the roses, and are always convinced that things are never good enough
- Too forgiving, thus, have a tendency to be a doormat
- **Impractical** and dreamy, rarely are their thoughts grounded in reality
- Overthink everything
- Needy and **dependant**, too easy-going and laid back
- **Lazy** and aimless
- **Indecisive**
- Lack independence, not a self-starter
- Inability to face up to reality and bite the bullet
- Only ever see the negatives in a situation, never the positives
- Never see their own flaws, only the flaws in others
- Tendency to hide/cover-up mistakes
- **Bleeding heart**, overly sympathetic, a tendency to be **gullible** or naïve
- Nostalgic and **sentimental** to the point of seemingly mostly living in the past
- Overly concerned about how people perceive them, **thin-skinned**
- Will do anything in the name of maintaining their reputation
- Tendency to push the blame to others
- **Overly-sensitive**
- Knowledgeable but unable to turn that knowledge into resourcefulness

The Indirect Resource Star 偏印星

The Indirect Resource Star is always the Resource Element that is of the same polarity as the Day Master.

Indirect Resource Star

日元 Day Master	偏印星 Indirect Resource Star
甲 Jia Yang Wood	壬 Ren Yang Water
乙 Yi Yin Wood	癸 Gui Yin Water
丙 Bing Yang Fire	甲 Jia Yang Wood
丁 Ding Yin Fire	乙 Yi Yin Wood
戊 Wu Yang Earth	丙 Bing Yang Fire
己 Ji Yin Earth	丁 Ding Yin Fire
庚 Geng Yang Metal	戊 Wu Yang Earth
辛 Xin Yin Metal	己 Ji Yin Earth
壬 Ren Yang Water	庚 Geng Yang Metal
癸 Gui Yin Water	辛 Xin Yin Metal

Positive Character Attributes Associated with the Indirect Resource Star

- Strong **intuition**
- Good gut-feel/instincts
- **Quick study** – grasp ideas and concepts quickly and intuitively
- Innate **sixth sense**
- Relaxed personality, **laid back** character
- **Non-judgmental**
- Usually religious or spiritually inclined, or interested in alternative/metaphysical fields and subjects
- **Unconventional** interests, can sometimes be **eccentric** or have unusual hobbies or interests
- Enjoy reading and researching pet subjects or hobby horses
- Varied and expansive knowledge about a range of subjects and topics
- **Dabblers** in a wide variety of interests
- Like to think out of the box
- Highly **innovative**, ultra-unique creativity
- Planners and strategic thinkers
- **Idealistic** and willing to chase after their dreams
- **Resourceful** but through unconventional means
- **Intellectually curious**
- Love new and unique experiences
- Mischievous and **impish**
- Highly imaginative
- Deep thinkers
- **Inventive**
- **Dreamers**

Negative Character Attributes Associated with the Indirect Resource Star

- **Hedonistic**
- Prone to living in imaginary worlds
- Unrealistic expectations out of life and people
- **Paranoid**, worrywart, prone to getting upset easily
- Suspicious-minded
- **Hyper-sensitive**
- **Over-sentimental**
- Excessively **introverted**
- Keep their feelings to themselves, extremely **secretive**
- Over-thinkers, prone to tinkering
- **Impractical**
- Make decisions without consideration for facts, figures or real life situations
- **Superstitious** to the point of extreme
- Avoids confrontation at all cost and has difficulty dealing with reality
- Prefers to take the path of least resistance
- Bleeding heart who sympathises with everyone
- Focuses on the trivial and minutiae, at the expense of the big picture
- **Flaky** and weird
- **Likes to cut corners**, use short-cuts, and is prone to guess-work
- Knowledge often lacks depth
- **Jack of all Trades**, Master of None
- Lazy and **procrastinators**

- Bleeding hearts, at times, overly sentimental
- Can be extremely naïve and gullible
- **Sloppy** with work and details
- **Solitary**, prefer their own company
- Resourceful by means of their ability to rely on other people, think Huckleberry Finn
- Tend to leave many lose-ends untied in their endeavours – **tardy** workers and **scatterbrained.**
- Prone to solitude or solitary moments – they are individuals who like their own space

The Rob Wealth Star 劫財星

Rob Wealth Star

The Rob Wealth Star is always the Companion Element that is of the opposite polarity to the Day Master.

日元 **Day Master**	劫財星 **Rob Wealth Star**
甲 *Jia* Yang Wood	乙 *Yi* Yin Wood
乙 *Yi* Yin Wood	甲 *Jia* Yang Wood
丙 *Bing* Yang Fire	丁 *Ding* Yin Fire
丁 *Ding* Yin Fire	丙 *Bing* Yang Fire
戊 *Wu* Yang Earth	己 *Ji* Yin Earth
己 *Ji* Yin Earth	戊 *Wu* Yang Earth
庚 *Geng* Yang Metal	辛 *Xin* Yin Metal
辛 *Xin* Yin Metal	庚 *Geng* Yang Metal
壬 *Ren* Yang Water	癸 *Gui* Yin Water
癸 *Gui* Yin Water	壬 *Ren* Yang Water

Positive Character Attributes Associated with the Rob Wealth Star

- **Talkative** and chatty
- Witty
- Happy go lucky, easy going
- Approachable and friendly
- Good **people skills**
- Love a good bit of gossip
- **Highly-competitive**
- **Generous**, at times to a fault
- Good social skills, fast to make friends
- **Altruistic** – will take one for the team
- Outgoing and extremely **extroverted**
- Naturally **charismatic**, life of the party types
- Great communicators and orators, excellent motivators
- Value friendships, place their friends above others
- Prone to telling white lies but this is usually to make someone feel better
- Possess a natural **gift of the gab**, are highly persuasive, good sales people
- May be willing to put the interests of friends above those of self
- Envious and easily jealous but this is used to spur them on to be more competitive, or to reach the next level
- Brave and **gutsy** although sometimes, they tend to be a bit too gung-ho
- Have a positive ego
- **Adaptive**, flexible individuals who have quick reflexes and quick witted – have MacGyver-like skills and are able to improvise and handle unexpected last-minute developments and changes well
- Great **networkers**
- Have an optimistic personality, and look at challenges in a positive light
- Honour their promises and undertakings but out of a sense of obligation rather than actual sense of responsibility

Negative Character Attributes Associated with the Rob Wealth Star

- Envious and **jealous**, but manifests it in a destructive or spiteful manner
- Utterly indiscreet, unable to keep ANY secrets
- Suffers from low self-esteem but projects an image of great confidence
- Treats friends blatantly better than family members, tends to have a distant relationship with family members
- Foot-in-mouth syndrome
- **Compulsive liars** or prone to telling frequent white lies
- Have trouble honouring promises
- Guilty of over-promising and under-delivering
- Boastful
- Ultimately selfish, although will disguise their intentions as for the greater good
- **Impulsive**, fly-by-the-seat-of-their-pants types
- Prone to reckless behaviour, often to just show-off
- Excessively **egotistical**
- **Indecisive** as they keep changing their mind or can't make up their minds
- **Spendthrift** and frivolous with money
- **Over-competitive**
- Accident and injury-prone
- Insecure and require constant assurance
- Users and abusers when it comes to friendships – don't know where to the draw the line when it comes to friendships
- Have lots of friends, but these tends to be superficial friendships

Friend Star

The Friend Star 比肩星

The Friend Star is always the Companion Element that is of the same polarity as the Day Master.

日元 Day Master	比肩星 Friend Star
甲 *Jia* Yang Wood	甲 *Jia* Yang Wood
乙 *Yi* Yin Wood	乙 *Yi* Yin Wood
丙 *Bing* Yang Fire	丙 *Bing* Yang Fire
丁 *Ding* Yin Fire	丁 *Ding* Yin Fire
戊 *Wu* Yang Earth	戊 *Wu* Yang Earth
己 *Ji* Yin Earth	己 *Ji* Yin Earth
庚 *Geng* Yang Metal	庚 *Geng* Yang Metal
辛 *Xin* Yin Metal	辛 *Xin* Yin Metal
壬 *Ren* Yang Water	壬 *Ren* Yang Water
癸 *Gui* Yin Water	癸 *Gui* Yin Water

Positive Character Attributes Associated with the Friend Star

- Firm but not pig-headed character
- Comfortable with who they are, with little or **no hang-ups** or complexes
- Believe in self-help and Do-It-Yourself
- Interested in evolving and bettering themselves to please themselves
- Possess **will-power** and the ability to self-motivate themselves
- Understand themselves from all angles, strengths and limitations
- Possess inherent grace and generosity
- **Competitive but with themselves**, rather than as a result of the achievements of others
- Do not see themselves as defined by those around them but by themselves
- Optimists, possess a **positive outlook** on life
- First amongst equals, leadership that emerges as a result of camaraderie and altruism rather than strength and authority
- Good sense of self-pride and **self-worth**
- Able to play well with others, and share equitably in all things in life
- Focused on looking good, and feeling good but not in a manner that indicates excessive vanity or over-indulgence
- Treats all friends equally and is able to afford unconditional friendship
- Decisive, clear-minded, and act upon their own views and principles with certainty
- Realists who don't complain but get on with the job
- Possess inherent inner strength and conviction
- Take responsibility for their own actions
- Highly and fiercely independent
- Quietly confident
- **Self-assured**
- Possess positive self-belief

Negative Character Attributes Associated with the Friend Star

- Play the blame game
- Avoid responsibility for their own actions and abdicate responsibility for themselves to others
- **Interfering** and nosy
- Self-centered and **narcissistic**
- Selfish – they are the most important person in this world.
- Over-value themselves, their contributions, their abilities
- Perceive themselves as unable to do any wrong
- My way or the highway is their motto
- Extremely stubborn and pig-headed – always convinced that they have to be right, and everyone needs to follow them.
- Lack the ability to consider all the options and viewpoints in a given situation
- Inflexible thinking, stubborn, one-track-mind
- Prone to extreme behaviour – they can be extreme workaholics, or extreme bums.
- **Poor social skills**, socially inept, or don't seem to know how to interact with people in an intelligent and emotionally balanced manner. Lack EQ
- Many friends, but no real true friendships. **A fair-weather friend**
- **Grumbler**, and often unable to see why people are unwilling to do things their way or insist on alternative options (the result of an over-inflated sense of self)
- Lacks a clear sense of identity thus will appear as all things to all people

- Exhibits confidence but in reality, is **deeply insecure**.
- Concerned about likeability and acceptance amongst those around them
- Feel small and thus, become a **petulant** character because they constantly think and feel they are **inferior** yet dislike that feeling
- **Lack self-worth** – as a result the person becomes tremendously self-conscious, shy and retiring or even a wallflower or shrinking violet
- Scatterbrained and have difficulty following instructions because their thoughts are disorganised
- Tend have 'convenient hearing' and 'convenient memories'

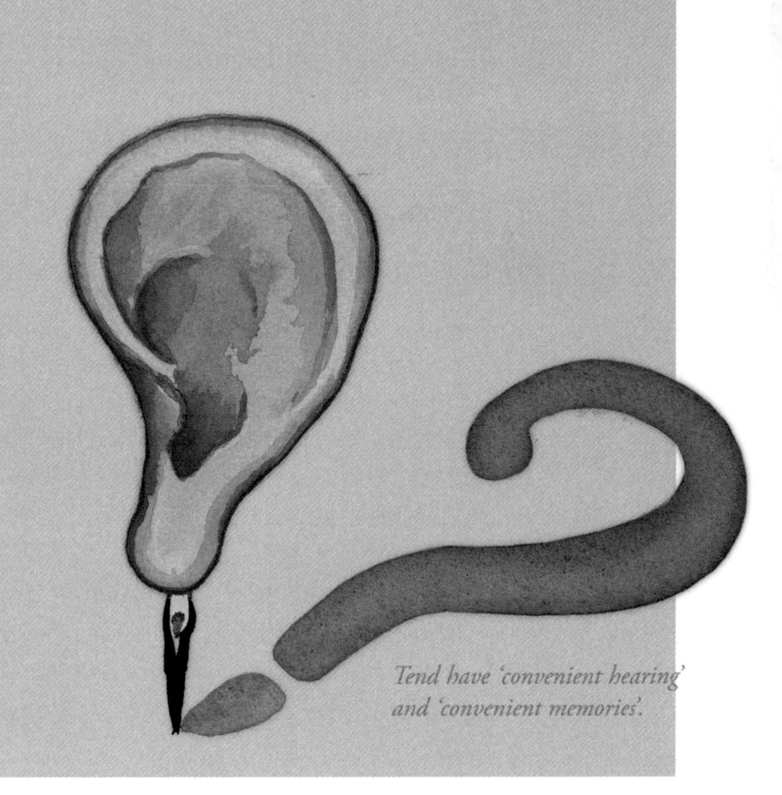

Tend have 'convenient hearing' and 'convenient memories'.

Mastering the Essentials

At this point, you will be eager to proceed to the next chapter, which explains how to utilise the information about the 10 Gods essentials provided here to analyse an individual's character based on their BaZi.

DO NOT GO TO THE NEXT CHAPTER.

Yet.

Instead, do yourself a favour and go back to the start of this chapter and re-read it. Do not proceed to the next chapter until you have committed to memory at least 5 of the positive and negative character attributes associated with all of the 10 Gods.

Before proceeding further, make sure that at the very least, you are familiar with a few bare basic attributes of each of the 10 Gods.

I have taught the 10 Gods to students all around the world and the most common stumbling block when it comes to making the leap from the bare basics, into the practical aspect of analysis, is a lack of familiarity with the essential attributes of the 10 Gods. Many students are only able to identify the 10 Gods that relate to their own Day Master (thus essentially ignoring the other 9 Day Masters) or they cannot commit to memory the essentials attributes of the 10 Gods. Thus, before proceeding further, make sure that at the very least, you are familiar with a few bare basic attributes of each of the 10 Gods.

For the industrious, hard-working types, this should be a piece of cake. For the readers who are all about the shortcuts, you will notice that some of the words in each of the character attribute sections has been bolded – these are the simple, basic keywords that most commonly are associated with each 10 God. For those inclined to the Indirect Resource method of learning, some mindmaps have been included at the back of this section. I recommend taking the time to be really familiar with the 10 Gods essentials before you progress to the next chapter as it will greatly speed up your ability to understand the analysis techniques that will be discussed in Chapter 4.

POSITIVE CHARACTER ATTRIBUTES ASSOCIATED WITH THE HURTING OFFICER STAR

imaginative **Outgoing** *Never-say-die* **Talkative** *Good communicators* *Highly intelligent* **inventive** *Bulldog tenacity* *Adores the limelight* *loves to* **debate** **always the center of attention** *Bends rules or looks for ways around the rules without overtly breaking them* **extroverted** *Charismatic speakers* **thinks outside the box** *highly individualistic* *Love a good challenge* *enjoy rising to the occasion* *Sharp-tongued* **dynamic** *Sees the world in the context of winners and losers* *Quick-witted* **Street smart** *Influential and persuasive through the power of speech or ideas or thoughts* **Opinionated** *sometimes to the point of obnoxious* *Fast learners* *highly adaptive*

NEGATIVE CHARACTER ATTRIBUTES ASSOCIATED WITH THE HURTING OFFICER STAR

Attention seeking **clingy** *Different for the sake of being different* **outrageous for the sake of being outrageous** *force their opinions upon other people* *Break the rules* **Impulsive** *hasty* **pig-headed** *extremely stubborn* *regard themselves as* **always right** *no respect for boundaries or conventions* *Argue for the sake of argument* *Victory at whatever cost* *My way or the highway attitude* **Lone rangers** **Temperamental** *prone to temper tantrums or diva-like behaviour* **Supremely egotistical** *Self-centered* *me-first mentality* *Suspicious-minded* **Interfering** *Excessively argumentative* **Tactless** *Ungracious in defeat* **Intolerant** *impatient* **Superiority complex**

POSITIVE CHARACTER ATTRIBUTES ASSOCIATED WITH THE EATING GOD STAR

Gentle *reserved* **Introverted** *Thoughtful* *Deep thinkers* *inward-looking* *all about the details* **extremely meticulous** *ultra-organised* *Long-term outlook* **Great strategists** *refined* *Artistic* *creative* *Highly analytical* **Classy** *Pleasure-centric* **hedonistic** *Value the finer things in life* *cultured* *Romantic* **Cultivated** *well-mannered* *Always refined* *Altruistic* *virtuous* **Gourmands** **Non-confrontational** *Good listeners with a very understanding and patient nature* **Perfectionists** *Quixotic* **eccentric** *Superior appreciation of aesthetics* *Love beautiful things* **Philosophical** *Open-minded*

NEGATIVE CHARACTER ATTRIBUTES ASSOCIATED WITH THE EATING GOD STAR

Aimless **daydreamers** *Divorced from reality Nitpickers* **Peter Pan syndrome** *Isolated Love to fiddle but never finish anything anti-social* **Weird** *extreme eccentricity ultra-unorthodox Over-thinkers Prone to over-complicating a problem* **dogmatic** *do not want to face reality or grow up lives in their own fantasy world Inability to focus wandering mind* **Lecherous** *lustful Prone to gluttony Over-analytical* **Pedantic** *Split hairs Excessive need for luxury in every facet of their life* **Calculative** *Churlish spiteful* **mean-spirited** *Keep their burdens and problems to themselves* **Impractical perfectionists** *Tinkerers Stubborn*

POSITIVE CHARACTER ATTRIBUTES ASSOCIATED WITH THE DIRECT WEALTH STAR

Responsible *Not the type to upset the apple cart* *Reasonable* **Reliable** *Absolutist outlook* **Trustworthy** *Strong value system* *Firm ideas of what is right and what is wrong* *Hard-working* *Workaholic* **Routine-driven** *Steady* *Law-abiding* **Practical** *Down to Earth* **Modest** *Fiscally responsible* *Sensible* **Prudent** *Supremely pragmatic* *Principled* **Conservative** *Sentimental* **Orthodox** *By-the-book*

NEGATIVE CHARACTER ATTRIBUTES ASSOCIATED WITH THE DIRECT WEALTH STAR

Calculative **Scrooge-like** *Extremely controlling Possessive Fixated on money Only motivated by material gains Risk adverse* **Over-planners** *Determines the basis of a relationship based on tangible advantages obtained from the relationship* **Small-minded** *Miserly Risk adverse* **Greedy** *Poor work-life Balance Hard taskmaster Rigid-minded* **ultra-conservative**

POSITIVE CHARACTER ATTRIBUTES ASSOCIATED WITH THE INDIRECT WEALTH STAR

Adrenaline-driven *all about the excitement the thrill and the high of a deal or an opportunity* **Wheeler-dealers** *Flamboyant* **action-oriented** *Extravagant* **Visionaries** *Fast-paced lifestyle* **Naturally entrepreneurial** *eye for opportunities, nose for great deals* **Quick-witted** *Good sense of judgment* **Multi-taskers** *See everything in the context of a negotiation and a deal* **Big Picture Types** *all about the art of the deal* **Generous** *Sharp-mind Natural negotiators* **business acumen**

NEGATIVE CHARACTER ATTRIBUTES ASSOCIATED WITH THE INDIRECT WEALTH STAR

Financially imprudent **not detail-orientated** *think in terms of revenue not profit* **Excessively generous** *impulsive spenders Calculative over the wrong things* **Poor sense of value** *Lack perseverance no persistence* **All about The Vision and The Grand Plan Only** *Easy-come-easy go when it comes to money Lack focus poor finishers* **Impulsive** *decision-makers Impatient No staying power Like to take short-cuts Throw money at problems rather than find the source of the problem* **Penny-wise Pound Foolish** *weak on ethics or principles*

POSITIVE CHARACTER ATTRIBUTES ASSOCIATED WITH THE DIRECT OFFICER STAR

Honourable *Righteous Principled Polite courteous well mannered* **Naturally authoritative** *Law-abiding ethical* **Honest** *upright Respectful of norms conventions and traditions* **Independent** *values integrity Even tempered Like to manage situations Dislikes chaos and disorder* **Take-charge types** *Responsible* **reliable** *See the world as black or white right or wrong* **Reasonable** *level-headed Command respect from those around them* **Disciplined** *a place for everything and everything in its place is their motto Planners* **Straight-shooters** *place a lot of emphasis on good reputation Conservative orthodox* **Organised**

NEGATIVE CHARACTER ATTRIBUTES ASSOCIATED WITH THE DIRECT OFFICER STAR

Rigid **unyielding** *inflexible* *Set in their ways and thoughts* *Uncompromising* *Ultra-orthodox* **ultra-conservative** *Fearful of change* *Unable to compromise or find a middle ground* **Fastidious** *Poor negotiators* *Unwilling to take risks or stick their neck out for anything* *Fearful* **timid** *nervous* **Lack leadership skills** *or the ability to step up* **Weak** *dependant on other people for guidance or direction* **subservient** *Lack initiative* **Shun responsibility** *Poor reputation* *Don't command much respect from those around them* **Indecisive** *hesitant* *Herd Mentality* *Tendency to pass the buck*

POSITIVE CHARACTER ATTRIBUTES ASSOCIATED WITH THE 7 KILLINGS STAR

Never-say-die attitude *Aggressive Go Getters Determined* **commanding presence charismatic** *Highly* **ambitious** *Thrive on power* **Over-achievers** *Likes to win See the world as divided into people who are either winners or losers* **Decisive** *unemotional in making decisions* **authoritative** *natural ability to judge risks* **Machiavellian** *believe the ends justify the means* **Edgy** *Thrive in pressure cooker situations* **Courageous** *fearless* **Strong leadership style** *like to make their own rules Sharp quick-witted* **swift thinkers**

NEGATIVE CHARACTER ATTRIBUTES ASSOCIATED WITH THE 7 KILLINGS STAR

Extremely unreasonable hasty **impulsive** **Spiteful** *ballistic temper or explosive emotional behaviour* **overly-aggressive** *have difficulty eliciting cooperation or assistance when they need it* **small-minded** *Warmongers* **troublemaker** *types* *Lone rangers* *Crack under pressure* **Abuse power** *Out of control* **mavericks** *Lack true courage* *Cowards at heart* *Little Napoleons* **Thoughtless** *Seek to win at all costs even if it means resorting to underhand methods* **Despotic** *Practice double standards* **Reckless** *Suspicious-minded* **petty**

POSITIVE CHARACTER ATTRIBUTES ASSOCIATED WITH THE DIRECT RESOURCE STAR

Knowledgeable *Comfortable with themselves and who they are* *Contented* **Patient** *Peace-loving* *Contemplative* **thoughtful** *Focused on self-cultivation and self-improvement* *Respects boundaries* *always appropriate* *Forgiving* **merciful** *Honours their word and fulfils their promises* *Compassionate* *benevolent* *sentimental* **Self-aware** *good empathy with others* *Loves learning new things* *Enjoys new experiences* **Optimistic** *Tolerant* *non-judgmental* *considerate* **Civilised** *Good-natured* *doesn't hold a grudge* *Gentle* **kind** **Resourceful** **cultured** *Prim and proper* *Well-mannered* **Curious** *Respectable* *refined* **Imaginative**

NEGATIVE CHARACTER ATTRIBUTES ASSOCIATED WITH THE DIRECT RESOURCE STAR

Overly-sensitive *Uncomfortable with themselves and who they are* **feel inadequate** *Knowledgeable but unable to turn that knowledge into anything useful* **Uncivilized** *ill-mannered uncouth Lack proper manners Inability to be content with anything* **Impractical** *dreamy Over-think everything Needy* **dependant** *too easy-going* **Lazy** *aimless* **Indecisive** *Lack independence not a self-starter* **Worriers** *Never see their own flaws only the flaws in others Tendency to hide/cover-up mistakes* **Bleeding heart** *overly sympathetic* **gullible** *naïve* **thin-skinned** *Tendency to push the blame to others* **Complainers**

POSITIVE CHARACTER ATTRIBUTES ASSOCIATED WITH THE INDIRECT RESOURCE STAR

Good intuition *naturally instinctive* *Deep thinkers* **Innate sixth sense** *Relaxed personality* **laid back** *Religious or spiritually inclined* **Unconventional Interests** *Can be eccentric* *Prone to unusual hobby* **Dreamers** *Varied and expansive knowledge about a range of subjects and topics* **Dabblers** *in a wide variety of interests* **Inventive** *ability to think out of the box* **Highly innovative** *uniquely creative* *Planners Strategic thinkers* **Idealistic** *willing to chase dreams* **Resourceful** *adventurous* **Intellectually curious** *Love new and unique experiences* *Playful* *Highly imaginative* **Quick study**

NEGATIVE CHARACTER ATTRIBUTES ASSOCIATED WITH THE INDIRECT RESOURCE STAR

Impractical *Often live in imaginary worlds Unrealistic expectations out of life and people* **Paranoid** *worrywart get upset easily* **Excessively introverted** *Suspicious-minded* **Hyper-sensitive** *superficial when it comes to knowledge Keep their feelings to themselves* **secretive** *Over-thinkers prone to tinkering* **Jack of all Trades** *Make decisions without consideration for facts figures or real life situations* **Hedonistic** *Prefers to take the path of least resistance Lazy* **procrastinators** **Flaky** *Focuses on the trivial and minutiae at the expense of the big picture* **Likes to cut corners** *prone to guess-work* **Over-sentimental** *always non confrontational* **Superstitious**

POSITIVE CHARACTER ATTRIBUTES ASSOCIATED WITH THE ROB WEALTH STAR

Talkative *chatty* **extroverted** *Happy-go-lucky Easy-going Good with people* **Altruistic** *Will take one for the team Outgoing* **charismatic** *life of the party Value friendships Place their friends above others* **Adaptive** *Possess a* **natural gift of the gab** *highly-persuasive Natural salesmen Approachable Friendly* **Highly-competitive** *Willing to put the interests of friends above those of self Brave* **gutsy** *Gung-ho Foolhardy Optimists* **social animals** *View challenges in a positive light* **Generous** *healthy ego* **Great networkers** *Witty*

NEGATIVE CHARACTER ATTRIBUTES ASSOCIATED WITH THE ROB WEALTH STAR

Envious **jealous** *Indiscreet Unable to keep secrets* **Spend-thrift** *Treats friends blatantly better than family members Foot-in-mouth Syndrome* **Compulsive liars** *Have trouble honouring promises Reckless behaviour show-offs* **egotistical** *Over-promise and under deliver* **Boastful** *Selfish* **Impulsive** *fly-by-the-seat-of-their-pants types Accident-prone* **Indecisive** *keep changing their mind or can't make up their minds Fair-weather friends* **Over-competitive** *Insecure Require constant assurance*

POSITIVE CHARACTER ATTRIBUTES ASSOCIATED WITH THE FRIEND STAR

Comfortable with who they are **no hang-ups** *Believe in self-help* **Do-It-Yourself Types** *Seek to improve and better themselves for their own advancement* **Strong will-power** *able to self-motivate Understand themselves inherent grace and generosity* **Competitive but with themselves** *not defined by those around them but by themselves* **positive outlook self-worth** *great inner strength Fierce conviction Take responsibility for their own actions Highly fiercely Always independent Quietly confident* **Self-assured** *positive self-belief* **No Complexes**

NEGATIVE CHARACTER ATTRIBUTES ASSOCIATED WITH THE FRIEND STAR

Poor social skills *Lack EQ* *Avoid responsibility* **Interfering** *Play the blame game* *Over-value themselvess their contributions, their abilities* **fair-weather friend** *Think they can never do wrong* **Conceited** *Self-centered* **narcissistic** *My way or the highway* *Inflexible thinking* *Stubborn* *One-track-mind* *Self-Centered* **Grumbler** *Obsessed with likeability and acceptance amongst those around them* *Feel small* **petulant** *Constantly think and feel* **inferior** *self loathing* **Lack self-worth** *Scatterbrained disorganised thinkers* *Bad at following instructions* **deeply insecure** *Tend have 'convenient hearing' and 'convenient memories'* *Frequently abdicate responsibility*

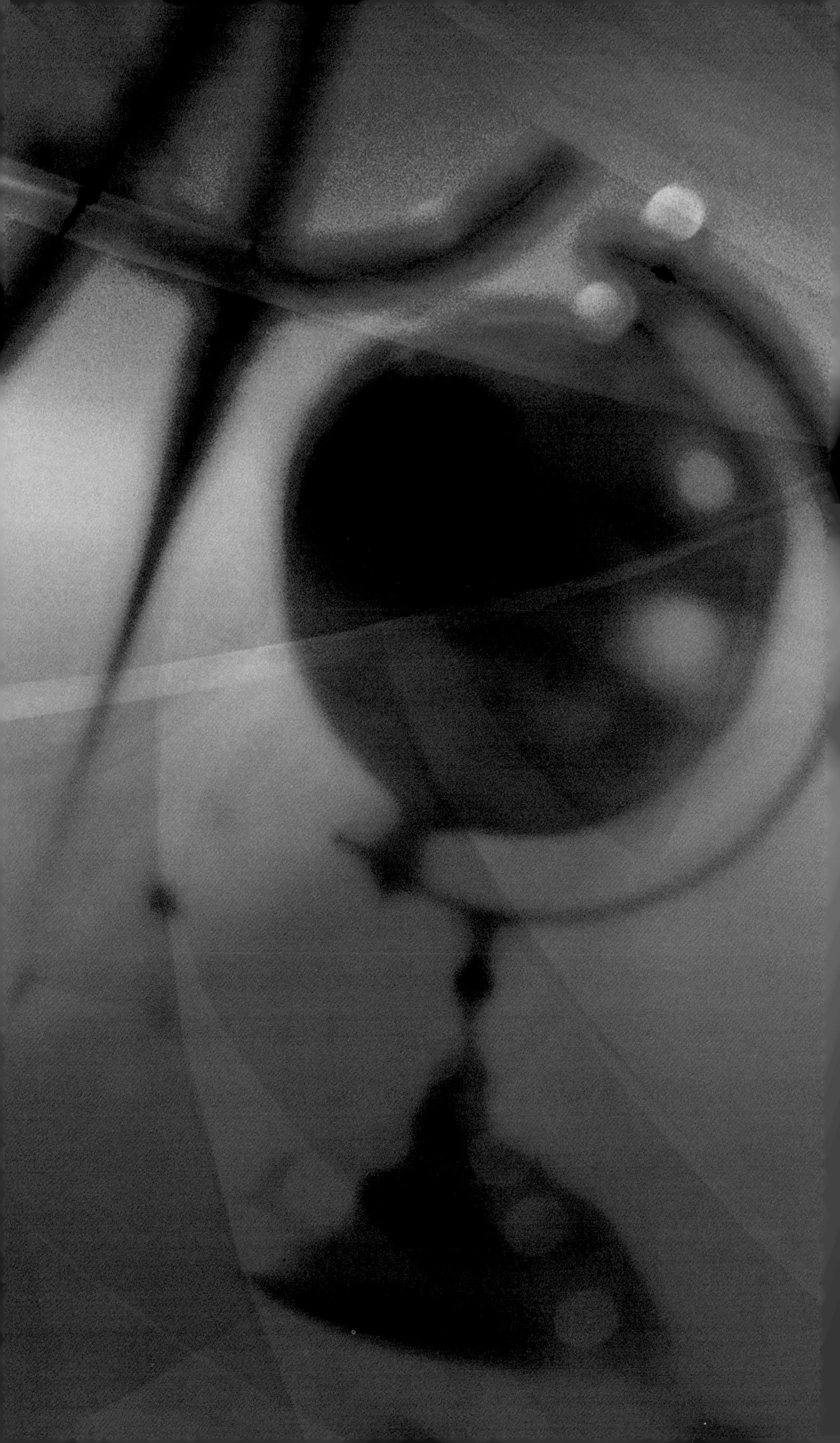

Chapter 4
Analysing Character through the 10 Gods

In his book, the Art of War, Sun Tzu states: "知彼知己，百戰不殆；不知彼而知己，一勝一負；不知彼，不知己，每戰必殆" which loosely translates as follows: *to know your enemy and know yourself, and you will always be victorious, know yourself but not your enemy, and you will both win and lose the battle, if you know neither your enemies nor yourself, every battle will be lost.*

This quotation aptly highlights the value of understanding character, both one's own and that of others. Sure, modern life is not a real war in any sense, but that doesn't mean that battles don't take place every day. In place of guns, we carry the weapons of our ambition and our dreams, and in place of defeat, there is disappointment or failure to achieve our goals in life. You could call this a modern application of Sun Tzu's above principle.

Character, at its most fundamental, is a composite of one's strengths and weaknesses, virtues and flaws, mindset, outlook, perceptions and attitude. In many ways, success and achievements in life come down to WHO YOU ARE as a person – what is your attitude, mindset, outlook and perception of the world around you? You can come from a great family, have a fantastic education, be given all the opportunities in the world but if your attitude in life is to be lazy, under-achieving, tardy and irresponsible, how far can you go?

Knowing, being aware and being conscious of our character in a 360-degree manner enables us to ensure that we are able to achieve the goals and dreams that we have. But more significantly, it also enables us to handle the disappointments and failures that comes with striving to achieve and succeed.

As Sun Tzu points out, it isn't however enough to just know yourself – you have also got to know others. In the era of the social network and where truly, fewer and fewer things can be achieved without the assistance, cooperation or involvement of others, knowing the character of the people around you (enemies and otherwise) is an invaluable advantage in the game of life.

Since one of the easiest things to read in a BaZi chart is character, BaZi is an invaluable tool in which to attain the advantage expounded by Sun Tzu and an excellent means in which to know yourself and know those around you.

The Reality of Knowing

Unless you live with someone 24/7/365, it is arguably impossible to truly know that person. How often have you been surprised by the actions of someone that you thought you knew or understood? How often do we hear the refrain 'but he's not like that' being raised in the defence of someone after they have done something that is apparently out of character?

Yet we often neglect to ask ourselves this - *if that's not who they are, or that's not their character, then why did they do it?*

It has to have been part of their character.

People have many reasons for not highlighting their true character or keeping certain facets of their character to themselves. Some people have learned the hard way that certain elements of their character don't gel with the society that they live in. Similarly, some people have learned the hard way that certain vices ought to be curtailed in the interest of personal advancement or just general, socially acceptable behaviour. That doesn't mean that those parts of their character disappear – rather, it just means that those parts of their character are kept more tightly under wraps, or will only become evident after many years of knowing the person, or when the person is placed in extra-ordinary circumstances. They say adversity brings out the best in a person, but by the same vein, it may well also reveal their true colours.

Now, it's important to appreciate that BaZi does not totally remove the surprise factor in life. It is not the case that just because you have seen someone's BaZi chart, that all bets are off. Even if we have analysed someone's character using BaZi and thus understand and have significant insight into their character, it is still possible for that person to surprise us with their actions. BaZi is after all, only 33% of the equation – recall the Cosmic Trinity discussed in *The Destiny Code*. And rarely are we able to analyse a BaZi, be it of a person that we know or don't know from Adam, with total honesty or absolute impartiality. Our personal biases and prejudices, views and thoughts, will always colour the interpretation slightly, thus allowing for that window of 'surprise'.

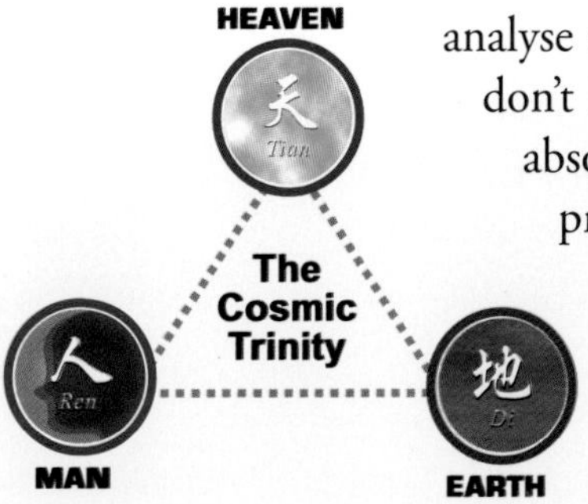

But, the advantage between being able to utilise BaZi and not being able to utilise BaZi lies in the ability to understand the motivations or the reason behind the surprises in life from the people around us who matter. In other words, we might still be surprised but there will definitely be fewer surprises. And we are less likely to be puzzled and surprised. Or disappointed and surprised. Or hurt and surprised.

We will never ever completely know a person. But that doesn't mean that there's no advantage to be conveyed by knowing and understanding them better, and with more depth, or to be able to seize up someone's character more quickly and speedily.

Facets of Character

In BaZi, a person's character can be loosely divided into two distinct facets: **External Character** and **Internal Character**. External Character is the classic first impression – it is what we judge a person's character to be upon first meeting them or it is what is termed 'the public face'. This is the impression that they may choose to give off. This first impression can sometimes be a reflection the person's Internal Character as well but it can also just be a superficial first impression, a veneer if you like that disguises the person's actual character.

Internal Character by contrast is what the person reveals themselves to be in private or to those who they are comfortable and familiar with. Internal Character can also be said to be the person's actual and inherent character, their true colours as it were.

It is possible to know a person for a long time and yet to find that what you have known all the while is only the External Character and not the Internal Character. Equally, it is possible in a very short period of time to ascertain a person's actual character quickly – in other words, that first impression was the Real McCoy. In such instances, the person is, as they say in Internet jargon, WYSIWYG – What You See is What You Get.

*In BaZi, a person's character can be loosely divided into two distinct facets: **External Character** and **Internal Character**.*

In BaZi, External Character is derived from the 10 Gods that are present in the Heavenly Stems of the chart only. The Heavenly Stems are sometimes referred to as 'Surface Qi' in the study of BaZi. Elements that appear in the Heavenly Stems (excepting the Day Master) are regarded as being of superficial or modest significance only. In other words, they don't carry much weight and are all about appearances only. Hence, the Heavenly Stems are regarded as offering up insight into a person's External Character, or the first impression of the person.

Internal Character is determined by the 10 Gods within the Hidden Stems of the Earthly Branches of a BaZi chart. Hidden Stems in the Earthly Branches have stronger Qi, and thus are regarded as being a truer representation of the person's character, as the energies in the Earthly Branches wield a greater influence in the chart.

It is said in the classics, [天干得三劫，不如地支一長生] which loosely translates to *one Growth Star in Branch is worth three in Stem.* This reflects the greater significance accorded to the elements (and by extension, the 10 Gods) that appear in the Earthly Branches, as opposed to those that appear in the Heavenly Stems.

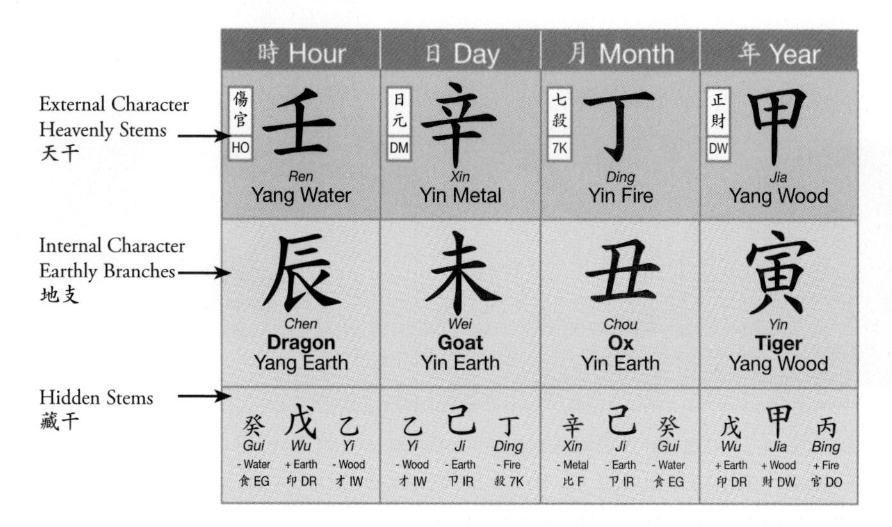

External Character
Heavenly Stems
天干
Internal Character
Earthly Branches
地支
Hidden Stems
藏干
時 Hour
日 Day
月 Month
年 Year
傷官 HO
壬
Ren
Yang Water
日元 DM
辛
Xin
Yin Metal
七殺 7K
丁
Ding
Yin Fire
正財 DW
甲
Jia
Yang Wood
辰
Chen
Dragon
Yang Earth
未
Wei
Goat
Yin Earth
丑
Chou
Ox
Yin Earth
寅
Yin
Tiger
Yang Wood
癸 Gui - Water 食 EG
戊 Wu + Earth 印 DR
乙 Yi - Wood 才 IW
乙 Yi - Wood 才 IW
己 Ji - Earth 卩 IR
丁 Ding - Fire 殺 7K
辛 Xin - Metal 比 F
己 Ji - Earth 卩 IR
癸 Gui - Water 食 EG
戊 Wu + Earth 印 DR
甲 Jia + Wood 財 DW
丙 Bing + Fire 官 DO

That being said, it is not the case that the Heavenly Stems should entirely be ignored from the equation either. The Heavenly Stems and Earthly Branches, viewed in unison, provide us with an accurate gauge of the person's Dominant Characteristics. Dominant Characteristics tell us what are the considerations or concerns or motivations or fears that primarily influence a person's thoughts and actions. Finally, building a portrait of a person's character is as much about knowing what makes up their character, as what is absent from their character, by looking at which 10 Gods are not present in the entire BaZi chart. Thus, whilst it is the case that the Earthly Branches represent Internal Character, the crux of a person's character, the innate and true self of a person, can only be derived from a 360-degree perspective of the chart, looking at the Stems and Branches in both isolation and unison.

Character Analysis Techniques: The Story So Far

In both the *Destiny Code* and the *Destiny Code Revealed*, I shared with you some simple ways to analyse Character using the elementary aspects of BaZi. In *Destiny Code* and the *Destiny Code Revealed*, we explored the 10 Day Masters and the integral characteristics that define each of the 10 Day Masters. From the information about the individual Day Masters alone, you would already have a little bit of insight into a person's character. *The Destiny Code Revealed* then explored the interactions (Clash, Combination, Harm, Punishment, Destructions) that maybe present in a given BaZi chart. Some of these interactions also provide insight into a person's character. Punishments for example, tend to make the person pessimistic or have a negative outlook on life and the people around them, especially the Ungrateful Punishment and Bullying Punishment.

Whilst the Day Master undoubtedly is of great value in giving us a snapshot of a person's character, in order to truly know and understand a person and their character, we must look at what the other 3 other Stems and 4 Branches in their BaZi chart reveal. The study of character, much like BaZi itself, is about subtleties, shades and layers, which can only come to light through the 10 Gods.

However, knowing and understanding a person's character is not as simple as looking at the 10 Gods that are present in a person's chart, and then listing the person's character attributes accordingly. Whilst that is a valuable start to the process of understanding a person's character and does yield some important information about the person's character, it is not the way to gain true insight into a person's character. Instead, using the 10 Gods to gain a deeper understanding of a person involves analysing the 10 Gods both individually in a chart, and analysing their collective presence within a given BaZi chart.

The analysis methods that will be shared with you here will endeavour to show you how to derive insight and understanding into a person's character by looking at the 10 Gods in unison as well as individually.

To make it easy to understand the techniques and also to provide some form of structure to the analysis, a question-based approach has been used here. We will start with analysis methods that look at the big picture, before examining the components of the chart in isolation.

Are you a simple person or a complex person?

As I have oft-stated in the *Destiny Code* and *The Destiny Code Revealed*, BaZi is never a numbers game. It isn't about how many elements you have in your chart, so much as what you have, and more importantly, the quality of the elements present in your chart and how well the Day Master is able to utilises the elements present in the chart. So when we are looking at the 10 Gods that are present in the chart, it is not as simple as having ALL the 10 Gods being the ideal and any chart with a few 10 Gods automatically relegated is as unfavourable or inferior.

That being said, the number of 10 Gods present in a chart can give us an important inkling about the person's character and by extension, their outlook in life, specifically, whether they are complex or simple individuals.

Charts where all 10 Gods are present or who have most of the 10 Gods (most here being 7-8 out of the 10) tend to have more complex and more layered personalities. They can be harder to understand or comprehend because they are multi-faceted individuals and their outlook is shaped by a number of considerations of varying significance depending on which characteristics dominate the chart.

時 Hour	日 Day	月 Month	年 Year	
偏印 IR 丙 Bing Yang Fire	日元 DM 戊 Wu Yang Earth	正印 DR 丁 Ding Yin Fire	比肩 F 戊 Wu Yang Earth	天干 Heavenly Stems
辰 Chen **Dragon** Yang Earth	戌 Xu **Dog** Yang Earth	巳 Si **Snake** Yin Fire	寅 Yin **Tiger** Yang Wood	地支 Earthly Branches
癸 Gui - Water 財 DW; 戊 Wu + Earth 比 F; 乙 Yi - Wood 官 DO	丁 Ding - Fire 印 DR; 戊 Wu + Earth 比 F; 辛 Xin - Metal 傷 HO	庚 Geng + Metal 食 EG; 丙 Bing + Fire 卩 IR; 戊 Wu + Earth 比 F	戊 Wu + Earth 比 F; 甲 Jia + Wood 殺 7K; 丙 Bing + Fire 卩 IR	藏干 Hidden Stems

This Wu Earth chart contains 8 out of 10 of the 10 Gods. As you can see from the chart, the Heavenly Stems show the presence of the Direct and Indirect Resource Stars and the Friend Star. In the Earthly Branches (including the Sub-Qi), we find the Direct Officer Star, Direct Wealth Star, Hurting Officer Star, Eating God Star, and the 7 Killings Star. As such it is clear that this chart belongs to an individual who is a more complex character, someone who has a personality that has many facets. Many matters shape this person's perspective of the world and as such, this person will not have a simplistic outlook on the world or be driven by just one or two emotions or motives or priorities in life.

Emotions? Motives? Priorities?

By contrast, charts which have a small number of 10 Gods (anywhere between 2-6) tend to indicate individuals with a more simplistic outlook in life. Their lives revolve around a smaller number of issues or considerations or emotions, their priorities are tightly restricted to few concerns and their mindset and perception of the world tends to be more absolute. Charts that have a small number of 10 Gods in them tend to usually denote individuals who have a more black and white outlook on the world.

時 Hour	日 Day	月 Month	年 Year	
比肩 F 辛 Xin Yin Metal	日元 DM 辛 Xin Yin Metal	比肩 F 辛 Xin Yin Metal	比肩 F 辛 Xin Yin Metal	天干 Heavenly Stems
卯 Mao Rabbit Yin Wood	卯 Mao Rabbit Yin Wood	卯 Mao Rabbit Yin Wood	卯 Mao Rabbit Yin Wood	地支 Earthly Branches
乙 Yi - Wood 才 IW	乙 Yi - Wood 才 IW	乙 Yi - Wood 才 IW	乙 Yi - Wood 才 IW	藏干 Hidden Stems

This Xin Metal chart is a rare illustration of a chart with only 2 of the 10 Gods present. Here, the chart only contains the Friend Star and the Indirect Wealth Star, represented by Yi Wood contained in the Rabbit (Mao). Hence, the person's character (and accordingly, outlook in life) can be summed up as being all about making money and taking care of their own needs since this is what the Indirect Wealth and Friend Stars represent. Accordingly, person will see everything in life through the prism of money and self.

What do Stems and Branches Reveal?

In this section, we will look at what information and insight about a person's character is revealed by analysing the Stems and Branches in the chart in isolation.

What do the Heavenly Stems reveal to be your External Character?

The elements that appear in the Stem are termed 'Surface Qi'. Thus the 10 Gods that appear in the Heavenly Stems and the characteristics they carry represent a person's External Character or the impression we get of someone when we first meet them.

For example Rob Wealth Star and the Hurting Officer Star both make a person extroverted in nature, amongst other things. Thus, if either the Rob Wealth Star or the Hurting Officer Star are present in the Heavenly Stems of an individual's BaZi chart, as in the examples below, then when we first meet this person, we will walk away with the impression that the person is an extroverted individual.

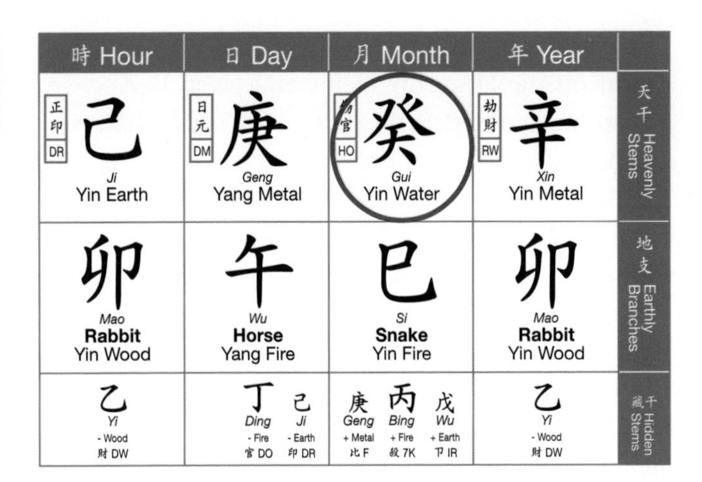

時 Hour	日 Day	月 Month	年 Year	
正印 DR 己 Ji Yin Earth	日元 DM 庚 Geng Yang Metal	傷官 HO 癸 Gui Yin Water	劫財 RW 辛 Xin Yin Metal	天干 Heavenly Stems
卯 Mao **Rabbit** Yin Wood	午 Wu **Horse** Yang Fire	巳 Si **Snake** Yin Fire	卯 Mao **Rabbit** Yin Wood	地支 Earthly Branches
乙 Yi - Wood 財 DW	丁 Ding - Fire 官 DO; 己 Ji - Earth 印 DR	庚 Geng + Metal 比 F; 丙 Bing + Fire 殺 7K; 戊 Wu + Earth 卩 IR	乙 Yi - Wood 財 DW	藏干 Hidden Stems

In this Geng Metal chart, the Hurting Officer Star, represented by Gui Water, appears only in the Month Stem.

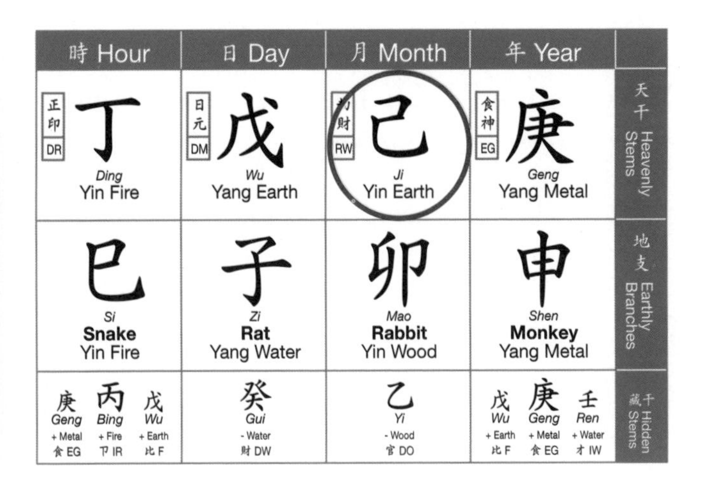

時 Hour	日 Day	月 Month	年 Year	
正印 DR 丁 Ding Yin Fire	日元 DM 戊 Wu Yang Earth	劫財 RW 己 Ji Yin Earth	食神 EG 庚 Geng Yang Metal	天干 Heavenly Stems
巳 Si **Snake** Yin Fire	子 Zi **Rat** Yang Water	卯 Mao **Rabbit** Yin Wood	申 Shen **Monkey** Yang Metal	地支 Earthly Branches
庚 Geng + Metal 食 EG; 丙 Bing + Fire 卩 IR; 戊 Wu + Earth 比 F	癸 Gui - Water 財 DW	乙 Yi - Wood 官 DO	戊 Wu + Earth 比 F; 庚 Geng + Metal 食 EG; 壬 Ren + Water 才 IW	藏干 Hidden Stems

In this Wu Earth chart, the Rob Wealth Star, represented by Ji Earth, appears only in the Month Stem.

The characteristics associated with the 10 Gods that appear on the Heavenly Stems of a given BaZi chart may or may not reflect the person's Internal Character. If a particular 10 God only appears in the Heavenly Stems, but is not reflected in the Hidden Stems of the Earthly Branches, then the characteristics associated with that 10 God are fleeting or superficial only.

Thus, if the Rob Wealth Star or Hurting Officer Star only appears in the Heavenly Stems, but do not appear in the Hidden Stems of the Earthly Branches, then the person is only superficially extroverted or only appears to be that way initially. Upon better getting to know the individual, they will not exhibit extroverted qualities.

What do the Earthly Branches reveal to be your Internal Character?

The elements that appear in the Earthly Branches are regarded as having more lasting and sustained Qi. Accordingly, the 10 Gods that appear in the Hidden Stems of the Earthly Branches (including the Sub-Qi) represent the true bedrock of a person's character. The characteristics carried by the 10 Gods that are present in the Hidden Stems of the Earthly Branches carry represent a person's Internal Character or character that becomes evident only when we get to know them or after a long period of interaction with the individual.

For example, the Direct Wealth Star amongst other things, indicates a hard-working, industrious and practical individual. If this Star only appears in the Earthly Branches of a BaZi chart (by extension, does not appear in any of the Heavenly Stems), then the person's industrious, hardworking and practical character will not be apparent on first meeting them or even upon the initial encounter. It is only after getting to know the person or perhaps working together with them, that their industrious, hard-working and practical manner becomes evident.

時 Hour	日 Day	月 Month	年 Year	
正印 DR 庚 Geng Yang Metal	日元 DM 癸 Gui Yin Water	食神 EG 乙 Yi Yin Wood	比肩 F 癸 Gui Yin Water	天干 Heavenly Stems
申 Shen **Monkey** Yang Metal	酉 You **Rooster** Yin Metal	丑 Chou **Ox** Yin Earth	巳 Si **Snake** Yin Fire	地支 Earthly Branches
戊 Wu + Earth 官 DO; 庚 Geng + Metal 印 DR; 壬 Ren + Water 劫 RW	辛 Xin - Metal 卩 IR	辛 Xin - Metal 卩 IR; 己 Ji - Earth 殺 7K; 癸 Gui - Water 比 F	庚 Geng + Metal 印 DR; 丙 Bing + Fire 財 DW; 戊 Wu + Earth 官 DO	藏干 Hidden Stems

In this Gui Water chart, the Direct Wealth Star, represented by Bing Fire, appears only in the Snake (Si) Earthly Branch, located in the Year Pillar. Thus, the qualities associated with the Direct Wealth Star will not be apparent upon first impression, but only become evident after getting to know the person or collaborating with them closely.

In addition to a person's Internal Character, the 10 Gods in the Earthly Branches may also indicate character traits which a person may themselves not be aware or conscious they possess. Typically, these are represented by 10 Gods that are located within the Sub-Qi of an Earthly Branch, particularly the Graveyard Branches.

時 Hour	日 Day	月 Month	年 Year	
傷官 HO 己 Ji Yin Earth	日元 DM 丙 Bing Yang Fire	偏印 IR 甲 Jia Yang Wood	偏印 IR 甲 Jia Yang Wood	天干 Heavenly Stems
亥 Hai **Pig** Yin Water	午 Wu **Horse** Yang Fire	戌 Xu **Dog** Yang Earth	辰 Chen **Dragon** Yang Earth	地支 Earthly Branches
壬 Ren + Water 殺 7K; 甲 Jia + Wood 卩 IR	丁 Ding - Fire 劫 RW; 己 Ji - Earth 傷 HO	丁 Ding - Fire 劫 RW; 戊 Wu + Earth 食 EG; 辛 Xin - Metal 財 DW	癸 Gui - Water 官 DO; 戊 Wu + Earth 食 EG; 乙 Yi - Wood 印 DR	藏干 Hidden Stems

In this Bing Fire chart, the Direct Wealth Star, represented by Xin Metal, appears only in the Sub-Qi of the Dog (Xu) Earthly Branch. Here, the person may not be aware that they possess the traits and qualities associated with the Direct Wealth Star as the element that represents the Star, which is Xin Metal, is buried deep inside the Sub-Qi of the Dog (Xu) Earthly Branch.

Packaging vs Substance

A good way to understand the difference between Stems and Branches is to look at it in the context of packaging and substance. The 10 Gods found in the Heavenly Stems essentially represent the person's packaging – how they present themselves, what they appear to be, what they project to the world, their External Character. What is found in the Earthly Branches on the other hand, represent the substance of the person, what is inherent within them, the Real McCoy, their Internal Character.

For example, the Eating God and Hurting Officer Stars both denote creative abilities and talents such as writing, painting, drawing, design, singing, song-writing, speaking and performance skills. These two Stars also mark a person out as an innovative problem-solver. However, if these two Stars only appear in the Stem but not the Branches, then the person only appears highly creative but is in reality, not much of an out-of-the-box thinker. Equally, if these two Stars only appear in the Branches but not in the Stems, then the person might be a creative or artistic genius, but guess what – no one readily sees these talents (they do appear eventually) but the person loses out on opportunities because no one immediately perceives their incredible creative skills and talents. They are people who are waiting to be discovered as it were.

時 Hour	日 Day	月 Month	年 Year	
正官 DO 庚 *Geng* Yang Metal	日元 DM 乙 *Yi* Yin Wood	偏印 IR 癸 *Gui* Yin Water	七殺 7K 辛 *Xin* Yin Metal	天干 Heavenly Stems
辰 *Chen* **Dragon** Yang Earth	卯 *Mao* **Rabbit** Yin Wood	巳 *Si* **Snake** Yin Fire	卯 *Mao* **Rabbit** Yin Wood	地支 Earthly Branches
癸 *Gui* - Water 卩 IR; 戊 *Wu* + Earth 財 DW; 乙 *Yi* - Wood 比 F	乙 *Yi* - Wood 比 F	庚 *Geng* + Metal 官 DO; 丙 *Bing* + Fire 傷 HO; 戊 *Wu* + Earth 財 DW	乙 *Yi* - Wood 比 F	藏干 Hidden Stems

In this Yi Wood chart, the Hurting Officer Star, represented by Bing Fire, appears only in the Snake (Si) Earthly Branch, located in the Month Pillar. Thus this person's creative skills and talents will not be immediately apparent and will only become obvious when the person is given an opportunity to showcase their skills.

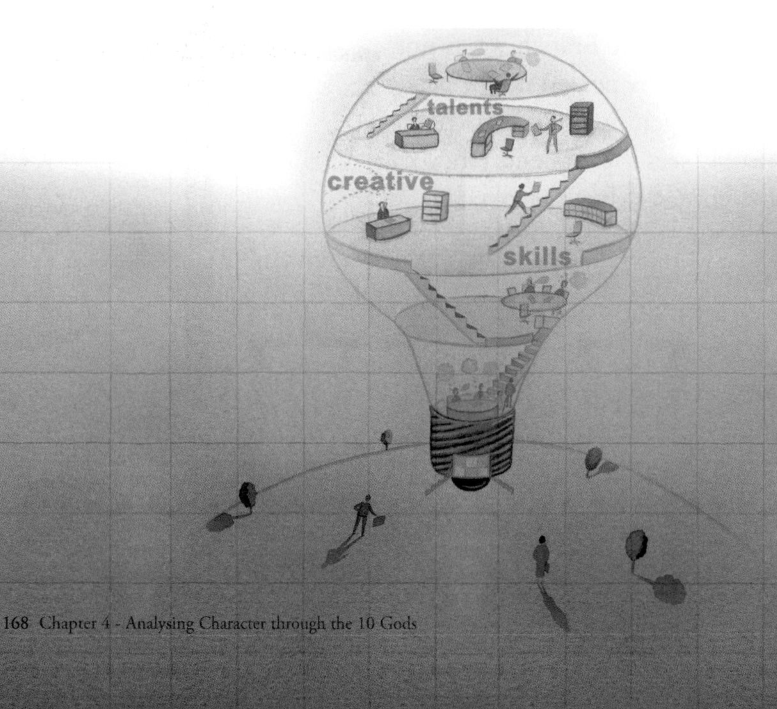

Now contrast the above example with the example below:

時 Hour	日 Day	月 Month	年 Year	
食神 EG 丁 *Ding* Yin Fire	日元 DM 乙 *Yi* Yin Wood	偏印 IR 癸 *Gui* Yin Water	偏財 IW 己 *Ji* Yin Earth	天干 Heavenly Stems
亥 *Hai* **Pig** Yin Water	丑 *Chou* **Ox** Yin Earth	酉 *You* **Rooster** Yin Metal	卯 *Mao* **Rabbit** Yin Wood	地支 Earthly Branches
壬 *Ren* + Water 印 DR; 甲 *Jia* + Wood 劫 RW	辛 *Xin* - Metal 殺 7K; 己 *Ji* - Earth 才 IW; 癸 *Gui* - Water 卩 IR	辛 *Xin* - Metal 殺 7K	乙 *Yi* - Wood 比 F	藏干 Hidden Stems

In this Yi Wood chart, the Eating God Star, represented by Ding Fire, appears only in the Heavenly Stems. Thus this person's creative skills and talents will be very evident to someone who meets them for the first time. But since the Star does not appear in the Earthly Branches, this denotes the person's creativity is superficial, or if we are to be generous, they are mildly creative.

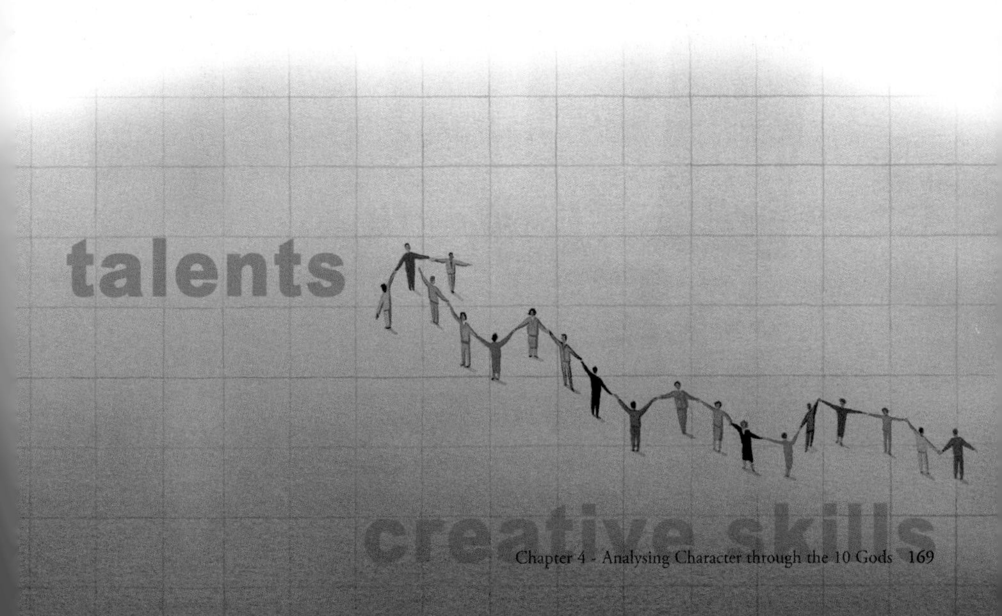

In the modern world, both packaging and substance are required to effectively succeed in life. Packaging is what makes people interested in you but to sustain that interest, you ultimately need substance. But all the substance in the world doesn't matter if you can't brand and market that substance in a meaningful and attractive manner – in short, the packaging. Innate traits and qualities of a positive nature are of no use if no one knows you possess them in the first place. Similarly, appearing to have certain positive attributes is of little value if you don't actually have these attributes in reality or these attributes lack substance.

Accordingly in BaZi, the Stems and the Branches need to be viewed not as separate and independent, but connected to each other. It is by looking at the connections between the Stems and Branches that we are able to discern an individual's Dominant Characteristics but also ascertain the trait that are absent in their character.

In the modern world, both packaging and substance are required to effectively succeed in life.

What do Stems and Branches viewed in unison Reveal?

Once we have determined a person's External and Internal Character, we must now build a coherent overall picture of the person's character, by deriving information about their Dominant Characteristics, and also by finding out what traits are missing from their character.

What are Dominant Characteristics?

Dominant Characteristics are essentially aspects of your character which are the most pronounced and most developed and form the central plank of your actions and thoughts. These are the traits and qualities which are present in the individual in both packaging and substance.

What is the difference between Dominant Characteristics and Internal Character? Internal Character (as indicated by the 10 Gods that are present in the Earthly Branches) refers to the traits and qualities that are at the heart of a person's character – the private face as it were. Internal Character is not always immediately evident upon the first encounter with a person.

Dominant Characteristics on the other hand, are traits and qualities which typically are present during the first impression and continue to be part of the lasting impression we have of an individual. Dominant Characteristics are evident in the person's public persona and private persona. It is the part of their character, the traits and abilities, and yes, the flaws and weaknesses, which the individual can't hide even if they tried. These are traits and qualities which someone meeting the person for the first time, and someone who has know the individual for 20 years, will both agree, form the central plank of the person's mindset, attitude and outlook on the world.

Dominant Characteristics are evident in the person's public persona and private persona.

How do you determine Dominant Characteristics?

The easiest way to determine a person's Dominant Characteristics is to identify which 10 Gods appear both in the Heavenly Stems and the Earthly Branches (including the Sub-Qi). For the more technical-minded readers, this is what is known as as 'rooting'.

The concept of Rooting is a very important one in BaZi and has an important impact on the question of the quality of an element and by extension, the 10 God represented by that element. 'Rooting' can manifest in many forms, with each different manner in which the element is rooted having an effect on the interpretation of the quality of that element. At this point and specifically in regard to the discussion on Dominant Characteristics, in order to keep things straightforward and uncomplicated, I have chosen to define the manner in which an element is rooted in a very strict manner. Readers however should be aware that there are many shades to the interpretation of the concept of rooting and this is a subject that we will

Roots

return to many times as we explore the 10 Gods in greater depth in subsequent *The Power of X* books.

For the purposes of the determination of Dominant Characteristics, an element and by extension the 10 God it represents, is regarded as rooted only if it appears in the following manner:

A) The element is rooted in the Main Qi or Sub Qi of the four Earthly Branches

B) The element on the Stem and its corresponding root must also be of the same polarity. In other words, Jia can only be rooted in Jia and not in Yi, Geng can only be rooted in Geng and not in Xin, and so on.

Examples:

時 Hour	日 Day	月 Month	年 Year	
正財 DW 甲 *Jia* Yang Wood	日元 DM 辛 *Xin* Yin Metal	正財 DW 甲 *Jia* Yang Wood	食神 EG 癸 *Gui* Yin Water	天干 Heavenly Stems
午 *Wu* **Horse** Yang Fire	巳 *Si* **Snake** Yin Fire	寅 *Yin* **Tiger** Yang Wood	卯 *Mao* **Rabbit** Yin Wood	地支 Earthly Branches
丁 *Ding* - Fire 殺 7K; 己 *Ji* - Earth 卩 IR	庚 *Geng* + Metal 劫 RW; 丙 *Bing* + Fire 官 DO; 戊 *Wu* + Earth 印 DR	戊 *Wu* + Earth 印 DR; 甲 *Jia* + Wood 財 DW; 丙 *Bing* + Fire 官 DO	乙 *Yi* - Wood 才 IW	藏干 Hidden Stems

Here, Jia Wood in the Month Stem is rooted in the Month Branch of Tiger (Yin) which has Jia Wood as its Main Qi.

時 Hour	日 Day	月 Month	年 Year	
食神 EG 己 Ji Yin Earth	日元 DM 丁 Ding Yin Fire	食神 EG 己 Ji Yin Earth	正印 DR 甲 Jia Yang Wood	天干 Heavenly Stems
酉 You Rooster Yin Metal	卯 Mao Rabbit Yin Wood	巳 Si Snake Yin Fire	午 Wu Horse Yang Fire	地支 Earthly Branches
辛 Xin - Metal 才 IW	乙 Yi - Wood 卩 IR	庚 Geng + Metal 財 DW; 丙 Bing + Fire 劫 RW; 戊 Wu + Earth 傷 HO	丁 Ding - Fire 比 F; 己 Ji Earth 食 EG	藏干 Hidden Stems

Here, Ji Earth in the Month Stem is rooted in the Year Branch of Horse (Wu) which has Ji Earth as its Sub-Qi.

時 Hour	日 Day	月 Month	年 Year	
正財 DW 丙 Bing Yang Fire	日元 DM 癸 Gui Yin Water	正官 DO 戊 Wu Yang Earth	劫財 RW 壬 Ren Yang Water	天干 Heavenly Stems
辰 Chen Dragon Yang Earth	酉 You Rooster Yin Metal	申 Shen Monkey Yang Metal	戌 Xu Dog Yang Earth	地支 Earthly Branches
癸 Gui - Water 比 F; 戊 Wu + Earth 官 DO; 乙 Yi - Wood 食 EG	辛 Xin - Metal 卩 IR	戊 Wu + Earth 官 DO; 庚 Geng + Metal 印 DR; 壬 Ren + Water 劫 RW	丁 Ding - Fire 才 IW; 戊 Wu + Earth 官 DO; 辛 Xin - Metal 卩 IR	藏干 Hidden Stems

Ren Water in the Year Stem is rooted in the Month Branch of Monkey (Shen) which has Ren Water as its Sub-Qi.

時 Hour	日 Day	月 Month	年 Year	
正官 DO 丁 *Ding* Yin Fire	日元 DM 庚 *Geng* Yang Metal	七殺 7K 丙 *Bing* Yang Fire	正財 DW 乙 *Yi* Yin Wood	天干 Heavenly Stems
亥 *Hai* **Pig** Yin Water	戌 *Xu* **Dog** Yang Earth	戌 *Xu* **Dog** Yang Earth	卯 *Mao* **Rabbit** Yin Wood	地支 Earthly Branches
壬 *Ren* + Water 食 EG; 甲 *Jia* + Wood 才 IW	丁 *Ding* - Fire 官 DO; 戊 *Wu* + Earth 卩 IR; 辛 *Xin* - Metal 劫 RW	丁 *Ding* - Fire 官 DO; 戊 *Wu* + Earth 卩 IR; 辛 *Xin* - Metal 劫 RW	乙 *Yi* - Wood 財 DW	藏干 Hidden Stems

Here, Ding Fire in the Hour Stem is rooted in the Day Branch of Dog (Xu) which has Ding Fire as its Sub-Qi. Bing Fire here would not be regarded as 'rooted' within a strict interpretation because there is no Bing Fire present in any of the Earthly Branches, including the Sub-Qi.

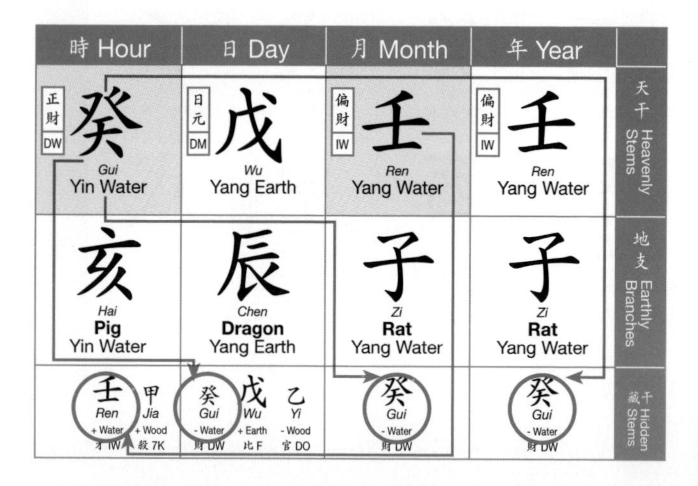

Here, Ren Water is rooted in Pig (Hai) located in the Hour Branch and Gui Water in the Hour Stem is Rooted in the Dragon (Chen) which contains Gui as part of its Sub-Qi and also rooted in the Rat (Zi) located in the Year and Month Branches.

Recall that we are using a 'strict' interpretation of rooting for the purposes of this discussion. A liberal interpretation of rooting would, for example, allow for rooting as long as the element on the Stem and Branch is the same element, irrespective of polarity. In such a liberal interpretation, Ren could claim roots in Gui or Ji could claim roots in Horse (Wu).

We will come back to the issue of rooting, and explore the implications of liberal vs strict interpretations and the instances where liberal interpretations can be used subsequently. We will also look at how rooting in the Main Qi vs the Sub-Qi produces a distinctly different effect and outcome. For now, adopt a 'strict' interpretation of rooting for the purposes of determining Dominant Characteristics.

When a particular 10 God appears in both the Heavenly Stems and the Earthly Branches (including the Sub-Qi), this means the characteristics associated with that 10 God are extremely prominent, evident and apparent. The traits and qualities associated with that 10 God will dominate the person's thinking, perceptions, attitude, mindset and actions. Hence the term 'Dominant Characeteristics'.

When we identify a person's Dominant Characteristics, the question of whether these characteristics are positive or negative in nature do not come into the equation. The focus is identifying the characteristics (ie: introverted, extroverted, passive, aggressive, thinkers or do-ers) rather than judging the person.

These examples illustrate how to identify Dominant Characteristics and define the Dominant Characteristics.

時 Hour	日 Day	月 Month	年 Year	
正印 DR 丁 Ding Yin Fire	日元 DM 戊 Wu Yang Earth	劫財 RW 己 Ji Yin Earth	食神 EG 庚 Geng Yang Metal	天干 Heavenly Stems
巳 Si Snake Yin Fire	子 Zi Rat Yang Water	卯 Mao Rabbit Yin Wood	申 Shen Monkey Yang Metal	地支 Earthly Branches
庚 Geng + Metal 食 EG; 丙 Bing + Fire 卩 IR; 戊 Wu + Earth 比 F	癸 Gui - Water 財 DW	乙 Yi - Wood 官 DO	戊 Wu + Earth 比 F; 庚 Geng + Metal 食 EG; 壬 Ren + Water 才 IW	藏干 Hidden Stems

This is the chart of a Wu Earth Day Master. In the Heavenly Stems, we have the Eating God Star, Rob Wealth Star and Direct Resource Star. In the Earthly

Branches, the Monkey (Shen) contains the Eating God Star, with the Direct Wealth Star and Friend Star in the Sub-Qi, the Rabbit (Mao) contains the Direct Officer Star alone, the Rat (Zi) contains the Direct Wealth Star and finally, the Snake (Si) contains the Indirect Resource Star, along with the Eating God Star and the Friend Star.

In this chart, only one of 10 Gods appears in both the Heavenly Stems and the Earthly Branches, namely, the Eating God Star, as represented by Geng Metal. The Eating God Star denotes, amongst other things, an introverted personality, a strategic thinker, a highly-creative, out of the box thinker, mildly eccentric personality and someone who prefers to be behind the scenes rather than in the limelight. Thus, the qualities and characteristics associated with the Eating God Star represent this individual's Dominant Characteristics. Although the Day Master, Wu Earth, is rooted Monkey (Shen) as well, we do not interpret the Friend Star to be accordingly rooted because the Day Master does not constitute one of the 10 Gods that appears on the Stem.

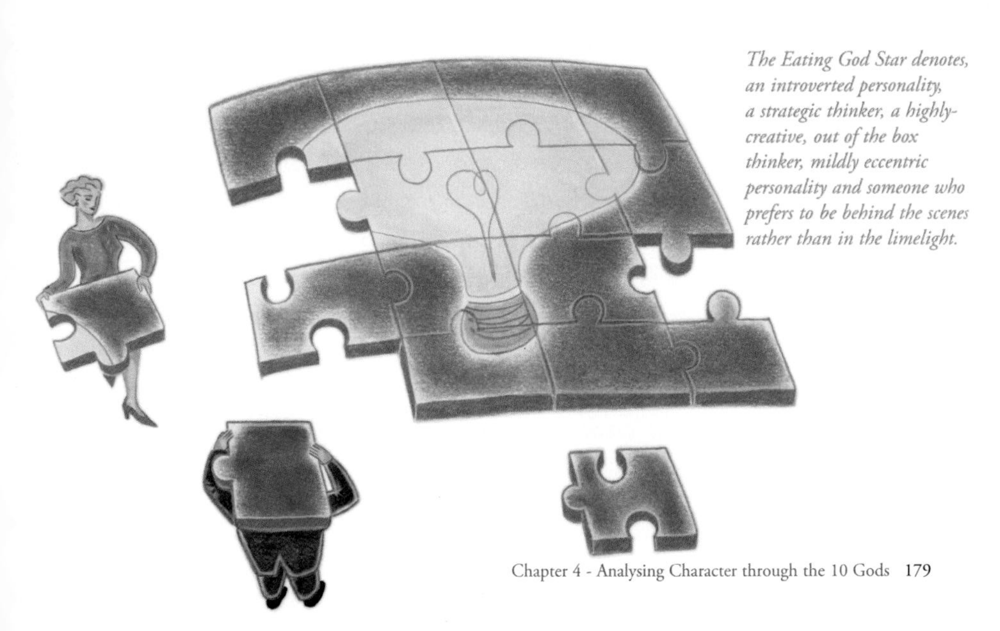

The Eating God Star denotes, an introverted personality, a strategic thinker, a highly-creative, out of the box thinker, mildly eccentric personality and someone who prefers to be behind the scenes rather than in the limelight.

It is possible for a person to have more than one set of Dominant Characteristics, as this example shows.

	時 Hour	日 Day	月 Month	年 Year
天干 Heavenly Stems	偏印 IR 己 *Ji* Yin Earth	日元 DM 辛 *Xin* Yin Metal	正財 DW 甲 *Jia* Yang Wood	食神 EG 癸 *Gui* Yin Water
地支 Earthly Branches	丑 *Chou* **Ox** Yin Earth	酉 *You* **Rooster** Yin Metal	子 *Zi* **Rat** Yang Water	亥 *Hai* **Pig** Yin Water
藏干 Hidden Stems	辛 *Xin* - Metal 比 F 己 *Ji* - Earth 卩 IR 癸 *Gui* - Water 食 EG	辛 *Xin* - Metal 比 F	癸 *Gui* - Water 食 EG	壬 *Ren* + Water 傷 HO 甲 *Jia* + Wood 財 DW

This is the chart of a Xin Metal Day Master. In the Heavenly Stems, we have the Eating God Star, Direct Wealth Star and Indirect Resource Star. In the Earthly Branches, the Pig (Hai) contains the Hurting Officer Star and Direct Wealth Star, the Rat (Zi) contains the Eating God Star alone, the Rooster (You) contains the Friend Star and finally, the Ox contains the Indirect Resource Star, along with the Eating God Star and the Friend Star.

In this chart, three 10 Gods present appear in both the Heavenly Stems and the Earthly Branches, namely, the Direct Wealth Star (Jia Wood), the Eating God Star and the Indirect Resource Star (Ji Earth). The Direct Wealth Star denotes an industrious attitude, an upright, practical and down to earth attitude to life. The Indirect Resource Star represents eccentricity, an imaginative mind, a tendency towards shortcuts and a person who has great intuition. The Eating God Star indicates a person who is introverted in nature, a strategic thinker, someone who has a long-term outlook, and a person who appreciates luxury and the finer things in life. So we can say that these characteristics, and the other traits and abilities associated with the the Direct Wealth Star, Eating God Star and Indirect Resource Star, represent this individual's Dominant Characteristics.

Determining the Absent Characteristics

It is rare to find a chart that contains all of the 10 Gods. Where there is a particular 10 God absent from the chart (and it is theoretically possible for up to 8 of the 10 Gods to be absent from a given BaZi chart), this is also very telling because it reveals the characteristics and traits that are **absent** from a person's character. Knowing what a person is NOT, is just as important as knowing what they ARE, which is why being able to discern the characteristics and traits that are absent from a person character is important.

For example, if a person's chart contains the Direct Wealth Star, but does not contain the Indirect Wealth Star, then we know that the characteristics and traits associated with the Indirect Wealth Star are not present in the person.

They will **not** be naturally entrepreneurial or business-minded, they won't have the free-wheeling, hustling, deal-maker tendency that typifies the entrepreneur, and they will lack the opportunistic eye conveyed by the Indirect Wealth Star. On the other hand, if the person's chart contains the Indirect Wealth Star only, but does not contain the Direct Wealth Star, then you have a slightly different scenario. The person will lack the practical, frugal character imbued by the Direct Wealth Star. The person will be rather shortcut driven (since Indirect Wealth is all about getting rich fast, maximum upside, minimum effort) and will be fiscally irresponsible. They will also have lack a careful, methodical approach to their work, since the Indirect Wealth Star's style is to do things quickly but not necessarily thoroughly.

You can also combine the information about what they ARE, with what they are NOT, to gain some extra insight into the person's character or to reinforce certain conclusions. The absence of a particular 10 God can sometimes amplify the effects of a particular10 God that is already present in the chart or it can result in a particular gap in the person's character becoming more apparent.

Indirect Wealth is all about getting rich fast, maximum upside, minimum effort

For example, if a person lacks the Direct Officer Star, and has the Indirect Resource Star and/or 7 Killings Star as their Dominant Characteristics, then not only is the person unlikely to follow the rules or be a principled, upright character, but they are MORE LIKELY to break the rules or go with shortcuts in order to get things done, even if those shortcuts are a little illegal or even very illegal! If for example, a person has the Eating God Star in their chart, and have the Indirect Resource Star as a Dominant Characteristic, and there is no Hurting Officer Star in the chart, then the introverted and loner traits of the Eating God and Indirect Resource Stars become amplified.

In the examples found in the subsequent section, I will allude to this approach periodically to show you how to combine information about absent 10 Gods and existing 10 Gods can be used to develop a clearer picture of the person. This is a little trickier to do and requires some left brain and right brain cooperation as well as an ability to connect the dots. Sometimes, the conclusions that are derived from this analysis technique are subtle insights but in some instances, they can also bring to fore glaring character deficiencies. For this reason, this technique requires a great deal of practice and experience and also, a good understanding of human psychology.

Figuring out the nexus between the 10 Gods that are present and absent certainly isn't something that you might want to try early in the process of analysing charts but something to give thought to as you advance through different charts.

Basic 10 Gods Character Analysis

Let's take a look at how to undertake a simple character analysis, using the techniques that have been explained in this Chapter.

In undertaking the analysis, we are trying to ascertain answers to the following questions:

- Is the person a complex person or a simple person?
- What is the first impression the person gives?
- What are their superficial qualities?
- What are their true inclinations?
- What are their innate inherent qualities?
- What are the characteristics and traits they DO NOT possess?
- What characteristics drive their actions/ thoughts/perceptions/attitudes?

In each of these examples, you will find there are some different methods being put into play, aside from the basic techniques that have been shared with you in this Chapter. These have been included to give you a broader perspective on character analysis and to expose you to some more advanced approaches to analysing character.

時 Hour	日 Day	月 Month	年 Year	
偏印 IR 己 *Ji* Yin Earth	日元 DM 辛 *Xin* Yin Metal	偏印 IR 己 *Ji* Yin Earth	七殺 7K 丁 *Ding* Yin Fire	天干 Heavenly Stems
亥 *Hai* **Pig** Yin Water	丑 *Chou* **Ox** Yin Earth	酉 *You* **Rooster** Yin Metal	酉 *You* **Rooster** Yin Metal	地支 Earthly Branches
壬 *Ren* + Water 傷 HO; 甲 *Jia* + Wood 財 DW	辛 *Xin* - Metal 比 F; 己 *Ji* - Earth 卩 IR; 癸 *Gui* - Water 食 EG	辛 *Xin* - Metal 比 F	辛 *Xin* - Metal 比 F	藏干 Hidden Stems

This is the chart of a Xin Metal Day Master. In the Heavenly Stems, the following 10 Gods are present: the 7 Killings Star and the Indirect Resource Star. In the Earthly Branches, the following 10 Gods are present in the Main Qi of the Four Earthly Branches: the Friend Star in the double Rooster (You), the Indirect Resource Star in the Ox (Chou) and the Hurting Officer Star in the Pig (Hai).

This table affords an at-a-glance look at the 10 Gods in this chart:

Hurting Officer Star	√
Eating God Star	√
Direct Wealth Star	√
Indirect Wealth Star	
Direct Officer Star	
7 Killings Star	√
Direct Resource Star	
Indirect Resource Star	√
Rob Wealth Star	
Friend Star	√

This chart contains 6 of the 10 Gods – we have the Indirect Resource Star, the Hurting Officer Star, the Direct Wealth Star, the Friend Star, the Eating God Star and the 7 Killings Star. So the person's isn't someone for whom life is simple and straightforward, but neither are they an overly-complex individual either.

Let's look now at the Stems. The Indirect Resource Star indicates eccentric personality, a person of unusual ideas, and also indicates a very sensitive personality. The 7 Killings Star denotes aggressive behaviour, leadership skills, but also indicates an intimidating personality, and an aggressive character. So we can say, the first impression of this Xin Metal Day Master is someone who is a little eccentric, has an unorthodox way of thinking, but can come across as something of a ruffian, and if provoked can be aggressive (since sensitive people are prone to over-reacting). Notably, this person also seems very temperamental since inconsistent behaviour is one of the hallmarks of both the Indirect Resource Star and the 7 Killings Star.

But this may not be the person's actual character and personality – it may merely be the impression they put forth, when we first meet them. To get a grasp of the person's true character, we must look at the 10 Gods that are present in the Earthly Branches. The Friend Star denotes a strong sense of self, a selfish, self-centric outlook in life, and a tendency to define the world based on one's own values. It also indicates inherent self-confidence. The Indirect Resource Star denotes eccentric personality, unusual ideas, strange hobby horses, sensitivity and idealistic character. The Hurting Officer Star denotes a rebellious personality, someone who loves the limelight, a highly opinionated person, and an outgoing, extroverted individual.

So we can say, deep down inside or upon getting to know the person, we find that they are self-preservationist, a person who will take care of himself first and foremost, someone who is quietly self confident, a sensitive, eccentric, dreamy character, but who is also full of ideas and opinions, and is the outspoken type.

The Hurting Officer Star denotes a rebellious personality, someone who loves the limelight, a highly opinionated person, and an outgoing, extroverted individual.

Let us now add some sophistication to the interpretation. Only the 7 Killings Star appears in the Stem alone. This also tells us an important fact about this person's character – that any aggressiveness in the person's character, or leadership skills, or courageous personality, are purely superficial. In other words, this is a person whose bark is worse than his bite. It's not real bravado but guts that are just for show. Remember, elements that appear on the Heavenly Stems represent surface Qi that is superficial at best. Thus, the qualities (positive and negative) that are associated with the 7 Killings Star do not form a significant or dominant part of the person's character.

時 Hour	日 Day	月 Month	年 Year	
偏印 IR 己 *Ji* Yin Earth	日元 DM 辛 *Xin* Yin Metal	偏印 IR 己 *Ji* Yin Earth	七殺 7K 丁 *Ding* Yin Fire	天干 Heavenly Stems
亥 *Hai* **Pig** Yin Water	丑 *Chou* **Ox** Yin Earth	酉 *You* **Rooster** Yin Metal	酉 *You* **Rooster** Yin Metal	地支 Earthly Branches
壬 *Ren* + Water 傷 HO; 甲 *Jia* + Wood 財 DW	辛 *Xin* - Metal 比 F; 己 *Ji* Earth 卩 IR; 癸 *Gui* - Water 食 EG	辛 *Xin* - Metal 比 F	辛 *Xin* - Metal 比 F	藏干 Hidden Stems

The Friend Star and the Hurting Officer Star appear in the Branches alone. Qi in the Earthly Branches is significantly stronger than that found in the Stems, which means that upon closer inspection or in private and in the company of familiar people, this person is argumentative, opinionated, outspoken, maybe tactless even, and very stubborn. They will put themselves first above everyone else, and make decisions based on self-interest first and foremost.

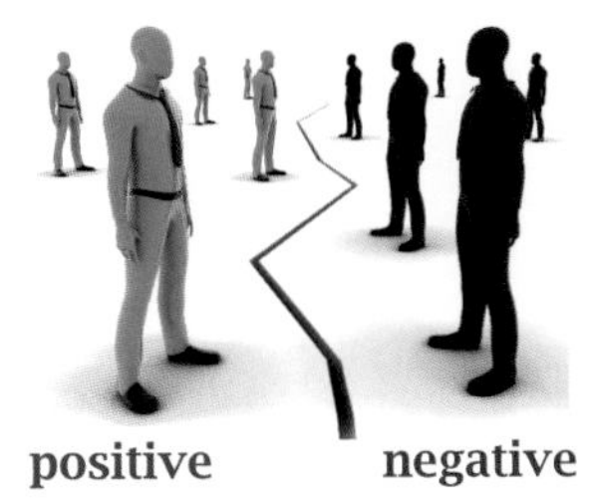

They have innate self-confidence, and a strong sense of their own values. The qualities (positive and negative) that are associated with the Friend and Hurting Officer Star will form a significant part of the person's character.

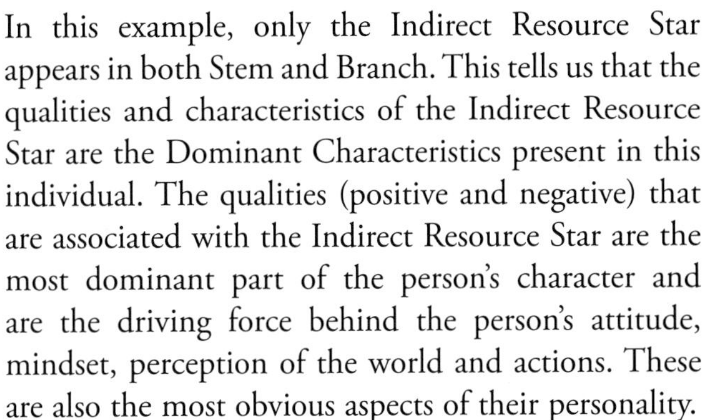

In this example, only the Indirect Resource Star appears in both Stem and Branch. This tells us that the qualities and characteristics of the Indirect Resource Star are the Dominant Characteristics present in this individual. The qualities (positive and negative) that are associated with the Indirect Resource Star are the most dominant part of the person's character and are the driving force behind the person's attitude, mindset, perception of the world and actions. These are also the most obvious aspects of their personality.

Finally – what's missing from the chart in terms of 10 Gods? The Direct Officer, Direct Resource, Indirect Wealth and Rob Wealth Stars are not present in this chart. Accordingly, all the characteristics and traits associated with these Stars will not be present in the person's character. The Direct Officer Star denotes an upstanding, honourable, upright and principled individual who is law-abiding and disciplined. The Rob Wealth Star denotes a spontaneous, witty character, who is very altruistic and happy to lucky, but also competitive. The Direct Resource Star denotes a learned cultured person, who is patient and good natured, civilised and well-behaved. Finally, the indirect Wealth Star denotes an entrepreneurial spirit, an opportunistic eye, a good negotiator/bargainer, and someone who is flamboyant and generous. All these qualities will NOT be present in this individual by and large.

時 Hour	日 Day	月 Month	年 Year	
傷官 HO 辛 *Xin* Yin Metal	日元 DM 戊 *Wu* Yang Earth	比肩 F 戊 *Wu* Yang Earth	七殺 7K 甲 *Jia* Yang Wood	天干 Heavenly Stems
酉 *You* **Rooster** Yin Metal	寅 *Yin* **Tiger** Yang Wood	辰 *Chen* **Dragon** Yang Earth	子 *Zi* **Rat** Yang Water	地支 Earthly Branches
辛 *Xin* - Metal 傷 HO	戊 *Wu* + Earth 比 F; 甲 *Jia* + Wood 殺 7K; 丙 *Bing* + Fire 卩 IR	癸 *Gui* - Water 財 DW; 戊 *Wu* + Earth 比 F; 乙 *Yi* - Wood 官 DO	癸 *Gui* - Water 財 DW	藏干 Hidden Stems

This is the chart of a Wu Earth Day Master. In the Heavenly Stems, the following 10 Gods are present: 7 Killings Star (Jia Wood), Friend Star (Wu Earth) and Hurting Officer Star (Xin Metal). In the Earthly Branches, the following 10 Gods are present in the Main Qi of the Four Earthly Branches: the Direct Wealth Star in Rat (Zi), the Friend Star in Dragon (Chen), the 7 Killings Star in Tiger (Yin) and the Hurting Officer Star in Rooster (You).

This table affords an at-a-glance look at the 10 Gods in this chart:

Hurting Officer Star	√
Eating God Star	
Direct Wealth Star	√
Indirect Wealth Star	
Direct Officer Star	√
7 Killings Star	√
Direct Resource Star	
Indirect Resource Star	√
Rob Wealth Star	
Friend Star	√

This chart also contains 6 of the 10 Gods – we have the Hurting Officer Star, the Direct Wealth Star, the Direct Officer Star, the 7 Killings Star, the Indirect Resource Star and the Friend Star. So the person's isn't someone for whom life is simple and straightforward, but neither are they an overly-complex individual either.

We start at the Stems, to determine the person's character upon first encounter. Here, the 7 Killings, Friend and Hurting Officer Starsz appear in the Stems. Accordingly, we can surmise that on first meeting, this person gives off the impression of being a very self-confident, certain person (Friend Star), is highly extroverted, opinionated and not afraid to say what's on their mind (Hurting Officer Star) and finally, is a go-getter, quite an aggressive personality, and someone who seems like a natural leader. But as we know, this might not be the person's actual character. So we must look at the 10 Gods present in the Earthly Branches to see what is true and what is merely packaging.

In the Branches (specifically only the Main Qi), we have the Direct Wealth Star, the Friend Star, the 7 Killings Star and the Hurting Officer Star. So upon better getting to know the person, we find that they are practical, hard-working, frugal and inherently sensible in nature, as a result of the Direct Wealth Star. The person is also very driven, aggressive, focused on success at all costs, and fearless, due to the 7 Killings Star. Finally, the Hurting Officer Star denotes an extroverted, strong-willed, argumentative and highly opinionated personality.

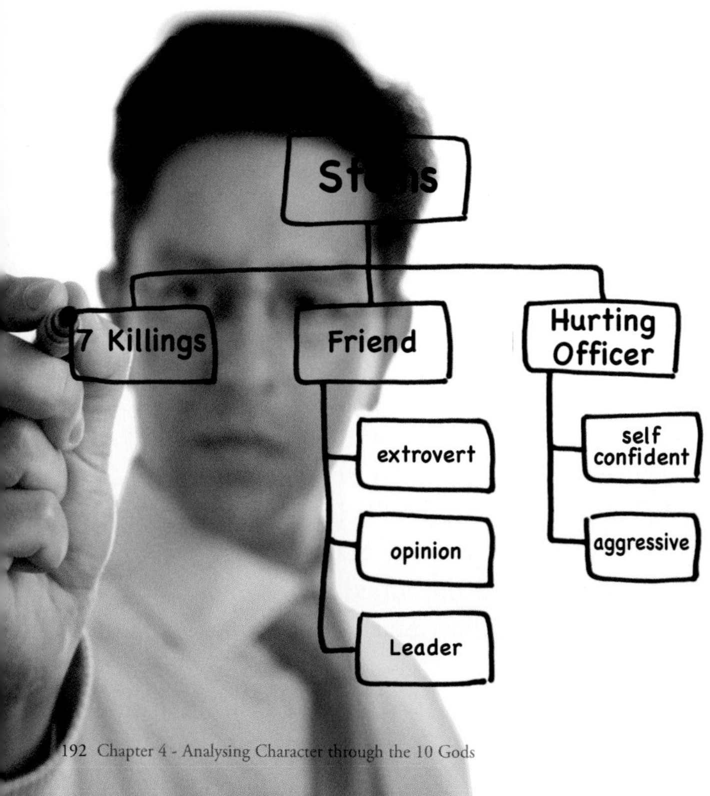

WYSIWYG
What You
See Is
What You
Get.

In this example, all three of the 10 Gods that appear on the Stem, are rooted in the Earthly Branches. So this person is someone who is really a case of WYSIWYG - *What You See Is What You Get*. The first impression you have of this person? That's the ONLY impression you'll get of them because they are who they say they are in every sense of the word. Whatever they seem to be in public, they are in private. Of course, there are additional characteristics that emerge when you get to know the person better, such as those associated with the Direct Wealth Star, which appears only in the Earthly Branches. But the main point is that this is a person who does not present a misleading or 'packaged' impression of themselves.

The qualities and characteristics of the Friend, 7 Killings and Hurting Officer Stars are the Dominant Characteristics present in this individual as these are the 10 Gods that are rooted in the chart. The qualities (positive and negative) that are associated with these Stars are a dominant part of the person's character and is the driving force behind the person's attitude, mindset, perception and actions.

The person will also exhibit a low level of patience as they lack the tolerant nature of the Direct Resource Star, and especially given the Hurting Officer Star is typically impatient, as is the 7 Killings Star.

To complete our analysis of this person's character, attention must be turned to the missing 10 Gods. There are 4 absent 10 Gods in this chart, namely, the Eating God, Indirect Wealth, Direct Resource and Rob Wealth Stars. Accordingly, this person is definitively not a gourmand or someone who will appreciate fine dining, nor are they particularly concerned with the finer things in life necessarily, due to the absence of the Eating God Star. They're also not likely to have a long-term outlook on matters, or adopt a strategic approach to doing things. The absence of the Rob Wealth Star denotes a person who doesn't make friends easily, although this tends to be common with Wu Earth Day Masters since Mountains tend to be solid and solitary (how often do you see two great mountains right next to each other?). The missing Direct Resource Star tells us that this is not a person who makes decisions based on facts and figures and that this person may come across as a bit uncouth or unrefined. The person will also exhibit a low level of patience as they lack the tolerant nature of the Direct Resource Star, and especially given the Hurting Officer Star is typically impatient, as is the 7 Killings Star.

時 Hour	日 Day	月 Month	年 Year	
正印 DR 癸 *Gui* Yin Water	日元 DM 甲 *Jia* Yang Wood	七殺 7K 庚 *Geng* Yang Metal	劫財 RW 乙 *Yi* Yin Wood	天干 Heavenly Stems
酉 *You* **Rooster** Yin Metal	子 *Zi* **Rat** Yang Water	辰 *Chen* **Dragon** Yang Earth	酉 *You* **Rooster** Yin Metal	地支 Earthly Branches
辛 *Xin* - Metal 官 DO	癸 *Gui* - Water 印 DR	癸 *Gui* - Water 印 DR; 戊 *Wu* + Earth 才 IW; 乙 *Yi* - Wood 劫 RW	辛 *Xin* - Metal 官 DO	藏干 Hidden Stems

This is the chart of a Jia Wood Day Master. In the Heavenly Stems, the following 10 Gods are present: Rob Wealth Star (Yi Wood), 7 Killings Star (Geng Metal), Direct Resource Star (Gui Water). In the Earthly Branches, the following 10 Gods are present in the Main Qi of the Four Earthly Branches: the Direct Officer Star in the two Roosters (You), the Indirect Wealth Star in the Dragon (Chen), the Direct Resource Star in the Rat (Zi).

This table affords an at-a-glance look at the 10 Gods in this chart:

Hurting Officer Star	
Eating God Star	
Direct Wealth Star	
Indirect Wealth Star	√
Direct Officer Star	√
7 Killings Star	√
Direct Resource Star	√
Indirect Resource Star	
Rob Wealth Star	√
Friend Star	

This chart contains 5 of the 10 Gods – we have the Indirect Wealth Star, the Direct Officer Star, the 7 Killings Star, the Direct Resource Star and the Rob Wealth Star. This would be a chart that leans on the simpler side in terms of outlook because the number of 10 Gods, although at 5 is exactly half, would still be regarded as on the 'less' rather than 'more' side.

On the Stems, we find the Rob Wealth, 7 Killings and Direct Resource Stars. The Rob Wealth Star denotes a spontaneous, witty, sociable, and very outgoing and extroverted personality. The 7 Killings Star denotes a person of charisma, an aggressive go-getter and indicates strong leadership skills. Finally, the Direct Resource Star denotes a person who is a good listener, patient, cultured, learned and non-judgmental.

Remember, these are only the qualities that the individual appears to possess or the impression the person leaves as a first impression. Thus, we must look to the Earthly Branches to dig a little deeper.

In the Earthly Branches, the Direct Officer Star is present in the two Roosters (You), the Direct Resource Star is present in the Rat (Zi) and the Dragon (Chen) has the Indirect Wealth Star as its Main Qi. The Direct Officer Star indicates a righteous, principled, upright and honourable person who abides by the rules and always plays nicely with everyone. The Direct Resource Star denotes a patient, kind, cultured, learned and relaxed nature, and the Indirect Wealth Star denotes entrepreneurial skills, flamboyance and an opportunistic eye for money-making. So, deep down inside, this person is really in a sense a bit of a goody-goody two shoes (thanks to the Direct Officer Star and Direct Resource Star), but has entrepreneurial ambitions and his goody-goody two shoes side has a spark of flamboyance to it, courtesy of the Indirect Wealth Star.

In this chart, the 7 Killings Star appears on the Stems, but is not rooted in the Earthly Branches. Indeed, the Star that exhibits the opposite characteristics and traits to the 7 Killings Star, the Direct Officer Star, is located in the Earthly Branches. As such, this is a person who only appears to be an aggressive go-getter, and only *seems* to be someone who is willing to break rules to get things done. The reality is that this is an individual who is all bark and no bite and who despite what he says, will not go against the order of things in order to achieve his goals. This is an individual who is actually entirely law-abiding at heart, even if he seems otherwise.

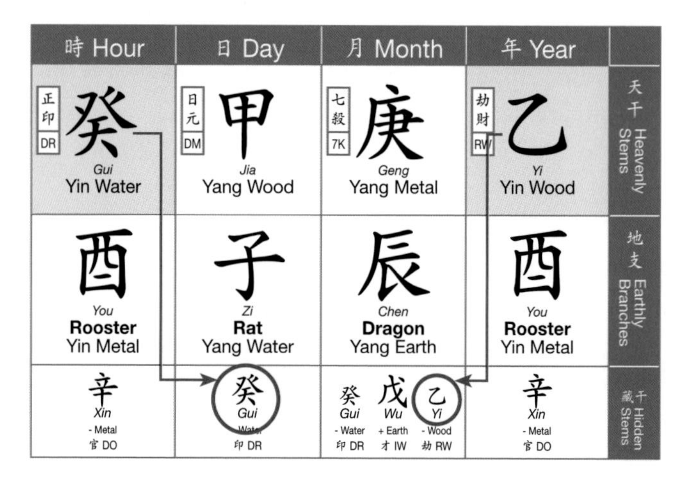

In this example, the Direct Resource Star and the Rob Wealth Star appear in both the Stem and Branch. This tells us that the qualities and characteristics of the Direct Resource Star are the Dominant Characteristics present in this individual. The qualities (positive and negative) that are associated with the Direct Resource Star are a dominant part of the person's character and is the driving force behind the person's attitude, mindset, perception and actions. Thus, this person is definitely a charming, witty, sociable character, and who is most certainly blessed with the gift of the gab. And although the person loves to talk and chat, they are also an excellent listener, being able to be non-judgmental and patient when it comes to listening to other people's problems. These and other traits associated with the Direct Resource and Rob Wealth Stars will be the bedrock of the person's character.

What can we learn from the 10 Gods that are absent in this chart? There are 5 of the Ten Gods missing from this chart – Direct Wealth, Indirect Resource, Friend, Hurting Officer and Eating God. It is the absence of the Eating God and Hurting Officer Stars in this chart that is most significant because it means that the Output Element (represented by the element of Fire) is entirely missing. The Output Element broadly relates to a person's communication skills, but also is closely connected to their ability to innovate, problem-solve and their work product. When this Element is entirely missing, the person's capacity to apply their knowledge is significantly compromised. Of course, the absence of the other three 10 Gods is not irrelevant, but the absence of the Output Element entirely overshadows the absence of the other three, because the chart still ultimately has a Wealth Element, a Resource Element and a Companion Element.

By looking at the 10 Gods that are Dominant Characteristics, and putting it alongside the absent 10 Gods, we also gain new insights. The Rob Wealth Star, which is rooted in this chart, will help to offset some of the disadvantage that arises from a missing Output Star from a communications standpoint. However, it is clear that this is likely to be a person who is all talk and not much in terms of delivery that lives up to the expectation, since the Output Element is missing. The Rob Wealth Star leads the person to promise the earth but the Output Element's absent means the performance does not live up to the promise. The presence of the Direct Resource Star, which relates to a person's education and denotes a learned person, is in many ways, completely undermined by the absence of the Output Element. This means the person is smart, but is not able to apply their knowledge effectively to solve problems or come up with ideas or solutions. This compounds and contributes to the problem of overpromising and under-delivering in their chart since the person may actually possess the knowledge or information required to deliver on their promise, but can't seem to actually apply that information well enough to meet the expectations that they have created.

時 Hour	日 Day	月 Month	年 Year	
傷官 HO 乙 *Yi* Yin Wood	日元 DM 壬 *Ren* Yang Water	七殺 7K 戊 *Wu* Yang Earth	比肩 F 壬 *Ren* Yang Water	天干 Heavenly Stems
巳 *Si* **Snake** Yin Fire	戌 *Xu* **Dog** Yang Earth	申 *Shen* **Monkey** Yang Metal	辰 *Chen* **Dragon** Yang Earth	地支 Earthly Branches
庚 *Geng* +Metal 卩 IR; 丙 *Bing* +Fire 才 IW; 戊 *Wu* +Earth 殺 7K	丁 *Ding* -Fire 財 DW; 戊 *Wu* +Earth 殺 7K; 辛 *Xin* -Metal 印 DR	戊 *Wu* +Earth 殺 7K; 庚 *Geng* +Metal 卩 IR; 壬 *Ren* +Water 比 F	癸 *Gui* -Water 劫 RW; 戊 *Wu* +Earth 殺 7K; 乙 *Yi* -Wood 傷 HO	藏干 Hidden Stems

This is the chart of a Ren Water Day Master. In the Heavenly Stems, the following 10 Gods are present: Friend Star (Ren Water), 7 Killings Star (Wu Earth), Hurting Officer Star (Yi Wood). In the Earthly Branches, the following 10 Gods are present in the Main Qi of the Four Earthly Branches: the 7 Killings Star in Dragon (Chen), the Indirect Resource Star in Monkey (Shen), the 7 Killings Star in Dog (Xu) and the Indirect Wealth Star in Snake (Si).

This table affords an at-a-glance look at the 10 Gods in this chart:

Hurting Officer Star	√
Eating God Star	
Direct Wealth Star	√
Indirect Wealth Star	√
Direct Officer Star	
7 Killings Star	√
Direct Resource Star	√
Indirect Resource Star	√
Rob Wealth Star	√
Friend Star	√

This chart contains 8 of the 10 Gods – we have the Hurting Officer Star, the Direct Wealth Star, the Indirect Wealth Star, the 7 Killings Star, the Direct Resource Star, the Indirect Resource Star, the Rob Wealth Star and the Friend Star. This would be a chart that leans on the complex side in terms of outlook because of the high number of 10 Gods present in the chart. This is a person with a sophisticated outlook, and who sees the world through a complex set of considerations.

The most immediate conclusion that can be derived about this person's character is that they are not duplicitous in any way. How does this conclusion arise? From the fact that all three of the 10 Gods that appear in the Stems are present also in the Earthly Branches. So there are no mixed signals from this person – they are who they say they are, and their public and private personas will not be that far apart. In this instance, it is not the case that the first impression of the person is necessarily deceptive, in so much as it is a question of determining what else there is to the person, other than what is obviously and clearly displayed via their Dominant Characteristics.

The Indirect Wealth Star for example does not appear in the Stem but appears in the Branch. This tells us that whilst the person may not indicate an overt interest in materialistic pursuits, making money, and making it fast (as is the nature of Indirect Wealth) is definitely on their mind.

The Eating God and Direct Officer Stars are missing in this chart. Accordingly the qualities associated with both these Stars will not be present in the person's character. Thus, the upright, honourable, principled and law-abiding qualities of the Direct Officer Star will not form a part of this person's outlook in life, or even influence their actions. Similarly, the strategic thinking and long-term outlook that are the hallmark of the Eating God Star will not be present in the person's character. Oh, and don't bother inviting them to a gourmet dinner either because that's not high on their list of priorities in life, given the missing Eating God.

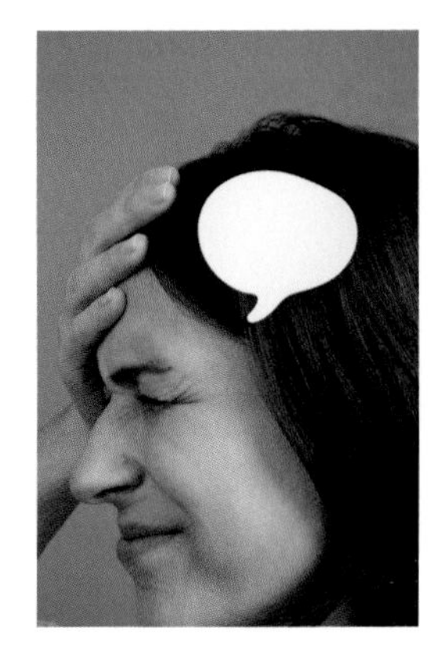

... strategic thinking and long-term outlook that are the hallmark of the Eating God Star will not be present in the person's character.

The Hurting Officer Star and 7 Killings Star have some common features, notably, a go-getter temperament, a denote a domineering personality and tremendous ambition.

In this example, the Indirect Resource Star, Hurting Officer Star and 7 Killings Star appear in both the Stem and Branch. This tells us that the qualities and characteristics of the Indirect Resource Star, Hurting Officer Star and 7 Killings Star are the Dominant Characteristics present in this individual. The qualities (positive and negative) that are associated with the Indirect Resource Star, Hurting Officer Star and 7 Killings Star are a dominant part of the person's character and is the driving force behind the person's attitude, mindset, perception and actions.

Let us try now to gain a clearer picture of the person's Dominant Characteristics by looking at any commonalities that cut across the three Stars that make up the Dominant Characteristics. The Hurting Officer Star and 7 Killings Star have some common features, notably, a go-getter temperament, a denote a domineering personality and tremendous ambition. Thus, this person will most definitely come across someone who will stop at nothing to get what they want.

Whilst the Indirect Resource Star's qualities – eccentricity, unorthodox ideas, tendency to resort to short-cuts or underhand methods – will exhibit strongly as well, the characteristics that are in tandem with the common characteristics of the Hurting Officer Star and 7 Killings Star will tend to be more prominent. For example, both the Hurting Officer Star and the 7 Killings Star make a person prepared to break the rules to achieve their goals. Thus, the traits and characteristics of the Indirect Resource Star that reinforce this characteristic will exhibit more, such as a tendency towards unorthodox ways of doing things (including underhand/illegal methods) or a habit of resorting to the path of least resistance, which again, could be an illegal or underhand method.

時 Hour	日 Day	月 Month	年 Year	
食神 EG 己 *Ji* Yin Earth	日元 DM 丁 *Ding* Yin Fire	偏印 IR 乙 *Yi* Yin Wood	七殺 7K 癸 *Gui* Yin Water	天干 Heavenly Stems
酉 *You* **Rooster** Yin Metal	丑 *Chou* **Ox** Yin Earth	丑 *Chou* **Ox** Yin Earth	卯 *Mao* **Rabbit** Yin Wood	地支 Earthly Branches
辛 *Xin* - Metal 才 IW	辛 *Xin* - Metal 才 IW; 己 *Ji* - Earth 食 EG; 癸 *Gui* - Water 殺 7K	辛 *Xin* - Metal 才 IW; 己 *Ji* - Earth 食 EG; 癸 *Gui* - Water 殺 7K	乙 *Yi* - Wood 𠃌 IR	藏干 Hidden Stems

This is the chart of a Ding Fire Day Master. In the Heavenly Stems, the following 10 Gods are present: 7 Killings Star (Gui Water), Indirect Resource Star (Yi Wood) and Eating God Star (Ji Earth). In the Earthly Branches, the following 10 Gods are present in the Main Qi of the Four Earthly Branches: Indirect Resource Star in Rabbit (Mao), the Eating God Star in the double Ox (Chou) and finally the Indirect Wealth Star in Rooster (You).

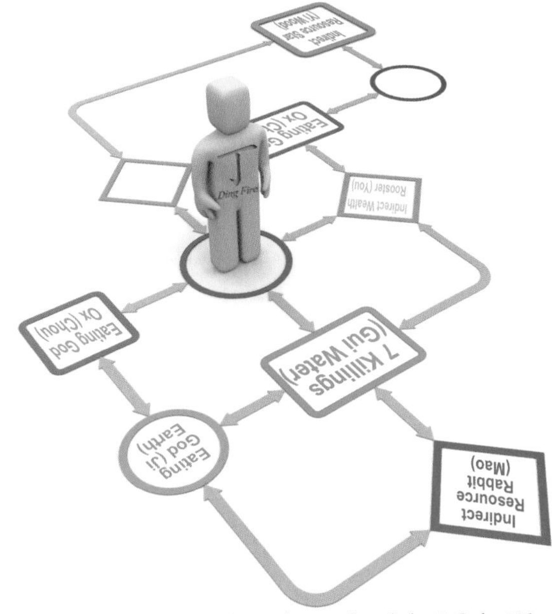

This table affords an at-a-glance look at the 10 Gods in this chart:

Hurting Officer Star	
Eating God Star	√
Direct Wealth Star	
Indirect Wealth Star	√
Direct Officer Star	
7 Killings Star	√
Direct Resource Star	
Indirect Resource Star	√
Rob Wealth Star	
Friend Star	

This chart contains 4 of the 10 Gods – we have the Eating God Star, the Indirect Wealth Star, the 7 Killings Star and the Indirect Resource Star. This would be a chart that clearly denotes a person with a more simplified outlook on the world. This is a person who sees the world in terms of black and white, rather than shades of gray.

What do we find on the Stems? We have the 7 Killings, Indirect Resource and Eating God Stars. So on the surface, this person appears to be highly erratic in nature, both idealistic and Machiavellian at the same time (Indirect Resource Star and 7 Killings Star). Yet, there is a craftiness about the person, born out of the strategic thinking tendencies of the Eating

God Star. This person would appear to be someone who should not be under-estimated, even though they are quiet and seemingly introverted.

But what is the true nature of the person? For that, we must look at the Branches. In this chart, the Indirect Resource, Eating God and Indirect Wealth Stars appear in the Branches. As such, this person is very much a born entrepreneur, a wheeler-dealer, hustler and opportunistic of the highest order, as a result of the Indirect Wealth Star. This person is someone who takes a calculated approach to everything that he or she does when it comes to entrepreneurial pursuits, thanks to the Eating God Star. Decision-making tends to be instinctive and based on gut-feel, sentiment or old-fashioned experience, rather than facts and figures, due to the presence of the Indirect Resource Star.

Now, let's try to develop a more sophisticated picture of the person's character. The Indirect Resource Star to a large degree compliments the Indirect Wealth Star, which tends to denote fast and furious decision-making, and sometimes a habit of being impulsive. However, because the Eating God is present in tandem, we can say that the person is not totally spontaneous or impulsive in their decision-making, because the Eating God moderates the impulsive nature of the Indirect Wealth and Indirect Resource Stars.

... this person is very much a born entrepreneur, a wheeler-dealer, hustler and opportunistic of the highest order, as a result of the Indirect Wealth Star.

時 Hour	日 Day	月 Month	年 Year	
食神 EG 己 *Ji* Yin Earth	日元 DM 丁 *Ding* Yin Fire	偏印 IR 乙 *Yi* Yin Wood	七殺 7K 癸 *Gui* Yin Water	天干 Heavenly Stems
酉 *You* **Rooster** Yin Metal	丑 *Chou* **Ox** Yin Earth	丑 *Chou* **Ox** Yin Earth	卯 *Mao* **Rabbit** Yin Wood	地支 Earthly Branches
辛 *Xin* - Metal 才 IW	辛 *Xin* - Metal 才 IW; 己 *Ji* - Earth 食 EG; 癸 *Gui* - Water 殺 7K	辛 *Xin* - Metal 才 IW; 己 *Ji* - Earth 食 EG; 癸 *Gui* - Water 殺 7K	乙 *Yi* - Wood 卩 IR	藏干 Hidden Stems

In this example, the Indirect Resource Star and Eating God Star appear in both the Stem and Branch. This tells us that the qualities and characteristics of the Eating God Star and Indirect Resource Star are the Dominant Characteristics present in this individual. The qualities (positive and negative) that are associated with the Indirect Resource and 7 Killings Stars are a dominant part of the person's character and is the driving force behind the person's attitude, mindset, perception and actions. Now put two and two together - this person is actually able to combine a crafty, long-term outlook, with gut feel and instinct for the market. There is innate wisdom in their decision-making, rather than just a decision born out of pure guesswork, which is typical of the Indirect Resource Star alone.

The characteristics and traits that are associated with the Rob Wealth Star, Friend Star, Direct Resource, Direct Officer, Direct Wealth and Hurting Officer Stars are not present in this person at all. Thus they lack the spontaneity and social skills that come with the Rob Wealth Star, or the innate confidence and sense of self that are associated with the Friend Star. They also lack the upright, principle, honourable and law-abiding qualities of the Direct Officer Star. They are not frugal or fiscally responsible, and lack the practical, down to earth nature of the Direct Wealth Star. This is not a person who makes decisions based on facts and figures, as the Direct Resource Star would have one, but goes with intuition or guesswork since only the indirect Resource Star is present (and is a Dominant Characteristic). Finally, this person will err on the side of introverted or very quiet, and have a preference for being behind the scenes or just staying unseen, as the Hurting Officer Star is not present.

Finally, this person will err on the side of introverted or very quiet, and have a preference for being behind the scenes or just staying unseen, as the Hurting Officer Star is not present.

Return of the Day Master

As the 10 Gods are derived from the Day Master, accordingly, it is expected that any conversation involving the 10 Gods necessarily include a reference to the Day Master. Indeed, interpreting character begins with the Day Master, with the 10 Gods then added onto the basic characteristics of the Day Master to give further colour and texture to our understanding of a person's character. From the *Destiny Code* and the *Destiny Code Revealed*, you would already have some information about how to interpret your basic character based on your Day Master. In the next chapter, I will show you how to marry information about the Day Master together with the basic 10 Gods character analysis, to analyse your own personal BaZi chart.

Chapter 5
Getting to know YOU (and Others)

This chapter contains a simple walk-through that will help you become familiar with the process of determining a person's character by analysing their BaZi chart. You should practice on your own chart first, then move on to practicing with friends or family members whom you are familiar with so as to enable you to confirm your analysis. Only after you have done about 20 charts of people who you are familiar with, should you then move on to total strangers.

It may seem as though this walk-through is rather long and tedious but it's important to follow a series of steps, a format or structure if you like, when you first start analysing a BaZi chart. In the absence of a format or structure, you will find that you are staring at all 8 characters, and your brain is unable to separate out the strands of information that it is receiving, to form a coherent picture of the person's character. As you get better, you'll find that your mind naturally will structure and arrange the information in an order that works best for you. But initially, follow the steps until you become very comfortable with the process.

For this section to be effective, you need to have a good familiarity with the basic traits of the 10 Day Masters, as has been discussed in *Destiny Code* and *The Destiny Code Revealed.* You also need to have memorised at least 10-15 of the traits and characteristics associated with each of the 10 Gods, covered in Chapter 3 of this book.

Step 1: Identify the Day Master and the qualities of the Day Master.

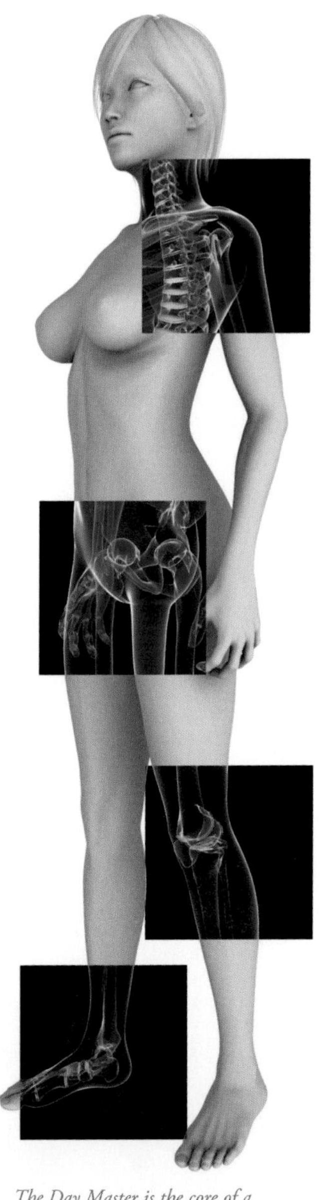

The Day Master is the core of a person's character and self. It is the skeleton of the person's character,

The Day Master is the core of a person's character and self. It is the skeleton of the person's character, in the way the 10 Gods is the flesh on the bones. The qualities of each of the 10 Day Masters has been discussed in *The Destiny Code Revealed* but here is a quick summary. These essential qualities of each of the 10 Day Masters provided here is by no means exhaustive. Thus as your understanding of BaZi grows, and your ability to perceive the 10 Day Masters in a pictoral manner becomes enhanced, add to your knowledge and the basics that have been provided here.

Day Master		Basic Qualities & Attributes
甲 *Jia* **Yang Wood**		Tall soaring trees. Solid, dependable, steady, one track mind, persevering type,
乙 *Yi* **Yin Wood**		Flowers, vines and twines. Flexible, adaptive, survivalist, cunning, fickle, non-committal, charming.
丙 *Bing* **Yang Fire**		Fire of the sun. Bold, magnanimous, generous, warm, spirited, routine-centric, charitable, independent.
丁 *Ding* **Yin Fire**		Candle fire, twinkling stars. Born leaders, fickle, able to rise to the occasion, love to learn new things, meticulous, motivating.
戊 *Wu* **Yang Earth**		Rocks, boulders, mountains. Solid, dependable, trustworthy, protective, inflexible, unmoving, stubborn, slow to act.
己 *Ji* **Yin Earth**		Soft soil, silt, mud, porous earth. Fertile, nurturing, motherly, giving, supportive, good hearted, understanding.
庚 *Geng* **Yang Metal**		Raw iron ore, axes, swords. Tough, hardy, hands-on types, altruistic and value friendship, loyal, justice minded.
辛 *Xin* **Yin Metal**		Fine jewellery, diamonds, penknives. Intellectually or physically vain, showy, love the spotlight, attention-grabbing, proud, opinionated.
壬 *Ren* **Yang Water**		River or sea water. Powerful, unforgiving, focused, unrelenting, always on the move, determined.
癸 *Gui* **Yin Water**		Rain water, mist, clouds, dew on the ground. Floaty, flighty, fleeting, mysterious, quixotic, temperamental, moody, nurturing.

Step 2: Identify and Label all the 10 Gods in the chart

This may seem like a very elementary step but it's important to make the effort to be aware of what are the 10 Gods that are present in the chart.

If you use my BaZi MingPan software, this step is already done for you, **www.masteryacademy.com/regbook**

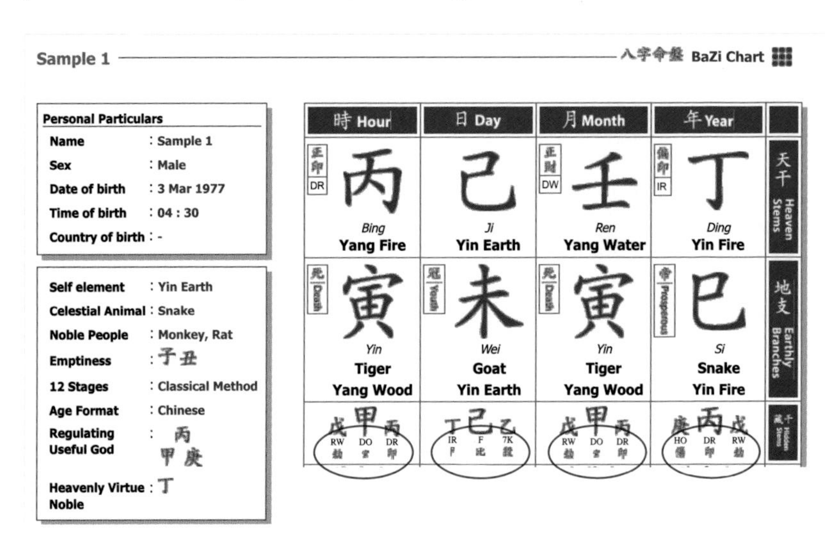

However, I would recommend just having a go at labelling the chart even if it's already done for you so as to speed up your ability to learn and commit to memory the 10 Gods.

If you are plotting the charts by hand, then this step is absolutely necessary. Use a Red Pen and label all the 10 Gods, including those in the Sub-Qi, with their abbreviated forms. (ie: F for Friend, DW for Direct Wealth, IR for Indirect Resource).

For quick and easy reference, you may also wish to draw and fill up a table similar to the one below:

Hurting Officer Star	
Eating God Star	
Direct Wealth Star	
Indirect Wealth Star	
Direct Officer Star	
7 Killings Star	
Direct Resource Star	
Indirect Resource Star	
Rob Wealth Star	
Friend Star	

Step 3: Determine if the person's inherent character is SIMPLE or COMPLEX.

By looking at the 10 Gods checklist, you will be able to determine if the person is a Simple individual or a Complex individual.

Step 4: List out the 10 Gods in the chart and their location.

Use a replica of the simple table below to help you keep everything at hand. To make it quicker, fill in the information using the abbreviations for each Star. Fill in the information starting from the right side of the chart, where the Year Pillar is located, and then move across to the left. Leave plenty of space below each section.

Hour Stem 10 God	Day Master	Month Stem 10 God	Year Stem 10 God
Hour Branch 10 God (Main Qi)	**Day Branch 10 God (Main Qi)**	**Month Branch 10 God (Main Qi)**	**Year Branch 10 God (Main Qi)**
Hour Branch 10 God (Sub-Qi)	**Day Branch 10 God (Sub-Qi)**	**Month Branch 10 God (Sub-Qi)**	**Year Branch 10 God (Sub-Qi)**

Step 5: My first impression of this person is....

List out 5 characteristics associated with each of the 10 Gods that appears on the Stem in the same table above. This will reveal the first impression of the person. You can put in both negative and positive characteristics, or if you just remember the positive ones, than just the positives ones.

Hour Stem 10 God	Day Master	Month Stem 10 God	Year Stem 10 God
Characteristics:	Characteristics:	Characteristics:	Characteristics:

Step 6: This person's actual innate character is...

Now list out 5 characteristics associated with each of the 10 Gods that appears in the Main Qi of each of the four Earthly Branches. This tells you what the person's character is actually like when they are in private company or after you have gotten to know them.

Hour Branc 10 God (Main Qi)	Day Branch 10 God (Main Qi)	Month Branch 10 God (Main Qi)	Year Branch 10 God (Main Qi)
Characteristics:	Characteristics:	Characteristics:	Characteristics:

Step 7: This person only seems to be...

Highlight characteristics associated with the 10 Gods that ONLY appear in the Stem, and are not rooted in the Branches at all (including the Sub-Qi).

Step 8: This person's strongest and most prominent characteristics are...

Highlight the Dominant Characteristics associated with the 10 Gods that appear in both the Stem and the Branch, based on the strict interpretation of the rooting principle.

Step 9: This person does not possess these characteristics....

Determine the 10 Gods that are absent from the chart so that you are able to determine the characteristics and traits that are NOT possessed by the individual. List down these characteristics separately.

PRACTICAL WALKTHROUGH

Using this example, I'll show you how to use the above walkthrough.

時 Hour	日 Day	月 Month	年 Year	
七殺 7K 壬 *Ren* Yang Water	日元 DM 丙 *Bing* Yang Fire	偏印 IR 甲 *Jia* Yang Wood	正財 DW 辛 *Xin* Yin Metal	天干 Heavenly Stems
辰 *Chen* **Dragon** Yang Earth	寅 *Yin* **Tiger** Yang Wood	午 *Wu* **Horse** Yang Fire	亥 *Hai* **Pig** Yin Water	地支 Earthly Branches
癸 *Gui* - Water 官 DO; 戊 *Wu* + Earth 食 EG; 乙 *Yi* - Wood 印 DR	戊 *Wu* + Earth 食 EG; 甲 *Jia* + Wood 卩 IR; 丙 *Bing* + Fire 比 F	丁 *Ding* - Fire 劫 RW; 己 *Ji* - Earth 傷 HO	壬 *Ren* + Water 殺 7K; 甲 *Jia* + Wood 卩 IR	藏干 Hidden Stems

Step 1: Identify the Day Master and the qualities of the Day Master.

This chart belongs to a Bing Fire Day Master. Bing Fire is the fire of the sun, and thus is imbued with the qualities of warmth, openness, magnanimity and generosity of spirit. Like the sun, which rises in the East and sets in the West, the Bing Fire person is a routine-centric person, who tends to have a pattern to his or her daily activities.

Step 2: Identify and Label all the 10 Gods in the chart

時 Hour	日 Day	月 Month	年 Year	
七殺 7K 壬 *Ren* Yang Water	日元 DM 丙 *Bing* Yang Fire	偏印 IR 甲 *Jia* Yang Wood	正財 DW 辛 *Xin* Yin Metal	天干 Heavenly Stems
辰 *Chen* **Dragon** Yang Earth	寅 *Yin* **Tiger** Yang Wood	午 *Wu* **Horse** Yang Fire	亥 *Hai* **Pig** Yin Water	地支 Earthly Branches
癸 *Gui* - Water 官 DO; 戊 *Wu* + Earth 食 EG; 乙 *Yi* - Wood 印 DR	戊 *Wu* + Earth 食 EG; 甲 *Jia* + Wood 卩 IR; 丙 *Bing* + Fire 比 F	丁 *Ding* - Fire 劫 RW; 己 *Ji* - Earth 傷 HO	壬 *Ren* + Water 殺 7K; 甲 *Jia* + Wood 卩 IR	藏干 Hidden Stems

For ease of reference, I recommend using the 10 Gods Checklist.

Star	
Hurting Officer Star	√
Eating God Star	√
Direct Wealth Star	√
Indirect Wealth Star	
Direct Officer Star	√
7 Killings Star	√
Direct Resource Star	√
Indirect Resource Star	√
Rob Wealth Star	√
Friend Star	√

Step 3: Determine if the person's inherent character is SIMPLE or COMPLEX.

Here, we have 9 out of the 10 Gods present in the chart. Although not all of these 10 Gods will exert a strong effect on the person's character, the fact is that this is a person who does not see the world in simple black and white terms. This is someone with a sophisticated though process and a complex outlook on the world.

Step 4: List out the 10 Gods in the chart and their location.

Hour Stem 10 God	Day Master	Month Stem 10 God	Year Stem 10 God
7K	丙 Bing Fire	IR	DW
Hour Branch 10 God (Main Qi)	**Day Branch 10 God (Main Qi)**	**Month Branch 10 God (Main Qi)**	**Year Branch 10 God (Main Qi)**
EG	IR	RW	7K
Hour Branch 10 God (Sub-Qi)	**Day Branch 10 God (Sub- Qi)**	**Month Branch 10 God (Sub-Qi)**	**Year Branch 10 God (Sub-Qi)**
DO, DR	F, EG	HO	IR

Step 5: My first impression of this person is….

Hour Stem 10 God (Main Qi)	Day Stem 10 God (Main Qi)	Month Stem 10 God (Main Qi)	Year Stem 10 God (Main Qi)
EG Characteristics: • Strategic thinker • Introverted • Philosophical • Eccentric • Non-confrontational	**IR** Characteristics: • Intuitive • Deep thinker • Idealistic • Dreamer • Laid-back	**RW** Characteristics: • Talkative and chatty • Sociable • Outgoing, extroverted • Generous • Competitive	**7K** Characteristics: • Authoritative and commanding • Charismatic • Aggressive, go-getter • Decisive • Achiever
Hour Branch 10 God (Main Qi)	**Day Branch 10 God (Main Qi)**	**Month Branch 10 God (Main Qi)**	**Year Branch 10 God (Main Qi)**
EG	IR	RW	7K
Hour Branch 10 God (Sub-Qi)	**Day Branch 10 God (Sub- Qi)**	**Month Branch 10 God (Sub-Qi)**	**Year Branch 10 God (Sub-Qi)**
DO, DR	F, EG	HO	IR

Step 6: This person's actual innate character is...

Hour Stem 10 God (Main Qi)	Day Stem 10 God (Main Qi)	Month Stem 10 God (Main Qi)	Year Stem 10 God (Main Qi)
EG Characteristics: • Strategic thinker • Introverted • Philosophical • Eccentric • Non-confrontational	**IR** Characteristics: • Intuitive • Deep thinker • Idealistic • Dreamer • Laid-back	**RW** Characteristics: • Talkative and chatty • Sociable • Outgoing, extroverted • Generous • Competitive	**7K** Characteristics: • Authoritative and commanding • Charismatic • Aggressive, go-getter • Decisive • Achiever

Step 7: This person only seems to be…

The Direct Wealth Star appears only in the Stem and is not rooted in the Earthly Branches. As such, the qualities and traits associated with this Star are superficial at best and a minimal influence on this person's mindset and thinking.

時 Hour	日 Day	月 Month	年 Year	
七殺 7K 壬 *Ren* Yang Water	日元 DM 丙 *Bing* Yang Fire	偏印 IR 甲 *Jia* Yang Wood	正財 DW 辛 *Xin* Yin Metal	天干 Heavenly Stems
辰 *Chen* **Dragon** Yang Earth	寅 *Yin* **Tiger** Yang Wood	午 *Wu* **Horse** Yang Fire	亥 *Hai* **Pig** Yin Water	地支 Earthly Branches
癸 *Gui* - Water 官 DO; 戊 *Wu* + Earth 食 EG; 乙 *Yi* - Wood 印 DR	戊 *Wu* + Earth 食 EG; 甲 *Jia* + Wood 卩 IR; 丙 *Bing* + Fire 比 F	丁 *Ding* - Fire 劫 RW; 己 *Ji* - Earth 傷 HO	壬 *Ren* + Water 殺 7K; 甲 *Jia* + Wood 卩 IR	藏干 Hidden Stems

Step 8: This person's strongest and most prominent characteristics are…

As this table shows, the 10 Gods that appear in both the Stem and Branch, which represent the Dominant Characteristics of the person, are the 7 Killings and Indirect Resource Stars.

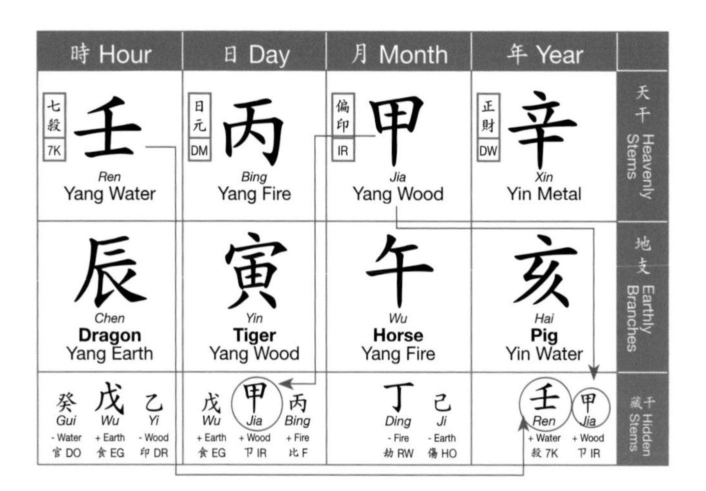

Hour Stem 10 God	Day Master	Month Stem 10 God	Year Stem 10 God
7K Characteristics: • Authoritative and commanding • Charismatic • Aggressive, go-getter • Decisive • Achiever	**丙 Bing Fire**	**IR** Characteristics: • Intuitive • Deep thinker • Idealistic • Dreamer • Laid-back	**DW** Characteristics: • Responsible • Reliable • Hard-working • Practical • Down to Earth

Hour Stem 10 God (Main Qi)	Day Stem 10 God (Main Qi)	Month Stem 10 God (Main Qi)	Year Stem 10 God (Main Qi)
EG Characteristics: • Strategic thinker • Introverted • Philosophical • Eccentric • Non-confrontational	**IR** Characteristics: • Intuitive • Deep thinker • Idealistic • Dreamer • Laid-back	**RW** Characteristics: • Talkative and chatty • Sociable • Outgoing, extroverted • Generous • Competitive	**7K** Characteristics: • Authoritative and commanding • Charismatic • Aggressive, go-getter • Decisive • Achiever

Step 9: This person does not possess these characteristics...

Out of all the 10 Gods, only one 10 God is absent from this chart and that is the Indirect Wealth Star. Accordingly, the natural qualities associated with the Indirect Wealth Star, namely, entrepreneurial mindset, wheeler-dealer, hustler, flamboyant personality and get-rich-quick mindset will not be part of the person's character.

Now, put everything from Step 1-9 together and you would get an analysis as follows:

You are a magnanimous, generous person, a charitable sort, a person who is a very open spirit. On first impression, you give the appearance of a slightly eccentric dreamer, an innovative individual but yet are someone who is hardworking, practical, down to earth. You exhibit a strong drive to succeed in life and are someone who likes winning at everything that you do. As people get to know you better, they realise that you actually have great social skills, are chatty and witty, and the life of the party, but there are also moments when you are introverted, and prefer to be left alone to your own thoughts. There's a strategic thinker side to you as well, and you have the innate ability to always see the long-term benefits of a given situation. Hard-work isn't really the path to success in your eyes – instead, it is about using contacts and connections, networking, and also, all about having the right strategy and playing the game right.

You are ultimately driven by big dreams and have grand ambitions, which you will stop at nothing to achieve but at the same time you also come across strongly as a dreamer, a big picture person, and a laid-back personality. You are not however a natural entrepreneur or a person who spots financial opportunities easily and you don't believe in get-rich-quick methods.

Everyone has 'issues' with themselves.

You will notice at this point that there are some contradictions in the above profile. For example, the person is both a go-getter, aggressive and ambitious (7 Killings Star) yet also is laid-back, relaxed, and a dreamer (Indirect Resource Star). The person seems spontaneous, outgoing and open (Rob Wealth Star) but yet is also introverted and a person who prefers their own company (Eating God Star) and has a tendency to be a loner (Indirect Resource Star).

Most people by and large, contain contradictions in their characters. Everyone has 'issues' with themselves. Very few charts will contain a set of qualities and traits that are entirely and absolutely in tandem with each other or are entirely without some form of contradiction. It's the contradictions in character that give rise to our foibles, flaws and conflicts that we have with ourselves. If you've ever wondered why you did something silly or which didn't seem to make sense in hindsight, these contradictions in character are probably to blame in a large number of those instances.

Making sense of the contradictions

At a more advanced level of BaZi, the analysis will focus on making sense of the contradictions, including determining the extent and degree of these contradictions. This helps us determine the extent in which a given BaZi chart fulfils an important requirement of chart quality, namely, clarity. A chart that has clarity (清) is regarded as superior to one that lacks clarity. Clarity is quite an abstract concept and it would not be appropriate to explore that subject at the moment. However, it's important to know that such a criteria exists. Further, determining clarity is also not easy. It requires a very good grasp of the 10 Gods and an understanding of which 10 Gods play better together and which 10 Gods make for strange bedfellows with each other. One also has to have the ability to perceive the chart at both a macro big picture and micro, detailed level, interchanging between the two perspectives. A detailed understanding of the Five Elements and the 10 Stems is also integral to being able to evaluate chart clarity. This is why clarity as a subject is generally not something that should be introduced into the mix too early for beginner and intermediate students of BaZi.

Clarity

A detailed understanding of the Five Elements and the 10 Stems is also integral to being able to evaluate chart clarity.

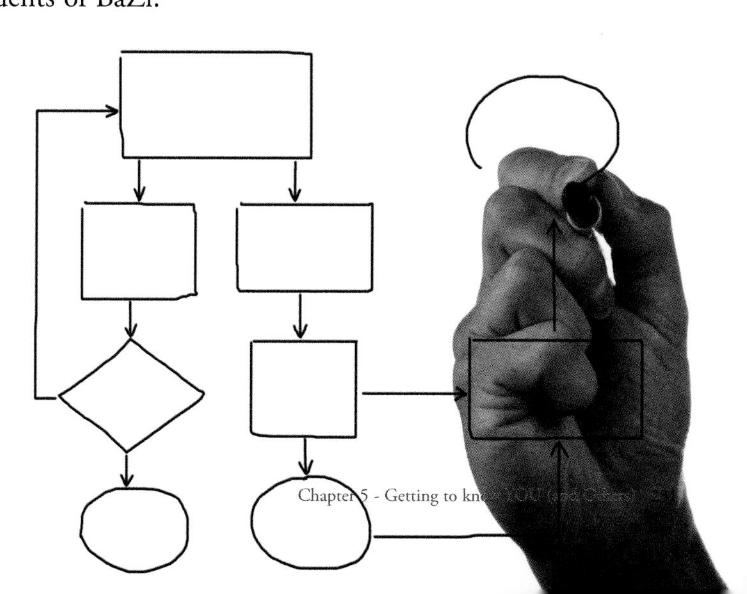

At this stage, you should just focus on being able to identify the 10 Gods that are present in a given BaZi chart, knowing the relevant positive and negative characteristics associated with the 10 Gods present in the chart, determining the person's Dominant Characteristics, and being able to identify the missing/absent aspects of a person's character.

In the next Chapter, we'll look at the question of making use of the information that you have obtained from the analysis of a person's character by ensuring that you take the right Action.

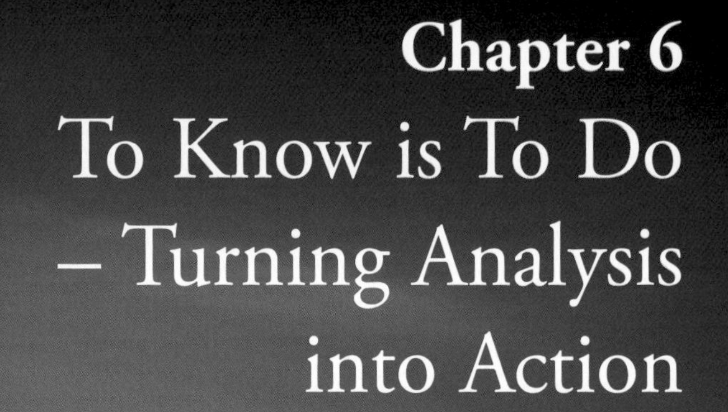

Chapter 6
To Know is To Do – Turning Analysis into Action

In the final chapter of *The Destiny Code*, I briefly explained the use of BaZi for the purposes of self-improvement, planning one's life and stress-avoidance by enabling individuals to manage their expectations. In this chapter, I want to discuss in a little more depth how to utilise the information obtained about one's character via analysing one's own BaZi to engage specifically in self-improvement and its necessary counterpart, expectation management.

At this point, you should have already analysed your personal BaZi chart and ascertained your character using the techniques discussed in Chapter 4 and the walk-through in Chapter 5. You may have even 'discovered' a few things about yourself that you never knew (or perhaps were reluctant to admit in the past). You are now aware of whether or not you are someone with a complex or simple outlook in life, what is the first impression people have of you upon first meeting you, what is your character like when you are with people you are familiar with, what are your Dominant Characteristics and finally, what traits are absent from your character. So let's now talk about what you do with this information.

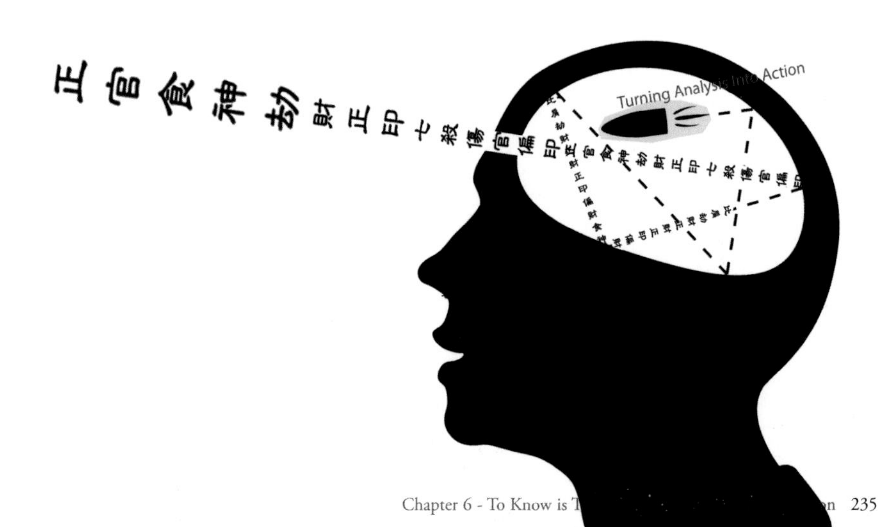

Beware over-promising and under-delivering

We have all experienced the person who over-promises and under-delivers. Recall the salesman who promises you the moon when trying to close the deal but conveniently ignores your phone calls after everything is signed, sealed and delivered. Or a member of staff who talks up their proposal to be the greatest thing since sliced bread, only to deliver a rather mediocre version of what was a grandiose vision. In today's world, it is very important to avoid over-promising and under-delivering. Delivering what you have promised demonstrates consistency between action and intent. It indicates reliability and reinforces a sense of honesty. Consistency, reliability and honesty are needed in order for trust to exist. If we can believe in someone or something, if we can rely on someone and something, and if we know they will not lie to us, then they have earned our trust. Trust is the foundation and essence of all successful relationships, business and personal, and often the basis for the failure of a relationship and the ensuing destructive outcome.

Consistency, reliability and honesty are needed in order for trust to exist.

Over-promising and under-delivering manifests in BaZi in a number of forms. The most common is the appearance of Stars which manifest positive traits on the Heavenly Stems, but which do not appear in the Earthly Branches.

For example, the Direct Officer Star denotes a person who is responsible, upright, honest, principled, and a person who follows the rules. These are generally regarded as positive traits to have. Now, imagine if a person only appears to be responsible but is actually an irresponsible person because the Direct Officer Star only appears in the Heavenly Stems but does not appear in the Earthly Branches of their chart? Such a person is immediately at risk of over-promising and under-delivering because they appear to be able to follow instructions but actually are not able to do so. Indeed, if the Hurting Officer Star appears in the Branches instead, you get someone who not only ignores instructions, but decides to do things their way.

時 Hour	日 Day	月 Month	年 Year	
正官 DO 丁 Ding Yin Fire	日元 DM 庚 Geng Yang Metal	正印 DR 己 Ji Yin Earth	劫財 RW 辛 Xin Yin Metal	天干 Heavenly Stems
丑 Chou **Ox** Yin Earth	子 Zi **Rat** Yang Water	亥 Hai **Pig** Yin Water	酉 You **Rooster** Yin Metal	地支 Earthly Branches
辛 Xin - Metal 劫 RW; 己 Ji - Earth 印 DR; 癸 Gui - Water 傷 HO	癸 Gui - Water 傷 HO	壬 Ren + Water 食 EG; 甲 Jia + Wood 才 IW	辛 Xin - Metal 劫 RW	藏干 Hidden Stems

In this chart, the Direct Officer Star appears in the Heavenly Stems, but does not appear in the Earthly Branches. Instead, in the Earthly Branches, we have the Hurting Officer Star.

Another example would be the Direct Wealth Star. This denotes a person who is hard-working, industrious, responsible, prudent and financially responsible. Now, imagine if a person only appears to be hard-working, industrious, prudent and financially responsible, but is actually a spendthrift character, who doesn't put in the hours and turns out to be quite lazy because the Direct Wealth Star only appears in the Heavenly Stems and not the Earthly Branches? Indeed, if there are Indirect or Direct Resource Stars or Rob Wealth Stars in the Earthly Branches instead, you'll find the person is anything BUT hard-working, industrious, responsible, prudent and financially responsible.

Direct Wealth Star does not appear in the Branches - spendthrift character

	時 Hour	日 Day	月 Month	年 Year
天干 Heavenly Stems	偏印 IR 己 Ji Yin Earth	日元 DM 辛 Xin Yin Metal	正財 DW 甲 Jia Yang Wood	食神 EG 癸 Gui Yin Water
地支 Earthly Branches	丑 Chou **Ox** Yin Earth	丑 Chou **Ox** Yin Earth	子 Zi **Rat** Yang Water	丑 Chou **Ox** Yin Earth
藏干 Hidden Stems	辛 Xin - Metal 比 F; 己 Ji - Earth 卩 IR; 癸 Gui - Water 食 EG	辛 Xin - Metal 比 F; 己 Ji - Earth 卩 IR; 癸 Gui - Water 食 EG	癸 Gui - Water 食 EG	辛 Xin - Metal 比 F; 己 Ji - Earth 卩 IR; 癸 Gui - Water 食 EG

In this chart, the Direct Wealth Star, represented by Jia Wood, appears in the Heavenly Stems, but does not appear in the Earthly Branches. This denotes that the person's 'industriousness' and 'hard-working temperament' is not part of their Internal Character. In fact, this person only looks hard-working but is actually lazy, since the Earthly Branches are dominated by the Indirect Resource Star, which typically marks a more laid-back character and a person who generally does not exhibit strong initiative or drive.

Now imagine if you had because of that first impression conveyed by the Direct Wealth Star, hired this person to be your accountant or financial controller? Instead of getting someone who knows how to manage your company's finances and do budgets, you have someone who only knows how to spend money (the Rob Wealth Star denotes spendthrift habits or an inability to save money) or worse, someone who does sloppy work since both the Rob Wealth and Indirect Resource Stars tend towards shortcuts and a lack of meticulousness.

時 Hour	日 Day	月 Month	年 Year	
偏印 IR 戊 Wu Yang Earth	日元 DM 庚 Geng Yang Metal	食神 EG 壬 Ren Yang Water	正財 DW 乙 Yi Yin Wood	天干 Heavenly Stems
子 Zi **Rat** Yang Water	戌 Xu **Dog** Yang Earth	午 Wu **Horse** Yang Fire	酉 You **Rooster** Yin Metal	地支 Earthly Branches
癸 Gui - Water 傷 HO	丁 Ding - Fire 官 DO; 戊 Wu + Earth 卩 IR; 辛 Xin - Metal 劫 RW	丁 Ding - Fire 官 DO; 己 Ji - Earth 印 DR	辛 Xin - Metal 劫 RW	藏干 Hidden Stems

In this chart, the Direct Wealth Star, represented by Yi Wood, appears in the Heavenly Stems but does not appear in the Earthly Branches. The Rob Wealth Star, represented by Xin Metal, does not appear in the Stems but appears in the Rooster (You) and Dog (Xu) Earthly Branches. On the surface, this person appears to be financially prudent and fiscally responsible, per the qualities of the Direct Wealth Star. However, in reality, this person is probably not as careful with money or as good at managing money as they seem, because their Internal Character does not reflect a Direct Wealth nature. Indeed, their Internal Character reflects a less

than prudent approach to money due to the presence of the Rob Wealth Star, which indicates a more spendthrift mindset or a less careful approach to money-matters.

The point that these examples illustrate is that we want to avoid creating misleading impressions (or 'false advertising') as much as possible, especially if these misleading impressions result in an inability to actually deliver on what has been promised. If for example, you find that in your own chart, you are at risk of creating a misleading impression of yourself, then you need to be extra careful to manage the expectations created properly.

Often, that simply translates into a greater awareness of your actions but also making conscious decisions to avoid putting yourself in a situation where your weakness can be exploited. If for example, you are someone who only appears to exhibit the traits of the Direct Officer Star (meaning, the Direct Officer Star is present only in the Heavenly Stems), but in fact, lean more towards the Hurting Officer Star in terms of Internal Character, then you may want to avoid taking a leadership position at work or a position that involves administration or deals with a lot of details. Instead, focus on a job or area that involves more idea generation or requires out of the box thinking or problem solving such as marketing.

Equally, you may wish to avoid joining a company that has a very conservative culture and go with an organisation that has a more entrepreneurial culture or a culture that respects people who are different or a company which encourages the expression of opinions openly. The presence of the Direct Officer Star in the Heavenly Stems *suggests* that you can work or be part of a conservative, orthodox organisation. But the reality is that you would not be suited for such a company the Direct Officer Star is not a part of your Internal Character.

It may not be immediately apparent to you what you need to do right now based on your chart. This is understandable because you may not have a high level of familiarity with the 10 Gods and you do not have a great deal of experience in connecting the dots of your personal character to the external environment of your workplace, your career, and your relationships, personal or otherwise. The solution-development aspect of BaZi will of course eventually come as you grow to understand the subject in a deeper and more advanced manner.

The objective here is to get you thinking about the question of whether or not the challenges that you have faced in the past or which you are facing at present and are likely to face in the future, are potentially connected to misleading impressions of who you really are and what are your true capabilities. In other words, have you somehow been *over-promising and under-delivering*? And in turn, are you hurting on your trustworthiness as a person and destroying rather than building relationships with people who matter?

Take a look at your BaZi chart and give some thought to what are the differences in the 10 Gods that appear in the Heavenly Stems and the 10 Gods that are present in the Earthly Branches. Look closely in particular at the 10 Gods that ONLY appear in the Heavenly Stems. Are the differences in External Character and Internal Character such that they may be the cause of miscommunications or misunderstandings or even false impressions? Are you indicating that you possess certain skills or abilities which are not actually a part of your Internal Character? Now ask yourself if there have been situations at work or in your personal life where such a misleading impression has resulted in a case of over-promising and under-delivering.

Of course, not everyone experiences this problem. Some people may exhibit a highly consistent External and Internal Character (where the Stars in the Heavenly Stems and Earthly Branches largely mirror each other), and thus are unlikely to face a problem of over-promising and under-delivering. Every person faces different challenges. The idea here is to be open to the possibility that you might be inadvertently engaged in 'misleading' advertising and thus, creating unnecessary problems for yourself.

Are you indicating that you possess certain skills or abilities which are not actually a part of your Internal Character?

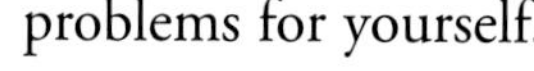

Summon forth your inner talents.

In the same vein that you may inadvertently be promoting or advertising abilities that you don't have through first impressions, equally, you may not be exhibiting your inner talents or abilities sufficiently. When an element appears in the Branches but does not correspondingly appear in the Stems, this means that that the qualities and traits associated with that element are not immediately apparent upon first meeting the person. Thus, in a first impression situation such as a job interview, business networking session or business presentation, your true abilities may simply not come to fore because there simply hasn't been enough time for people to discover your Internal Character.

Having analysed your own BaZi chart using the walk-through in Chapter 5, you should be aware of your Internal Character and thus accordingly conscious of what are the traits and characteristics you inherently possess as part of your Internal Character. Now, spend a moment to reflect on whether or not you are really bringing forth those traits and characteristics in your day-to-day dealings with people or at work.

leadership skills

For example, if you have a Direct Officer or 7 Killings Star in the Branches of your chart, but not in the Stems, this means that you have inherent leadership skills but these leadership skills may not come to the fore quickly or strongly. Equally, if you have Hurting Officer Stars in the Branches of your chart, but not in the Stems, then your creative skills, your capacity for innovation, your ability to generate unique ideas and your communication skills may be under-exhibited. If you have Indirect Wealth Stars in the Branches of your chart but these do not appear in the Stems of your chart, then your entrepreneurial skills may not be immediately obvious and you may lose out on business opportunities because you're do not seem like obvious entrepreneur material. Alternatively, you may find that you lose out on job opportunities that require demonstrable deal-making and negotiation skills, in spite of having the haggling talents of a carpet-seller.

Of course, there are some 'talents' which you may wisely not want to exhibit. For example, a gift for unorthodox and unconventional problem-solving, the ability to find shortcuts or even an insightful sixth sense or intuition, as bestowed by the Indirect Resource Star, are probably skills and traits you don't want to advertise directly to prospective employers. There's nothing wrong with having these traits and abilities and certainly, the Indirect Resource Star affords many traits and characteristics that are useful in a job or in life generally. But there may also be traits related to that Star which you do not want to prominently advertise.

Generally speaking however, if you have a talent or an ability (and each of the 10 Stars conveys something unique in terms of talent or ability), then as far as possible, you want to make sure that talent or ability is a known-quality. And whilst that talent or ability may be a known quality to your friends or family, the fact is that your talents and abilities must be known by the people that matter as well, such as employers, business partners or people who you rely upon to earn an income or make a living.

So what can you do to bring out your inner talents? Being aware of what those talents are is the first step. Learning to talk up your skills at every opportunity you get is another step. Training yourself to exhibit those abilities all the time, 24/7, would also be another logical step. Remember the 30% in life that constitutes Man Luck? This is what is meant by Man Luck – the pro-active moves that **you** make in order to achieve your goals.

Thus if for example, leadership skills are part of your Internal Character, then you should seize opportunities to demonstrate these skills, no matter small or big. You should discuss your leadership skills in any job interview you attend. And you should consciously make sure that you exhibit these leadership skills and traits all the time. You should be constantly improving and enhancing your leadership skills through courses or reading books on the subject because even inherent talents and skills need to be improved.

If creative skills are part of your Internal Character, then you should be in a job that involves making use of these skills or take up hobbies or pastimes that involve creativity or innovation or communication or artistic endeavours. You need to be open to constantly improving your creative abilities by pushing yourself to get better at what you do.

Whether it is in small ways or big ways, you should strive to always be doing something with these inner talents. Practice them, nurture them, enhance them, perfect them, but most importantly, make sure they are visible and on display for all the world to see.

Seize opportunities to demonstrate your leadership skills

Nurturing your hidden talents and abilities

The 10 Gods that are found in the Sub-Qi of Earthly Branches are regarded as representative of hidden or latent talents, traits and abilities. However, the 10 Gods that are present as the Sub-Qi within Graveyard Storage Branches and Growth Branches are regarded as more significant by way of hidden or latent talents, traits and abilities. This is because the Graveyard-Storage Branches or 墓庫星 (sometimes termed the 'Vault') are the end point of each of the four seasons. But the Graveyard-Storage Branches are also one component of the Three Harmony Combination.

As such, each Graveyard-Storage Branch contains an element that is weak and diminishing, but also an element that is nascent. Thus, in each Graveyard-Storage Branch, the Sub-Qi represents a weak hidden talent, trait or ability, and a nascent or latent hidden talent, trait or ability.

四墓 The 4 Graveyards

辰	戌	丑	未
Chen **Dragon** Yang Earth	*Xu* **Dog** Yang Earth	*Chou* **Ox** Yin Earth	*Wei* **Goat** Yin Earth
癸 *Gui* - Water 食 EG; 戊 *Wu* + Earth 印 DR; 乙 *Yi* - Wood 才 IW	丁 *Ding* - Fire 殺 7K; 戊 *Wu* + Earth 印 DR; 辛 *Xin* - Metal 比 F	辛 *Xin* - Metal 比 F; 己 *Ji* - Earth 卩 IR; 癸 *Gui* - Water 食 EG	乙 *Yi* - Wood 才 IW; 己 *Ji* - Earth 卩 IR; 丁 *Ding* - Fire 殺 7K

Earthly Branch	Weak/ Diminishing Element (termed 'in Graveyard')	Nascent Element (termed 'in storage')
Dragon 辰 (Chen)	Wood	Water
Goat 未 (Wei)	Fire	Wood
Dog 戌 (Xu)	Metal	Fire
Ox 丑 (Chou)	Water	Metal

Specific Sub-Qi of the Growth Branches 四生星 on the other hand, expressly represent latent talent, traits and abilities. This is because each of the Growth Branches is the start point of each of the four seasons, and is a component of the Three Harmony Combinations. However, unlike the Graveyard-Storage Branches, which contain elements that are both weak and diminishing as well as nascent, the focal point of the Growth Branches is the element in the Sub-Qi that is rising and nascent.

四生 The Four Growths

寅 Yin **Tiger** Yang Wood	申 Shen **Monkey** Yang Metal	巳 Si **Snake** Yin Fire	亥 Hai **Pig** Yin Water
戊 Wu + Earth 印 DR; 甲 Jia + Wood 財 DW; 丙 Bing + Fire 官 DO	戊 Wu + Earth 印 DR; 庚 Geng + Metal 劫 RW; 壬 Ren + Water 傷 HO	庚 Geng + Metal 劫 RW; 丙 Bing + Fire 官 DO; 戊 Wu + Earth 印 DR	壬 Ren + Water 傷 HO; 甲 Jia + Wood 財 DW

Earthly Branch	Element in Growth
Tiger 寅 (Yin)	Fire 火
Snake 巳 (Si)	Metal 金
Monkey 申 (Shen)	Water 水
Pig 亥 (Hai)	Wood 木

For example, in Tiger (Yin), Bing Fire is regarded as being 'in growth'. Thus the Star (and the accompanying traits, abilities and talents) represented by the element of Bing Fire constitute latent talents within the person – talents that are present but not fully developed yet. With cultivation, nurturing and encouragement, the traits, abilities and talents associated with this Star will come to the fore more strongly and within a shorter period of time.

As general rule, a Star that regarded as an Element in Growth inside a Growth Branch is considered to be a superior manifestation of a latent talent compared to a Star hidden inside a Graveyard-Storage Branch. Stars hidden in the Growth Branches denote potential that is on the uptick and which eventually will emerge at full strength if it is well-nurtured. Stars hidden inside Graveyard Branches on the other hand denote potential that is present but may require a lot of effort to bring forth and the potential of those traits and abilities being beneficial is limited.

Whilst it is a good idea to nurture both Stars hidden in the Growth and Graveyard Branches, strategically, you want to focus on nurturing the talents hidden in the Growth Branches, since these are easier to bring forth and represent strongly nascent Qi. Stars hidden in the Graveyard Branches tend to be more difficult to bring forth (as they are hidden deep inside the Earth elements) or may represent weakened Qi (if the Star happens to be the element 'in Graveyard'.

Chart A:

時 Hour	日 Day	月 Month	年 Year	
正印 DR 乙 Yi Yin Wood	日元 DM 丙 Bing Yang Fire	偏印 IR 甲 Jia Yang Wood	正財 DW 辛 Xin Yin Metal	天干 Heavenly Stems
未 Wei **Goat** Yin Earth	申 Shen **Monkey** Yang Metal	午 Wu **Horse** Yang Fire	酉 You **Rooster** Yin Metal	地支 Earthly Branches
乙 Yi - Wood 印 DR; 己 Ji - Earth 傷 HO; 丁 Ding - Fire 劫 RW	戊 Wu + Earth 食 EG; 庚 Geng + Metal 才 IW; 壬 Ren + Water 殺 7K	丁 Ding - Fire 劫 RW; 己 Ji - Earth 傷 HO	辛 Xin - Metal 財 DW	藏干 Hidden Stems

In this chart, the 7 Killings Star of Bing Fire, which is Ren Water, is hidden in the Growth Branch of the Monkey (Shen). This denotes a person with hidden or latent leadership abilities, especially the more aggressive, corporate-raider kind.

Chart B:

時 Hour	日 Day	月 Month	年 Year	
正財 DW 癸 Gui Yin Water	日元 DM 戊 Wu Yang Earth	劫財 RW 己 Ji Yin Earth	劫財 RW 己 Ji Yin Earth	天干 Heavenly Stems
丑 Chou **Ox** Yin Earth	午 Wu **Horse** Yang Fire	巳 Si **Snake** Yin Fire	未 Wei **Goat** Yin Earth	地支 Earthly Branches
辛 Xin - Metal 傷 HO; 己 Ji - Earth 劫 RW; 癸 Gui - Water 財 DW	丁 Ding - Fire 印 DR; 己 Ji - Earth 劫 RW	庚 Geng + Metal 傷 HO; 丙 Bing + Fire 印 DR; 戊 Wu + Earth 劫 RW	乙 Yi - Wood 官 DO; 己 Ji - Earth 劫 RW; 丁 Ding - Fire 印 DR	藏干 Hidden Stems

In this chart, the Direct Officer Star of Wu Earth, which is Yi Wood, is hidden in the Graveyard Branch of the Goat (Wei). Whilst this denotes hidden management skills or leadership skills, as the Direct Officer Star is in the Graveyard Branch, it will be harder for this person to nurture and bring forth this ability compared to Chart A.

時 Hour	日 Day	月 Month	年 Year	
七殺 7K 乙 Yi Yin Wood	日元 DM 己 Ji Yin Earth	劫財 RW 戊 Wu Yang Earth	七殺 7K 乙 Yi Yin Wood	天干 Heavenly Stems
亥 Hai **Pig** Yin Water	酉 You **Rooster** Yin Metal	寅 Yin **Tiger** Yang Wood	卯 Mao **Rabbit** Yin Wood	地支 Earthly Branches
壬 Ren + Water 財 DW; 甲 Jia + Wood 官 DO	辛 Xin - Metal 食 EG	戊 Wu + Earth 劫 RW; 甲 Jia + Wood 官 DO; 丙 Bing + Fire 印 DR	乙 Yi - Wood 殺 7K	藏干 Hidden Stems

In this chart, the Direct Resource Star of Ji Earth, which is Bing Fire, is hidden in the Growth Branch of the Tiger (Yin). The Direct Resource Star represents a person's learning, education and knowledge and paper qualifications. The Hidden quality of this Star in the Growth Branch denotes that the person is marshalling their knowledge and continuously adding to their learning, and that eventually, that knowledge and learning will come to fruition. In this chart, it is also notable that the Direct Resource Star is also the Useful God, which makes the Direct Resource Star all the more favourable to the Day Master.

The Direct Resource Star represents a person's learning, education and knowledge and paper qualifications.

At some point, these hidden or latent talents, traits and abilities will come to the fore but in some people, it takes so long for them to realise these talents, traits and abilities that by the time they decide to do something or make use of these abilities, they may have already lost out on valuable opportunities. That is why it is important to nurture these hidden or latent talents, traits and abilities. They may not pay off right now, but the quicker you can bring them out from within you, the sooner you'll be able to make use of them to achieve your goals or advance yourself in life.

You might be wondering: how do I nurture my latent traits, abilities and talents? From the 10 Gods essentials in Chapter 3, you should be able to identify certain traits, abilities or mindsets and attitudes that epitomise each of the 10 Gods. Nurturing your latent traits, abilities or talents then becomes a case of using your Man Luck to help nudge these talents, abilities and traits out into the open. For example, if leadership skills (represented by the 7 Killings or Direct Officer Stars) are part of your latent traits, abilities and talents, then seeking out opportunities to utilise leadership skills (ie: joining an association where you get to organise activities or participating in team sports) or taking classes where you learn about leadership skills are some examples of the things that you can do to nurture these latent traits, abilities and talents.

Equally, if creative skills (represented by the Hurting Officer or Eating God Stars) are part of your latent traits, abilities or talents, then you should be taking up lots of creative activities, or endeavour to find a creative element or innovation element to your job to help nurture those skills to the fore.

Many of the 10 Gods essentials highlighted in Chapter 3 represent attitudes or traits. By making these attitudes or traits part of your core values, you are also nurturing these abilities. If for example, if you want to nurture your Direct Wealth Star, then making the traits and attitudes connected with the Direct Wealth Star (such as prudence, orthodoxy, self-discipline, a devout sense of responsibility) a part of your day-to-day practice will help you nurture this Star. It could be something as simple as sticking to a gym routine or regularly cleaning your apartment since both these activities represent a form of self-discipline.

The point to remember about Hidden Stars is that they represent talents, traits and abilities that you already possess. They just need a little helping hand along the way to blossom and fulfil their potential, and in turn, help you fulfil your fullest potential.

Downplaying the Disadvantages

Too often people are focused on what they are good at doing or what they can do and not enough thought is sometimes given to what they are NOT good at doing or what they shouldn't be doing. Many times in a professional BaZi consultation, clients consciously avoid getting information about the less favourable aspects of their chart. There is perhaps this notion, in this age of positive thinking and motivational speakers, that we should all have a gung-ho can-do attitude and that life should not be about what we can't but be focused on what we can.

Unfortunately, many pitfalls and perils in life occur because people have a false perception of what they can do or are capable of achieving. Disappointments then ensue and frustration occurs because a person is unable to rationalise why their endeavour failed, when the answer may well be very simple: they are not equipped to do that, skills-wise.

Whatever Stars are absent in your chart will provide you with an indication of the traits and abilities which are not part of your inherent character make-up. Attempting then to enter into a field or profession or career choice that requires utilising such traits or abilities is arguably unwise seeing as one is then competing against other individuals who have such traits and abilities and are thus able to naturally harness such traits and abilities better. In such a situation, you're not just competing against people who already have an advantage because they possess certain Stars that you may

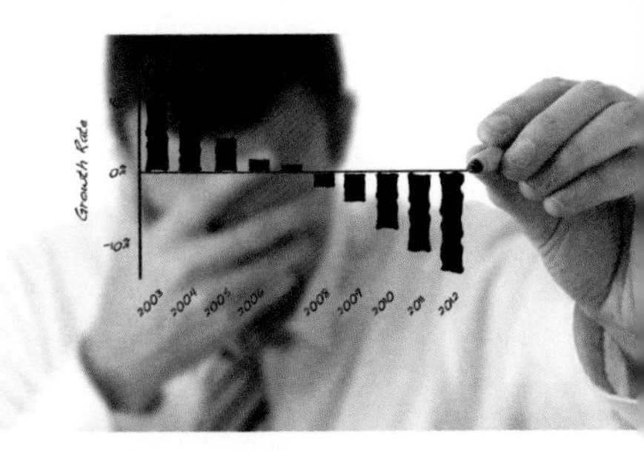

Disappointments and frustration occurs because a person is unable to rationalise why their endeavour failed.

not have, but you are also competing against people who possess the same Stars, but of a superior quality.

For example, the Indirect Wealth Star usually denotes entrepreneurial skills, deal-making ability and an opportunistic eye for financial opportunities. The presence of the Indirect Wealth Star is conventionally regarded as one of the indicators of a person's suitability to start/own a business or to be an entrepreneur.

If a chart does not contain the Indirect Wealth Star, typically this indicates a limited capacity for business ownership. Individuals who do not have the Indirect Wealth Star in their chart are usually only suited for very orthodox businesses with limited upside and steady returns, such as franchises, mini-markets, stationary stores, petrol stations or family-owned businesses. Alternatively, they are professionals businesses such as doctors, dentists or accountants.

If your chart does not contain the Indirect Wealth Star and you want to start a business that is neither highly-orthodox nor a professional business, then you need to be aware that you are already starting out with a ***disadvantage***. There are very few businesses out there which do not require skills such as deal-making and negotiation, the instant ability to see financial upsides in a given situation, an inherent instinct for revenue-generating opportunities and a hustler mindset.

If a chart does not contain the Indirect Wealth Star, typically this indicates a limited capacity for business ownership.

Not only are you starting with a disadvantage, but it is a significant disadvantage.

Comparing the individual who does not possess the Indirect Wealth Star with the individual who does possess the Indirect Wealth Star reveals just one part of the disadvantage equation. Now compare the individual who does not possess the Indirect Wealth Star and the individual who possesses a superior quality Indirect Wealth Star, or someone for whom the Indirect Wealth Star is a Useful God or Favourable Element.

The individual who does not possess the Indirect Wealth Star is already at a severe disadvantage as he or she will lack the skills needed to succeed in running an entrepreneurial venture. Such an individual is also entirely dependant on a favourable Luck Pillar cycle in order to achieve a measure of financial success via a business venture. By contrast, the individual with the superior quality Indirect Wealth Star or with the Indirect Wealth Star as their Useful God will already enjoy a measure of entrepreneurial financial success and their Luck Pillar cycle will simply determine the extent of their financial success.

The individual with the superior quality Indirect Wealth Star, will enjoy a measure of entrepreneurial financial success.

These three examples illustrate the point above aptly.

Chart A:

時 Hour	日 Day	月 Month	年 Year	
正印 DR 戊 *Wu* Yang Earth	日元 DM 辛 *Xin* Yin Metal	正財 DW 甲 *Jia* Yang Wood	正印 DR 戊 *Wu* Yang Earth	天干 Heavenly Stems
子 *Zi* **Rat** Yang Water	酉 *You* **Rooster** Yin Metal	子 *Zi* **Rat** Yang Water	午 *Wu* **Horse** Yang Fire	地支 Earthly Branches
癸 *Gui* - Water 食 EG	辛 *Xin* - Metal 比 F	癸 *Gui* - Water 食 EG	丁 *Ding* - Fire 殺 7K; 己 *Ji* - Earth 卩 IR	藏干 Hidden Stems

Chart A only contains the Direct Wealth Star, and has no Indirect Wealth Star. Thus this person will clearly be disadvantaged if he or she decided to start an entrepreneurial venture.

Chart B:

時 Hour	日 Day	月 Month	年 Year	
七殺 7K 壬 *Ren* Yang Water	日元 DM 丙 *Bing* Yang Fire	正印 DR 乙 *Yi* Yin Wood	偏印 IR 甲 *Jia* Yang Wood	天干 Heavenly Stems
辰 *Chen* **Dragon** Yang Earth	寅 *Yin* **Tiger** Yang Wood	亥 *Hai* **Pig** Yin Water	子 *Zi* **Rat** Yang Water	地支 Earthly Branches
癸 *Gui* - Water 官 DO; 戊 *Wu* + Earth 食 EG; 乙 *Yi* - Wood 印 DR	戊 *Wu* + Earth 食 EG; 甲 *Jia* + Wood 卩 IR; 丙 *Bing* + Fire 比 F	壬 *Ren* + Water 殺 7K; 甲 *Jia* + Wood 卩 IR	癸 *Gui* - Water 官 DO	藏干 Hidden Stems

Chart B contains no Wealth Stars – neither the Direct Wealth or Indirect Wealth Stars are present. This person will be even more disadvantaged if he or she decided to start an entrepreneurial venture compared to Chart A since they have no affinity with the Wealth Star at all.

Chart C:

時 Hour	日 Day	月 Month	年 Year	
正印 DR 戊 Wu Yang Earth	日元 DM 辛 Xin Yin Metal	偏印 IR 己 Ji Yin Earth	偏財 IW 乙 Yi Yin Wood	天干 Heavenly Stems
戌 Xu **Dog** Yang Earth	巳 Si **Snake** Yin Fire	卯 Mao **Rabbit** Yin Wood	亥 Hai **Pig** Yin Water	地支 Earthly Branches
丁 Ding - Fire 殺 7K; 戊 Wu + Earth 印 DR; 辛 Xin - Metal 比 F	庚 Geng + Metal 劫 RW; 丙 Bing + Fire 官 DO; 戊 Wu + Earth 印 DR	乙 Yi - Wood 才 IW	壬 Ren + Water 傷 HO; 甲 Jia + Wood 財 DW	藏干 Hidden Stems

Chart C not only contains the Indirect Wealth Star, but the Indirect Wealth Star is a Dominant Characteristic as Yi Wood in the Year Stem is rooted in the Rabbit (Mao) month. On a more advanced level of interpretation, Wood element in this chart, which is the Wealth Element for Xin Metal, is supported by a partial Three Harmony Wood Combination and also by the season of Birth. This chart has a superior quality Indirect Wealth Star. Accordingly, if three of these above individuals embarked on an entrepreneurial venture, the likelihood for success is significantly higher in the case of Chart C than Chart A or Chart B.

What is the moral of the story here? Trying to do something that you are ill-equipped to achieve is a form of setting yourself up for failure. Ignoring your weaknesses or denying that you don't have certain inherent skills needed to succeed in certain fields is patently unwise. Whilst there is of course room in life to push your luck, one must in the first place, have the seeds of possibility planted within one's chart.

Now it is the case today that most professions are made up of a mix of skills – in other words, multiple 10 Gods may be required in order to succeed at that profession. However, there is, in almost all the cases, one 10 God that is specifically required to attain a measure of success or achievement and which is not optional in every given field or profession. For example, if you want to pursue a career as a professional manager in a top company, the Direct Officer Star or 7 Killings Star is most certainly required. If you want to be a good salesperson, then the Rob Wealth Star is most certainly required. If you want to succeed in an artistic field, the Hurting Officer Star or Eating God Star are mandatory Stars to possess in your chart.

It is smart and strategic to be realistic about what are your weaknesses and then to avoid situations where you might be forced to call on skills or traits that you don't have. Instead of trying your luck, focus on finding alternative ways to achieve your personal goals either by utilising Stars that you do have in your chart or looking at your Dominant Characteristics. It may require some retooling of your objectives or a recognition that your skills lie elsewhere from where you thought they did but it is better than banging your head against the wall. As I mentioned earlier, the complexity of the working world today means that most jobs and professions involve a mixture of skill sets, so perhaps it is just a case of finding where you truly fit in your industry or profession of choice. As with the example of the Indirect Wealth Star above, the absence of such a Star does not mean an inability to start or own a business but simply puts restrictions or limitations on the type of business that can be owned.

I personally am a great believer in the power of motivational and positive thinking but as I say to my students, there is positive thinking and there is positively bluffing yourself. Ignoring your inherent weaknesses is positively bluffing yourself in the biggest way possible.

By analysing your BaZi, and looking at what are the traits that you do not possess (based on what 10 Gods are absent in your chart), you are taking an important step towards removing obstacles from the path to success because you now understand where these obstacles lie. And by following the advice to summon forth your inner talents, you are opening the door to success, rather than failure.

Always Bring Your 'A' GAME

You will recall that in Chapter 3 on the 10 Gods Essentials, it was explained that each of the 10 Gods contains both positive and negative traits and characteristics. At this point, I have not touched on the topic of evaluating the quality of each of the 10 Gods in a BaZi chart. This is because evaluating the quality of each of the 10 Gods is quite a lengthy topic and thus deserving of a book on the subject. Evaluating the quality of the 10 Gods in a BaZi chart thus will be the subject of the next book in the *Power of X* series. The quality of an individual 10 God is what determines whether a 10 God manifests more of its positive traits and characteristics or more of its negative traits and characteristics, amongst other things.

However, even without being able to evaluate the quality of the 10 Gods in your BaZi chart, you know one thing for certain: that every 10 God has positive and negative traits and your character will accordingly will contain both positive and negative traits and characteristics. You are simply unable to determine, through an analysis of the BaZi chart, whether the positive or negative traits are manifesting more strongly. (Of course, if you are self-conscious of your own character, you might have already sort of worked this out by now).

Positive

Negative

In all of our endeavours, we should strive to always bring what the Americans call, your 'A' Game or one's personal best. In the context of BaZi, bringing your 'A' Game essentially is about playing up your positive traits and characteristics and keeping the negative traits and characteristics to a minimum. This is particularly the case when it comes to your Dominant Characteristics.

The Dominant Characteristics, as you will recall from Chapter 5, are traits and characteristics which are the most pronounced aspects of a person's character and which significantly influence a person's mindset, attitude and outlook on the world. Your Dominant Characteristics will manifest in every aspect of your life and influence almost all of your decisions, actions and choices. Now, since it is possible that you will manifest both negative and positive aspects of your Dominant Characteristics, its essential to be conscious of the need to try to exude the positive aspects more, and downplay the negative aspects.

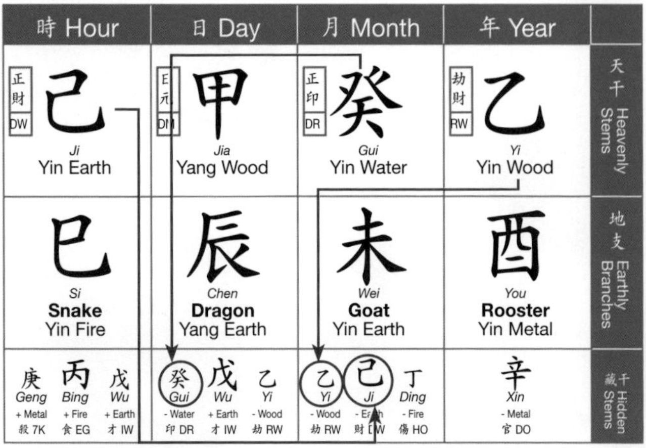

時 Hour	日 Day	月 Month	年 Year	
正財 DW 己 Ji Yin Earth	日元 DM 甲 Jia Yang Wood	正印 DR 癸 Gui Yin Water	劫財 RW 乙 Yi Yin Wood	天干 Heavenly Stems
巳 Si **Snake** Yin Fire	辰 Chen **Dragon** Yang Earth	未 Wei **Goat** Yin Earth	酉 You **Rooster** Yin Metal	地支 Earthly Branches
庚 Geng + Metal 殺 7K; 丙 Bing + Fire 食 EG; 戊 Wu + Earth 才 IW	癸 Gui - Water 印 DR; 戊 Wu + Earth 才 IW; 乙 Yi - Wood 劫 RW	乙 Yi - Wood 劫 RW; 己 Ji - Earth 財 DW; 丁 Ding - Fire 傷 HO	辛 Xin - Metal 官 DO	藏干 Hidden Stems

In this Jia Wood example, the Dominant Characteristics are the Direct Wealth Star, the Indirect Resource Star and the Rob Wealth Star, as all three of these Stars appear in the Heavenly Stems and are rooted in the Earthly Branches. Each of these three Stars has positive and negative aspects to them. For example, the Direct Wealth Star can denote a fiscally responsible person or a miser. The Indirect Resource Star can denote a resourceful person or someone who is just lazy and resorts to the path of least resistance. Finally, the Rob Wealth Star denotes a spontaneous character but can also denote a person with a habit of doing things at the last-minute with little preparation. This person must be careful to make sure that they emphasise and bring out the positive traits (fiscal responsibility, resourcefulness, spontaneous character) or chose the right moments to bring out the right traits. For example, spontaneity might be good for friends and family but perhaps less appropriate in the workplace.

時 Hour	日 Day	月 Month	年 Year	
偏財 IW 丁 Ding Yin Fire	日元 DM 癸 Gui Yin Water	正印 DR 庚 Geng Yang Metal	傷官 HO 甲 Jia Yang Wood	天干 Heavenly Stems
巳 Si **Snake** Yin Fire	卯 Mao **Rabbit** Yin Wood	午 Wu **Horse** Yang Fire	申 Shen **Monkey** Yang Metal	地支 Earthly Branches
庚 Geng + Metal 印 DR; 丙 Bing + Fire 財 DW; 戊 Wu + Earth 官 DO	乙 Yi - Wood 食 EG	丁 Ding - Fire 才 IW; 己 Ji - Earth 殺 7K	戊 Wu + Earth 官 DO; 庚 Geng + Metal 印 DR; 壬 Ren + Water 劫 RW	藏干 Hidden Stems

In this Gui Water example, the Dominant Characteristics are the Direct Resource Star and Indirect Wealth Star. The Direct Resource Star's positive traits include knowledge and patience, whilst its negative traits include laziness and procrastination. The Indirect Wealth Star's positive traits are entrepreneurialism and negotiation skills, whilst its negative traits include out of control spending and a lack of focus. Thus, this person should focus on their 'A' Game which is the entrepreneurialism, negotiation skills, knowledge and patience and try avoid procrastination or losing focus in what they do.

The Direct Resource Star's negative traits include laziness and procrastination.

Taking the first step

Much of what has been suggested to you in this Chapter by way of action is very wide-ranging and broad. It is not practical or sensible to attempt to do everything suggested here. Instead, look at the courses of action suggested in this chapter and pick something that most closely connects with **what you want to achieve at this very moment in time.** Periodically revisit your goals and objectives in life and ask yourself which course of action would better serve that purpose. For example, if misunderstandings or miscommunications seem to be the problem you constantly face, then it could be you are over-promising and under-delivering. If you don't seem to be able to make people realise what you are good at doing, then summoning forth your inner talents and nurturing your hidden talents is what you need to pay attention towards. If you're trying to get to the next level, then bringing your 'A' game out every day might be what you need to do.

Each person's BaZi chart is unique. Accordingly, each person's needs and requirements at a given time are special to them. Analyse your chart, be realistic and as grounded as you can about what are the things that you need to do. And then make sure you take action. Remember, improvements that you make don't have to be big – they can be small but most importantly, they must be consistently implemented in order to achieve true and lasting change.

Chapter 7
Using the 10 Gods and Character for Relationship, Wealth and Career Matters

This Chapter will demonstrate to you how to obtain practical useful information about yourself and other people, utilising the 10 Gods Essentials in Chapter 3 and the basic analysis techniques for the 10 Gods discussed in Chapter 4. The objective here is to show you some simple approaches to obtaining useful and insightful information about yourself or other people with regards relationship, wealth and career matters. Not everything that you will learn about yourself or other people will necessarily be positive of course but it is important to appreciate that insight into one's flaws is as valuable as insight into one's virtues.

It must be made clear that the techniques discussed here are not the be-all-and-end-all when it comes to analysing those three subjects. Some readers might regard the information they obtain from the analysis as rather simple and basic. In this respect, I think there is a lack of understanding of the value of certain basic answers when it comes to matters of relationship, wealth or career. For example, with wealth matters, the most common question BaZi clients pose is how they can make more money or conversely, why they never have enough money. With career matters, clients are often flummoxed by their inability to proceed forward with their career, despite by their own estimates, much effort. These are simple basic questions that frequently can be answered with simple basic answers. A basic answer to their question in turn provides an already valuable starting point towards understanding what needs to be DONE in order to improve the situation. So don't under-rate the simple and basic. Sometimes, that's all it takes!

In this section, you will notice that health will not be covered. This is because the issue of health is not quite so closely-connected to the subject matter of character. Indeed, Health is an entire subject on its own and is difficult to cover within a limited context. Accordingly, the focal point of this section will be on matters relating to Career, Relationships and Wealth.

✓	**Career**
✓	**Relationships**
✓	**Wealth**
✗	**Health**

The 10 Gods and Career Matters

In this section, I will show you how to utilise the information about the 10 Gods from Chapter 3 and combine it with the analysis methods discussed in Chapter 4 to gain certain insight into a person's career prospects and how their character can create specific career-related challenges. The analysis methods here will not delve into what industries or jobs are suitable for a person as that is beyond the scope of the analysis methods discussed here. Rather, the focal point will be on the 10 Gods that are most relevant to career-related matters and also a broad discussion of how certain Dominant Characteristics can pose difficulties with regards career matters.

Excepting routine administrative jobs or drone jobs such as manual labour or working in a factory, most jobs require a composite of skills. The average employee these days needs to be able to communicate well, both in terms of spoken and written skills, needs to be able to network and build relationships, is expected to show initiative, exercise responsibility, demonstrate leadership skills and of course, be learned and knowledgeable in their field of expertise. And in certain jobs, you must also show an ability to handle budgets and financial matters. If you think about it, that's practically all of the 10 Gods that need to be involved.

In Chapter 5, I eluded to the value of understanding if someone is a simple person or a complex person. When it comes to careers, some people are multi-taskers and able to handle a job with many different aspects. Others are a bit more specialised, and thus tend to be more suited for what are known as vertical jobs, meaning, jobs with a narrow scope of expertise.

By and large, if you don't have very many 10 Gods in your chart (and by very many, I mean 5 or less than 5), then chances are you are not a versatile and thus accordingly have limited job mobility. You likely need to be in a highly-specialised industry or do a job that involves a very narrowly defined set of skills. Given the limited capacity for job mobility, it is important to ensure that you have high-value skills or some form of trade skills (such as plumbing, carpentry, cooking).

Further, when there are 5 or less 10 Gods (as shown by the examples below) there is a 50-50 chance that the chart will also have a Missing Element. Accordingly, one of the Five Factors will be missing. This thus compounds the risk of limited job mobility and emphasises the need to ensure a clear set of high-value skills or a trade skill.

時 Hour	日 Day	月 Month	年 Year	
比肩 F 辛 *Xin* Yin Metal	日元 DM 辛 *Xin* Yin Metal	正印 DR 戊 *Wu* Yang Earth	正印 DR 戊 *Wu* Yang Earth	天干 Heavenly Stems
卯 *Mao* **Rabbit** Yin Wood	未 *Wei* **Goat** Yin Earth	午 *Wu* **Horse** Yang Fire	戌 *Xu* **Dog** Yang Earth	地支 Earthly Branches
乙 *Yi* - Wood 才 IW	乙 *Yi* - Wood 才 IW; 己 *Ji* - Earth 卩 IR; 丁 *Ding* - Fire 殺 7K	丁 *Ding* - Fire 殺 7K; 己 *Ji* - Earth 卩 IR	丁 *Ding* - Fire 殺 7K; 戊 *Wu* + Earth 印 DR; 辛 *Xin* - Metal 比 F	藏干 Hidden Stems

In this Xin Metal example, the chart only contains 5 out of the 10 Gods, namely, Friend, Direct Resource, Indirect Resource, 7 Killings and Indirect Wealth. Note that the element of Water, which represents the Output Element for Xin Metal, is entirely missing. In such an instance, the person will do well to avoid jobs which require the skills imbued by the Hurting Officer or Eating God Stars such as communication skills, strategic thinking or creativity and innovation.

	時 Hour	日 Day	月 Month	年 Year
天干 Heavenly Stems	偏印 IR 壬 *Ren* Yang Water	食神 EG 丙 *Bing* Yang Fire	劫財 RW 乙 *Yi* Yin Wood	比肩 F 甲 *Jia* Yang Wood
地支 Earthly Branches	辰 *Chen* **Dragon** Yang Earth	寅 *Yin* **Tiger** Yang Wood	亥 *Hai* **Pig** Yin Water	子 *Zi* **Rat** Yang Water
藏干 Hidden Stems	癸 *Gui* - Water 印 DR; 戊 *Wu* + Earth 才 IW; 乙 *Yi* - Wood 劫 RW	戊 *Wu* + Earth 才 IW; 甲 *Jia* + Wood 比 F; 丙 *Bing* + Fire 食 EG	壬 *Ren* + Water 卩 IR; 甲 *Jia* + Wood 比 F	癸 *Gui* - Water 印 DR

In this Bing Fire example, the chart only contains 6 out of the 10 Gods, namely, Friend, Direct Resource, Indirect Resource, 7 Killings, Direct Officer and Eating God. Note that the element of Metal, which represents the Wealth Element for Bing Fire, is entirely missing. In such an instance, the person will find it hard to thrive in a job that involves fiscal prudence or financial management or any form of budgeting. He or she should also avoid jobs that require entrepreneurialism or opportunism such as business development.

時 Hour	日 Day	月 Month	年 Year	
劫財 RW 戊 Wu Yang Earth	日元 DM 己 Ji Yin Earth	七殺 7K 乙 Yi Yin Wood	七殺 7K 乙 Yi Yin Wood	天干 Heavenly Stems
辰 Chen **Dragon** Yang Earth	卯 Mao **Rabbit** Yin Wood	酉 You **Rooster** Yin Metal	丑 Chou **Ox** Yin Earth	地支 Earthly Branches
癸 Gui - Water 才 IW; 戊 Wu + Earth 劫 RW; 乙 Yi - Wood 殺 7K	乙 Yi - Wood 殺 7K	辛 Xin - Metal 食 EG	辛 Xin - Metal 食 EG; 己 Ji - Earth 比 F; 癸 Gui - Water 才 IW	藏干 Hidden Stems

In this Ji Earth example, the chart only contains 5 out of the 10 Gods, namely, Friend, 7 Killings, Indirect Wealth, Eating God and Rob Wealth. Note that the element of Fire, which represents the Resource Element for Ji Earth, is entirely missing. In such an instance, the person will do well to avoid jobs which require the skills imbued by the Direct Resource or Indirect Resource Stars. Accordingly, jobs that require a lot of professional qualifications or intellectual activity or high levels of academic qualification are not suited for this person – they may be better off doing a job that involves hands-on skill, such as a craft or a trade.

If your chart contains a Missing Element or has very few 10 Gods, you shouldn't be trying for a job or be in a job that involves the skills or traits that the Missing Elements or absent 10 Gods require. Not only will you not be effective in these jobs, chances are you'll also be deeply unhappy because of the fact that you're not particularly good at what you do.

Of course, there are exceptions to this, such as in the case of a Special Structure chart. Whilst few charts with missing elements or with 5 or less 10 Gods will fall into this category, it is important to be aware of the possibility that a chart may fall into such a unique category.

For example, Donald Trump's chart (below) does not have a single drop of Water in it. As he is a Ji Earth Day Master, this means the Wealth Element is missing. However, his chart qualifies as a Special Structure, hence the normal rules of interpretation do not apply to his chart.

時 Hour	日 Day	月 Month	年 Year	
食神 EG 辛 Xin Yin Metal	日元 DM 己 Ji Yin Earth	正官 DO 甲 Jia Yang Wood	正印 DR 丙 Bing Yang Fire	天干 Heavenly Stems
未 Wei **Goat** Yin Earth	未 Wei **Goat** Yin Earth	午 Wu **Horse** Yang Fire	戌 Xu **Dog** Yang Earth	地支 Earthly Branches
乙 Yi - Wood 殺 7K; 己 Ji - Earth 比 F; 丁 Ding - Fire 卩 IR	乙 Yi - Wood 殺 7K; 己 Ji - Earth 比 F; 丁 Ding - Fire 卩 IR	丁 Ding - Fire 卩 IR; 己 Ji - Earth 比 F	丁 Ding - Fire 卩 IR; 戊 Wu + Earth 劫 RW; 辛 Xin - Metal 食 EG	藏干 Hidden Stems

Donald Trump's BaZi chart

However, the criteria to qualify as a Special Structure is very stringent and only a few charts actually meet the criteria. Broadly speaking, most charts would not be considered Special Structures just because they have 5 or less 10 Gods or missing elements. Thus it is best NOT to assume a chart is a Special Structure unless proven otherwise.

What if you have a high number of 10 Gods in your chart (5 or more)? This denotes a greater capacity for versatility and job mobility. However, in such individuals, there is a risk of being a jack-of-all trades and a master of none. As such, if you have a complex chart, it is all the more important to know what are your Dominant Characteristics and to also understand your Internal Character. Your Dominant Characteristics and your Internal Character collectively represent what you are best at doing because it comes naturally to you. The goal then is to find a position or job which plays to those Dominant Characteristics, rather than a job that utilises non-Dominant Characteristics. (for more on this, see Chapter 6, the section entitled 'Bring your 'A' Game')

A jack-of-all trades and a master of none

時 Hour	日 Day	月 Month	年 Year	
正官 DO 癸 Gui Yin Water	日元 DM 丙 Bing Yang Fire	食神 EG 戊 Wu Yang Earth	正印 DR 乙 Yi Yin Wood	天干 Heavenly Stems
巳 Si **Snake** Yin Fire	戌 Xu **Dog** Yang Earth	寅 Yin **Tiger** Yang Wood	卯 Mao **Rabbit** Yin Wood	地支 Earthly Branches
庚 Geng + Metal 才 IW; 丙 Bing + Fire 比 F; 戊 Wu + Earth 食 EG	丁 Ding - Fire 劫 RW; 戊 Wu + Earth 食 EG; 辛 Xin - Metal 財 DW	戊 Wu + Earth 食 EG; 甲 Jia + Wood 卩 IR; 丙 Bing + Fire 比 F	乙 Yi - Wood 印 DR	藏干 Hidden Stems

In this Bing Fire example, the chart contains 8 out of the 10 Gods – only the Hurting Officer and 7 Killings Stars are absent. In such an instance, the person will do well to focus on their Dominant Characteristics, and in particular, look to emphasis the positive aspects of their Dominant Characteristics. Here, the Direct Resource and Eating God Stars are clearly the Dominant Characteristics, denoting a person with a high level of intellectual ability since the Direct Resource Star denotes strong academic ability and the Eating God Star indicates strategic thinking skills. As such, the person should focus on career opportunities related to strategy, planning, training or research and development.

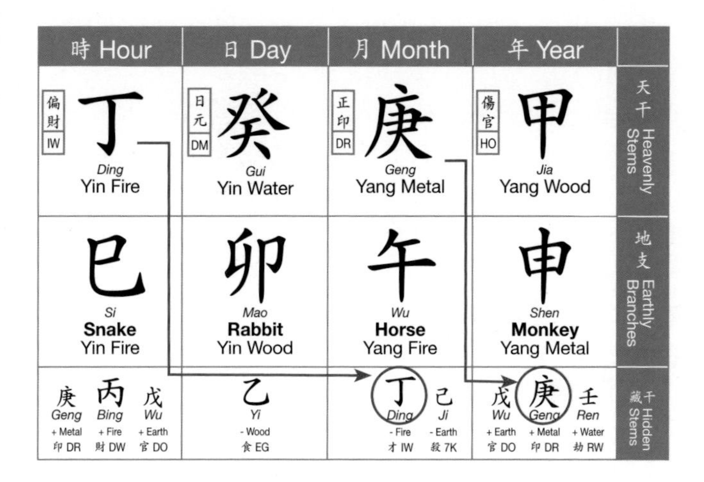

時 Hour
日 Day
月 Month
年 Year
偏財 IW
丁
Ding
Yin Fire
日元 DM
癸
Gui
Yin Water
正印 DR
庚
Geng
Yang Metal
傷官 HO
甲
Jia
Yang Wood
天干 Heavenly Stems
巳
Si
Snake
Yin Fire
卯
Mao
Rabbit
Yin Wood
午
Wu
Horse
Yang Fire
申
Shen
Monkey
Yang Metal
地支 Earthly Branches
庚 Geng + Metal 印 DR
丙 Bing + Fire 財 DW
戊 Wu + Earth 官 DO
乙 Yi - Wood 食 EG
丁 Ding - Fire 才 IW
己 Ji - Earth 殺 7K
戊 Wu + Earth 官 DO
庚 Geng + Metal 印 DR
壬 Ren + Water 劫 RW
藏干 Hidden Stems

In this Gui Water example, the chart contains 9 out of the 10 Gods – only the Indirect Resource Star is absent. In such an instance, the person will do well to focus on their Dominant Characteristics, and in particular, look to emphasis the positive aspects of their Dominant Characteristics. Here, the Indirect Wealth and Direct Resource Stars are clearly the Dominant Characteristics, denoting a person with poise, calm, and a patient temperament from the Direct Resource Star whilst the Indirect Wealth Star indicates strong negotiation skills and business acumen. As such, the person could be suited to running their own business or look at career opportunities related to business development or a job which demands an entrepreneurial and opportunistic mindset such as a sales or marketing job where remuneration is tied to how much business the person brings in.

The Character and Career Connection

Bad attitude comes from character, which dictates mindset and outlook and influences actions, all which composite together to form this thing called 'attitude'.

You might be wondering – how does my character affect my career? Well, if there is one thing employers universally dislike, it's an employee with a **bad attitude**. The definition of a bad attitude varies because there are cultural considerations that come into play. But I am sure most employers (or managers) will agree that tardiness, lackadaisical approach to work, irresponsibility constitute a bad attitude. Employees who are extremely argumentative, excessively opinionated, unable to function in a consensus driven environment, who 'talk back' to superiors and who refuse to follow instructions may also be considered employees with bad attitude. Where does bad attitude come from? It comes from character, which dictates mindset and outlook and influences actions, all which composite together to form this thing called 'attitude'.

So what character traits give rise to a bad attitude at work? If you have the Hurting Officer, Direct Resource or Indirect Resource Stars as your Dominant Characteristics (or both together), then you are at risk of being someone who may be labelled with a 'bad attitude'.

Let's look at the Hurting Officer Star first.

The Hurting Officer Star gives a person innovation skills, creativity, charisma, wit and great communication skills but it also indicates a highly individualistic, opinionated, rebellious individual who enjoys debating, non-conformist and can be very stubborn. In the study of the Five Elements, the Hurting Officer Star always clashes with the Direct Officer Star. As you learn later on in the *Power of X* series, the Direct Officer Star represents superiors, bosses and clients. Thus, the presence of a Hurting Officer Star denotes a person who is always going against the order, or going against the establishment.

If the Hurting Officer Star is a Dominant Characteristic, there is a risk that the person will be labelled as having a bad attitude because of their opinionated, non-conformist and individualistic style of doing things. Hurting Officer Stars also usually indicate individuals who are not so good at following instructions or like to do things their own way. In an organisation that is very orthodox and conventional or where there is a very strict hierarchy, such individuals will become seen as mavericks. Their disruptive ways accordingly get them labelled as bad employees because they are 'anti-establishment'.

Hurting Officer Stars usually indicate individuals who are not so good at following instructions or like to do things their own way.

時 Hour	日 Day	月 Month	年 Year	
傷官 HO 甲 Jia Yang Wood	日元 DM 癸 Gui Yin Water	偏財 IW 丁 Ding Yin Fire	比肩 F 癸 Gui Yin Water	天干 Heavenly Stems
寅 Yin **Tiger** Yang Wood	丑 Chou **Ox** Yin Earth	巳 Si **Snake** Yin Fire	酉 You **Rooster** Yin Metal	地支 Earthly Branches
戊 Wu + Earth 官 DO; 甲 Jia + Wood 傷 HO; 丙 Bing + Fire 財 DW	辛 Xin - Metal 卩 IR; 己 Ji - Earth 殺 7K; 癸 Gui - Water 比 F	庚 Geng + Metal 印 DR; 丙 Bing + Fire 財 DW; 戊 Wu + Earth 官 DO	辛 Xin - Metal 卩 IR	藏干 Hidden Stems

Gui Water's Hurting Officer Star is represented by Jia Wood – Jia Wood appears in the Hour Stem and is rooted in the Hour Branch. This is clearly a chart where the Hurting Officer Star is a Dominant Characteristic.

Now the Hurting Officer Star as one's Dominant Characteristic is not *always* detrimental to one's career. It's usually only a problem if you are in an organisation that is very conservative or orthodox or hierarchical or you work in a very conventional or traditional industry (such as banking or accounting). In other words, it is usually a problem of a mismatch between corporate culture and the individual's character rather than anything else.

Nonetheless, there can be instances when the Hurting Officer Star as a Dominant Characteristic causes a problem even in an organisation that welcomes highly individualistic personalities. This typically occurs in two instances: when the Hurting Officer Star is excessively Dominant OR the Direct Officer Star are both Dominant Characteristics and both the Stars are located side-by-side in what is known as the *Hurting Officer sees Direct Officer Formation.*

When a star is excessively Dominant, the negative qualities of the Star influence the person's character and pervade their actions and thoughts. The concept of excessively Dominant Characteristics will be delved into in the next *Power of X* series, where we'll look at the question of evaluating the quality of the 10 Gods. For now, focus on the Dominant Characteristics first.

傷官見官 or *Hurting Officer sees Direct Officer Formation* is a formation that originates from the BaZi saying: "傷官見官，爲禍百端" which translates into '*Hurting Officer See Direct Officer, Chaos and Conflict Rules*'. Such a formation typically denotes a career filled with lots of ups and downs and replete with challenges holding on to a job for long term due to an inability to effectively work with one's superiors.

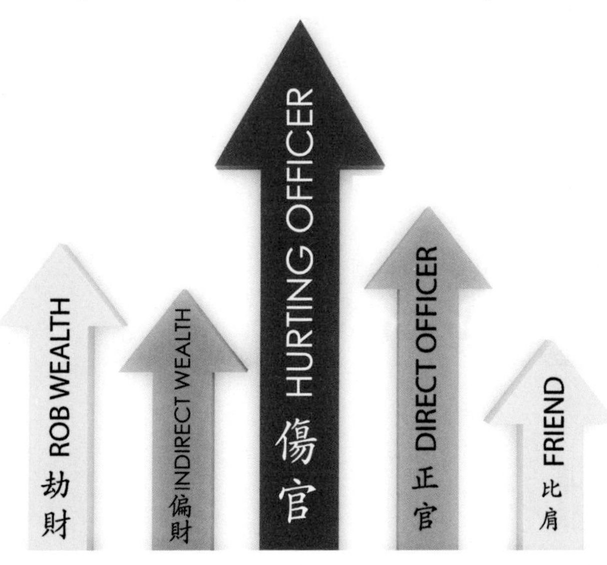

時 Hour	日 Day	月 Month	年 Year	
偏財 IW 辛 Xin Yin Metal	日元 DM 丁 Ding Yin Fire	傷官 HO 戊 Wu Yang Earth	正官 DO 壬 Ren Yang Water	天干 Heavenly Stems
亥 Hai **Pig** Yin Water	巳 Si **Snake** Yin Fire	申 Shen **Monkey** Yang Metal	戌 Xu **Dog** Yang Earth	地支 Earthly Branches
壬 Ren + Water 官 DO; 甲 Jia + Wood 印 DR	庚 Geng + Metal 財 DW; 丙 Bing + Fire 劫 RW; 戊 Wu + Earth 傷 HO	戊 Wu + Earth 傷 HO; 庚 Geng + Metal 財 DW; 壬 Ren + Water 官 DO	丁 Ding - Fire 比 F; 戊 Wu + Earth 傷 HO; 辛 Xin - Metal 才 IW	藏干 Hidden Stems

Ding Fire's Hurting Officer Star is represented by Wu Earth and Ding Fire's Direct Officer is represented by Ren Water In this chart, Wu Earth and Ren Water are rooted, thus making the Hurting Officer Star and Direct Officer Star Dominant Characteristics. Notice in this chart how the two stars appears side-by-side in the Heavenly Stems? This is clearly a chart with a Hurting Officer sees Direct Officer Formation and a chart where the person will have a tendency to experience career upheavals or a lot of challenges on the job.

時 Hour	日 Day	月 Month	年 Year	
偏印 IR 己 Ji Yin Earth	日元 DM 辛 Xin Yin Metal	傷官 HO 壬 Ren Yang Water	正官 DO 丙 Bing Yang Fire	天干 Heavenly Stems
亥 Hai Pig Yin Water	巳 Si Snake Yin Fire	辰 Chen Dragon Yang Earth	戌 Xu Dog Yang Earth	地支 Earthly Branches
壬 Ren + Water 傷 HO; 甲 Jia + Wood 財 DW	庚 Geng + Metal 劫 RW; 丙 Bing + Fire 官 DO; 戊 Wu + Earth 印 DR	癸 Gui - Water 食 EG; 戊 Wu + Earth 印 DR; 乙 Yi - Wood 才 IW	丁 Ding - Fire 殺 7K; 戊 Wu + Earth 印 DR; 辛 Xin - Metal 比 F	藏干 Hidden Stems

Xin Metal's Hurting Officer Star is represented by Ren Water and Xin Metal's Direct Officer is represented by Bing Fire. In this chart, Ren Water and Bing Fire are rooted, thus making the Hurting Officer Star and Direct Officer Star Dominant Characteristics. Notice in this chart how the two stars appears side-by-side in the Heavenly Stems? This is also clearly a chart with a Hurting Officer sees Direct Officer Formation. Accordingly, this person will most definitely be someone who has issues with superiors at work, and may well be regarded as a person with a 'bad attitude' due to their tendency to fight or rebel against the order or hierarchy of the workplace.

Unique formations as well as excessively Dominant Characteristics represent a slightly more advanced approach of looking at the Dominant Characteristics and we will be looking at more of these methods throughout the *Power of X* series. For now, focus your attention on the Dominant Characteristics first.

So what other types of Dominant Characteristics contribute to challenges in the career sphere? Having Direct Resource or Indirect Resource as a Dominant Characteristic can also give rise to a person having a bad attitude at work.

Let's look at Direct Resource first to understand why this is the case.

From Chapter 3, you will know that the Direct Resource Star indicates a patient, tolerant, respectful, upright, curious, imaginative and resourceful person. However, individuals with the Direct Resource Star can also manifest traits such as procrastination, an inability to make decisions, a habit of over-thinking things and complacency. When the Direct Resource Star is a Dominant Characteristic, there is a risk that the person will be tardy, lackadaisical with their work, shirk responsibilities and basically, just about earn their salary. They do the bare minimum required of them and do not exhibit initiative to go above and beyond.

When the Direct Resource Star is a Dominant Characteristic, there is a risk that the person will be tardy, lackadaisical with their work, shirk responsibilities and basically, just about earn their salary.

Of all the 10 Gods, the Indirect Resource Star most closely connects to the concept of 'vacation'.

Now, if you have the Direct Resource Star as a Dominant Characteristic, this doesn't mean you are de facto an employee who falls into the tardy and lazy category BUT there will be a measure of this type of attitude in your manner at work. If this is the only Dominant Characteristic in your chart, then it is time to scrutinise your attitude towards your job and your career closely. It's time to ask yourself if the reason why you're not making much headway is because you simply don't exhibit any interest to get ahead or advance in the workplace or you are simply too contented with where you are now to make an effort?

So what about the Indirect Resource Stars? Again, from Chapter 3, we know that individuals with Indirect Resource Stars are relaxed and laid-back, intuitive, quick studies, inventive and resourceful but they can also be prone to short-cuts, lack meticulousness, turn in sloppy work, lack care and attention when it comes to the details and are superficial when it comes to their knowledge and expertise. They are also complainers and perpetually wonder about when they can retire. Of all the 10 Gods, the Indirect Resource Star most closely connects to the concept of 'vacation'. So individuals with Indirect Resource as a Dominant Characteristic have the greatest risk of being labelled 'bad attitude' employees because of their tendency to be lazy or lackadaisical, their habit of delivering work late or incomplete, and their refusal to go the distance on the job.

時 Hour	日 Day	月 Month	年 Year	
正印 DR 己 *Ji* Yin Earth	日元 DM 庚 *Geng* Yang Metal	偏印 IR 戊 *Wu* Yang Earth	七殺 7K 丙 *Bing* Yang Fire	天干 Heavenly Stems
卯 *Mao* **Rabbit** Yin Wood	辰 *Chen* **Dragon** Yang Earth	戌 *Xu* **Dog** Yang Earth	戌 *Xu* **Dog** Yang Earth	地支 Earthly Branches
乙 *Yi* - Wood 財 DW	癸 *Gui* - Water 傷 HO; 戊 *Wu* + Earth 卩 IR; 乙 *Yi* - Wood 財 DW	丁 *Ding* - Fire 官 DO; 戊 *Wu* + Earth 卩 IR; 辛 *Xin* - Metal 劫 RW	丁 *Ding* - Fire 官 DO; 戊 *Wu* + Earth 卩 IR; 辛 *Xin* - Metal 劫 RW	藏干 Hidden Stems

In this Geng Metal chart, the Indirect Resource Star is clearly a Dominant Characteristic. As such, this person runs the risk of being labelled an employee with a bad attitude because they will be tardy, lackadaisical with their work and maybe even lazy. Whilst they will be well-liked in the office (as Indirect Resource denotes non-judgmental, kind and tolerant individuals), they won't be seen as reliable for work-related matters. If we analyse this from a slightly more advanced perspective, in this chart, the Indirect Resource Star is an excessively Dominant Characteristic. Notice how 3 out of 4 of the Earthly Branches contain the Indirect Resource Star? As such, the tendency is to manifest the negative qualities of the Indirect Resource Star, notably, a habit of procrastination, a tendency to be slipshod, resort to shortcuts, lack a sense of urgency with work-related matters and a tendency to be a jack-of-all-trades, master of none. The tendency for

procrastination is also typically high in individuals with more than 2 Graveyard Earthly Branches as these Branches contain Earth as their Main Qi. Earth, as we know, is ponderous, slow and immovable. When the Earth element also represents a person's Indirect Resource Stars, this denotes that the person has a habit of thinking very slowly and ponderously as well, and that they are very stubborn when it comes to shifting their position on any matter since Indirect Resource governs one's thoughts and feelings.

If you have the Hurting Officer Star or Direct Resource Star or Indirect Resource Star as one of your Dominant Characteristics, then you are at heightened risk of being a bad attitude employee. However, you could also simply be facing a mismatch between the corporate culture of the organisation and your own character, or a job mismatch. For example, individuals with Direct Resource as their Dominant Characteristic tend to suit slower paced organisations or mature companies better than start-ups or companies that are in the growth stage and are ill suited for entrepreneurial roles. Individuals with Indirect Resource as their Dominant Characteristic are more suited for soft-skill positions which are more focused on services or intangibles like customer relationship management. Thus, when analysing the issue of Career, it is important to look at whether the problem is due to the employee's character alone, or a mixture of the person and the organisation they are working for.

However, if you have two of more of the above Stars as your Dominant Characteristic, particularly both the Direct and Indirect Resource Stars are your Dominant Characteristics (see examples below), the likelihood is that it is the person has issues rather than the organisation.

時 Hour	日 Day	月 Month	年 Year	
正印 DR 癸 Gui Yin Water	日元 DM 甲 Jia Yang Wood	正官 DO 辛 Xin Yin Metal	偏印 IR 壬 Ren Yang Water	天干 Heavenly Stems
酉 You **Rooster** Yin Metal	辰 Chen **Dragon** Yang Earth	亥 Hai **Pig** Yin Water	子 Zi **Rat** Yang Water	地支 Earthly Branches
辛 Xin - Metal 官 DO	癸 Gui - Water 印 DR; 戊 Wu + Earth 才 IW; 乙 Yi - Wood 劫 RW	壬 Ren + Water 卩 IR; 甲 Jia + Wood 比 F	癸 Gui - Water 印 DR	藏干 Hidden Stems

In this Jia Wood Day Master example, the Indirect Resource Star, represented by Ren Water and Direct Resource Star, represented by Gui Water, are rooted. This person accordingly is at risk of being an employee with a bad attitude, due to his or her tardiness, general laid-back attitude towards work and an absence of initiative.

時 Hour	日 Day	月 Month	年 Year	
偏印 IR 己 *Ji* Yin Earth	日元 DM 辛 *Xin* Yin Metal	偏財 IW 乙 *Yi* Yin Wood	傷官 HO 壬 *Ren* Yang Water	天干 Heavenly Stems
丑 *Chou* **Ox** Yin Earth	卯 *Mao* **Rabbit** Yin Wood	巳 *Si* **Snake** Yin Fire	申 *Shen* **Monkey** Yang Metal	地支 Earthly Branches
辛 *Xin* - Metal 比 F; 己 *Ji* - Earth 卩 IR; 癸 *Gui* - Water 食 EG	乙 *Yi* - Wood 才 IW	庚 *Geng* + Metal 劫 RW; 丙 *Bing* + Fire 官 DO; 戊 *Wu* + Earth 印 DR	戊 *Wu* + Earth 印 DR; 庚 *Geng* + Metal 劫 RW; 壬 *Ren* + Water 傷 HO	藏干 Hidden Stems

In this Xin Metal Day Master example, the Indirect Resource Star, represented by Ji Earth Water and Hurting Officer Star, represented by Ren Water, are rooted. Thus, these two stars are Dominant Characteristics in this person's chart. This person thus has the potential to be a bad attitude employee because they have a habit of talking back to their superiors, being argumentative and confrontational, but at the same time, the person is prone to taking shortcuts with their work and having a short-attention span. In this chart, the Indirect Wealth Star, which is also a Dominant Characteristic, exaggerates the effects of the Indirect Resource Star because both these Stars have common characteristics, namely, a lack of focus, a tendency towards looking at the big picture only, and a preference for shortcuts. This increases the likelihood that this person will manifest a bad attitude as an employee.

do I have a bad attitude towards my work and career?

In such an instance, a good hard self-assessment is required and the person will do well to pose this question to themselves and to the people around them: *do I have a bad attitude towards my work and career?*

Let's say you don't have the Hurting Officer, Direct Resource or Indirect Resource Stars as Dominant Characteristics in your chart. Sometimes, an employee doesn't have a bad attitude but unfortunately gives off the impression that he or she has a bad attitude. In this instance, differences between the person's External and Internal Character is the cause of the misunderstanding.

You will recall from Chapter 4 that the Stems reveal External Character and the Branches reveal Internal Character.

Accordingly, if you have the Hurting Officer, Direct Resource or Indirect Resource Stars or a combination of two of these Stars on the Heavenly Stems of your BaZi chart (but none of these Stars appear in the Earthly Branches, thus are not Dominant Characteristics), you may be giving off bad attitude vibes despite your true nature or Internal Character at the workplace.

The result is that you get lumped into the same barrel as the rotten apples, even if you have nothing in common with them. In fact, you may even have a very good attitude towards your work and job. Appearing to have a bad attitude, in some respects, is worse than actually having a bad attitude. This is because you now have to work against the (negative) first impression in the minds of your co-workers and superiors.

時 Hour	日 Day	月 Month	年 Year	
正印 DR 己 Ji Yin Earth	日元 DM 庚 Geng Yang Metal	傷官 HO 癸 Gui Yin Water	七殺 7K 丙 Bing Yang Fire	天干 Heavenly Stems
卯 Mao Rabbit Yin Wood	寅 Yin Tiger Yang Wood	巳 Si Snake Yin Fire	申 Shen Monkey Yang Metal	地支 Earthly Branches
乙 Yi - Wood 財 DW	戊 Wu + Earth 卩 IR; 甲 Jia + Wood 才 IW; 丙 Bing + Fire 殺 7K	庚 Geng + Metal 比 F; 丙 Bing + Fire 殺 7K; 戊 Wu + Earth 卩 IR	戊 Wu + Earth 卩 IR; 庚 Geng + Metal 比 F; 壬 Ren + Water 食 EG	藏干 Hidden Stems

In this Geng Metal Day Master example, the Hurting Officer Star and Direct Resource Star appear in the Stems but do not appear in the Branches. Thus, upon first impression, this person may seem to exhibit something of a bad attitude in the workplace – they will seen to be rebellious and unable to follow instructions, and might even appear to lack initiative. However, note that the Hurting Officer Star and the Direct Resource Star are not rooted. So the person's actual attitude and demeanour towards work matters may well be very different.

時 Hour	日 Day	月 Month	年 Year	
七殺 7K 丁 *Ding* Yin Fire	日元 DM 辛 *Xin* Yin Metal	傷官 HO 壬 *Ren* Yang Water	正印 DR 戊 *Wu* Yang Earth	天干 Heavenly Stems
酉 *You* **Rooster** Yin Metal	巳 *Si* **Snake** Yin Fire	戌 *Xu* **Dog** Yang Earth	子 *Zi* **Rat** Yang Water	地支 Earthly Branches
辛 *Xin* - Metal 比 F	庚 *Geng* + Metal 劫 RW; 丙 *Bing* + Fire 官 DO; 戊 *Wu* + Earth 印 DR	丁 *Ding* - Fire 殺 7K; 戊 *Wu* + Earth 印 DR; 辛 *Xin* - Metal 比 F	癸 *Gui* - Water 食 EG	藏干 Hidden Stems

In this Xin Metal Day Master example, the Hurting Officer Star and Direct Resource Star appear in the Stems. However, the Hurting Officer Star is notably NOT rooted. Thus, upon first impression, this person may seem be a rebel rouser and someone who is excessively opinionated. He or she may seem disruptive initially in the workplace. However, as the Hurting Officer Star is not rooted, it is clear that the person only appears this way, and their actual work temperament may well be quite different.

時 Hour	日 Day	月 Month	年 Year	
傷官 HO 丁 Ding Yin Fire	日元 DM 甲 Jia Yang Wood	偏印 IR 壬 Ren Yang Water	七殺 7K 庚 Geng Yang Metal	天干 Heavenly Stems
卯 Mao **Rabbit** Yin Wood	戌 Xu **Dog** Yang Earth	午 Wu **Horse** Yang Fire	戌 Xu **Dog** Yang Earth	地支 Earthly Branches
乙 Yi - Wood 劫 RW	丁 Ding - Fire 傷 HO; 戊 Wu + Earth 才 IW; 辛 Xin - Metal 官 DO	丁 Ding - Fire 傷 HO; 己 Ji - Earth 財 DW	丁 Ding - Fire 傷 HO; 戊 Wu + Earth 才 IW; 辛 Xin - Metal 官 DO	藏干 Hidden Stems

In this Jia Wood Day Master example, the Hurting Officer Star and Indirect Resource Star appears in the Stems. However, the Indirect Resource Star is notably NOT rooted. Thus, upon first impression, this person may seem be lazy or lack initiative or appear to be tardy. However, as the Indirect Resource Star is not rooted, and the Branches actually contain the Direct and Indirect Wealth Stars, this person only appears to be tardy or lacking in initiative but is in fact, a very hard-working person.

This is not to say that having the other Stars (Direct Wealth, Indirect Wealth, Eating God, Rob Wealth, Friend, 7 Killings and Direct Officer) as your Dominant Characteristics do not give rise to problems in the workplace. However, the issues presented by the Direct Resource, Indirect Resource and Hurting Officer Stars are easier for most employers and employees to identify with and also, tend to exemplify traits that are easier to identify and see in an individual. Further, the challenges thrown up by the other sets of Stars involve assessing their interaction with other Stars (such as the 7 Killings Star with the Eating God Star) and accordingly, are beyond the scope of the 10 Gods analysis methods discussed in this book.

The issues presented by the Direct Resource, Indirect Resource and Hurting Officer Stars are easier for most employers and employees to identify with.

As you work your way through the *Power of X* series and you learn more about the 10 Gods in detail, you may wish to independently revisit this topic and see what conclusions you arrive at about how other types of Dominant Characteristics impact on a person's progress and opportunities in the workplace.

The 10 Gods and Relationship Matters

In this section, I will show you how to utilise the information about the 10 Gods from Chapter 3 and combine it with the analysis methods discussed in Chapter 4 to gain certain some insights into a person's relationship matters. Naturally when it comes to relationship matter, we are primarily interested in the Spouse Stars. As you would have already learnt in Chapter 7 of *The Destiny Code*, the Spouse Stars are represented by different Five Factors, depending on the gender of the person in question. To briefly recap, the Spouse Star for males is represented by the Wealth Element and the Spouse Star for females is represented by the Influence Element.

財星
Wealth Element
Spouse Star
官殺
Influence Element

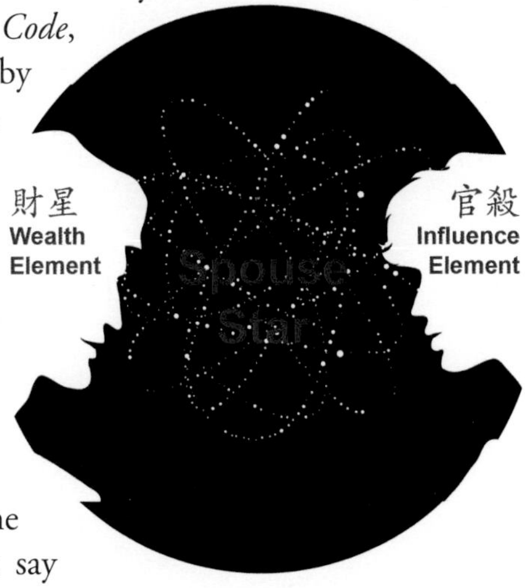

Now, this IS a book about the 10 Gods, and BaZi is the art of the specific. So it's not enough to just say the Influence Element represents the Spouse Star of the woman – after all, there are two Stars that make up the Influence Element! Similarly, there are two Stars that make up the Wealth Element – do they both represent a Spouse?

In the traditional BaZi, only the Direct Wealth Star and Direct Officer Star represented the spouses for males and females respectively. The Indirect Wealth Star was reserved for mistresses and concubines and the 7 Killings Star essentially was regarding as indicating a woman would marry a riff-raff rather than a nobleman or someone of status. In modern

In the traditional BaZi, only the Direct Wealth Star and Direct Officer Star represented the spouses for males and females respectively.

BaZi, which accounts for the sophistication of relationships between the sexes in this day and age, the Direct Wealth Star is still regarded as the true Spouse Star (ie: wife) whilst the Indirect Wealth Star is now regarded as representing girlfriends or relationships prior to marriage, or ex-wives in some instances. For women, the Direct Officer Star continues to be regarded as the true Spouse Star (ie: husband) but the 7 Killings Star now just references boyfriends or relationships prior to marriage or sometimes, ex-husbands. Accordingly, the Direct Wealth and Direct Officer Stars are in modern circumstances regarded as the Primary Spouse Star and the Indirect Wealth Star and 7 Killings Star are termed the Secondary Spouse Stars.

In the absence of the Direct Wealth and Direct Officer Stars, the Secondary Spouse Stars (Indirect Wealth Star and 7 Killings Star) are interpreted to represent the Spouse Stars for males and females respectively.

There are subtle but significant differences in the interpretation when the Indirect Wealth and 7 Killings Stars are used to represent the Spouse Stars due to the absence of the 'true' Spouse Stars, Direct Wealth and 7 Killings. However at this point, don't be too concerned about those issues yet. For now, view the Indirect Wealth and 7 Killings Stars as permissible substitutes in the event the Direct Wealth and Direct Officer Stars are not present in the chart. However, if the Direct Wealth or Direct Officer Stars are present in a chart, these Stars then should rightly be referenced as the Spouse Stars.

Spouse Stars appear only on the Stem

Broadly speaking, this is considered acceptable, as long as the Spouse Star (only Direct Wealth for men, Direct Officer for women) is directly next to the Day Master, either on the left or right side, although the Month Stem is preferred. Such a formation is regarded as being somewhat favourable because it denotes relative ease when it comes to getting married because the Spouse Star is obvious and apparent. This is particularly the case if the Day Master also happens to combine with the Spouse Star on the Stems.

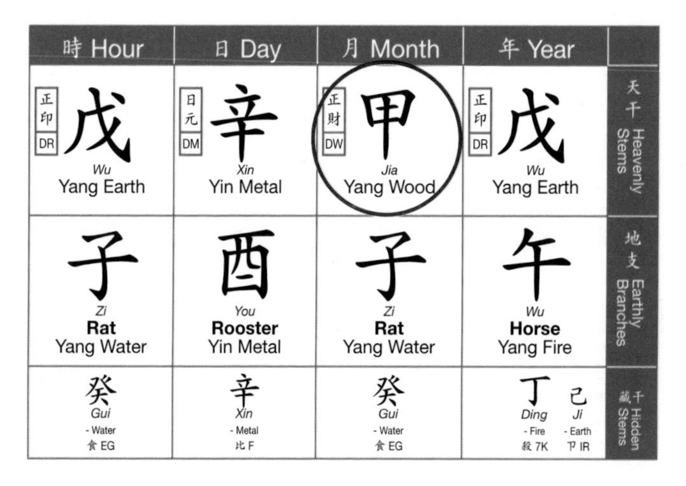

時 Hour	日 Day	月 Month	年 Year	
正印 DR 戊 *Wu* Yang Earth	日元 DM 辛 *Xin* Yin Metal	正財 DW 甲 *Jia* Yang Wood	正印 DR 戊 *Wu* Yang Earth	天干 Heavenly Stems
子 *Zi* **Rat** Yang Water	酉 *You* **Rooster** Yin Metal	子 *Zi* **Rat** Yang Water	午 *Wu* **Horse** Yang Fire	地支 Earthly Branches
癸 *Gui* - Water 食 EG	辛 *Xin* - Metal 比 F	癸 *Gui* - Water 食 EG	丁 *Ding* - Fire 殺 7K; 己 *Ji* - Earth 卩 IR	藏干 Hidden Stems

In this male Xin Metal example, the Direct Wealth Star (the Spouse Star for a man) is present only in the Month Branch but is located right next to the Day Master. This is considered a moderately favourable feature to have in a chart from a relationship standpoint.

時 Hour	日 Day	月 Month	年 Year	
正官 DO 癸 *Gui* Yin Water	日元 DM 丙 *Bing* Yang Fire	食神 EG 戊 *Wu* Yang Earth	正印 DR 乙 *Yi* Yin Wood	天干 Heavenly Stems
巳 *Si* **Snake** Yin Fire	戌 *Xu* **Dog** Yang Earth	寅 *Yin* **Tiger** Yang Wood	卯 *Mao* **Rabbit** Yin Wood	地支 Earthly Branches
庚 *Geng* + Metal 才 IW; 丙 *Bing* + Fire 比 F; 戊 *Wu* + Earth 食 EG	丁 *Ding* - Fire 劫 RW; 戊 *Wu* + Earth 食 EG; 辛 *Xin* - Metal 財 DW	戊 *Wu* + Earth 食 EG; 甲 *Jia* + Wood 卩 IR; 丙 *Bing* + Fire 比 F	乙 *Yi* - Wood 印 DR	藏干 Hidden Stems

In this female Bing Fire example, the Direct Officer Star is present only in the Hour Stem but is located right next to the Day Master. This is also considered a moderately favourable feature to have in a chart from a relationship standpoint.

時 Hour	日 Day	月 Month	年 Year	
正官 DO 壬 *Ren* Yang Water	日元 DM 丁 *Ding* Yin Fire	正財 DW 庚 *Geng* Yang Metal	偏財 IW 辛 *Xin* Yin Metal	天干 Heavenly Stems
寅 *Yin* **Tiger** Yang Wood	卯 *Mao* **Rabbit** Yin Wood	寅 *Yin* **Tiger** Yang Wood	酉 *You* **Rooster** Yin Metal	地支 Earthly Branches
戊 *Wu* + Earth 傷 HO; 甲 *Jia* + Wood 印 DR; 丙 *Bing* + Fire 劫 RW	乙 *Yi* - Wood 卩 IR	戊 *Wu* + Earth 傷 HO; 甲 *Jia* + Wood 印 DR; 丙 *Bing* + Fire 劫 RW	辛 *Xin* - Metal 才 IW	藏干 Hidden Stems

In this female Ding Fire example, the Direct Officer Star, represented by Ren Water, is present only in the Hour Stem but is located right next to the Day Master. This is also considered a moderately favourable feature to have in a chart from a relationship standpoint. Notably in this case, there is also a Stem Combination between the Day Master and the Direct Officer Star, which makes the positioning of the Direct Officer Star a little more advantageous.

時 Hour	日 Day	月 Month	年 Year	
傷官 HO 辛 Xin Yin Metal	日元 DM 戊 Wu Yang Earth	正財 DW 癸 Gui Yin Water	七殺 7K 甲 Jia Yang Wood	天干 Heavenly Stems
酉 You **Rooster** Yin Metal	寅 Yin **Tiger** Yang Wood	酉 You **Rooster** Yin Metal	寅 Yin **Tiger** Yang Wood	地支 Earthly Branches
辛 Xin - Metal 傷 HO	戊 Wu + Earth 比 F; 甲 Jia + Wood 殺 7K; 丙 Bing + Fire 卩 IR	辛 Xin - Metal 傷 HO	戊 Wu + Earth 比 F; 甲 Jia + Wood 殺 7K; 丙 Bing + Fire 卩 IR	藏干 Hidden Stems

In this male Wu Earth example, the Direct Wealth Star represented by Gui Water is present only in the Month Stem and is located right next to the Day Master. This is also considered a favourable feature to have in a chart from a relationship standpoint.

The Spouse Star appearing on the Stem is only ideal however if the Spouse Star is **next** to the Day Master. If the Spouse Star is located a distance from the Day Master on the Stem, then this is regarded as less favourable, as in the following example.

時 Hour	日 Day	月 Month	年 Year	
偏印 IR 己 *Ji* Yin Earth	日元 DM 辛 *Xin* Yin Metal	偏印 IR 己 *Ji* Yin Earth	七殺 7K 丁 *Ding* Yin Fire	天干 Heavenly Stems
亥 *Hai* **Pig** Yin Water	丑 *Chou* **Ox** Yin Earth	酉 *You* **Rooster** Yin Metal	酉 *You* **Rooster** Yin Metal	地支 Earthly Branches
壬 *Ren* + Water 傷 HO; 甲 *Jia* + Wood 財 DW	辛 *Xin* - Metal 比 F; 己 *Ji* - Earth 卩 IR; 癸 *Gui* - Water 食 EG	辛 *Xin* - Metal 比 F	辛 *Xin* - Metal 比 F	藏干 Hidden Stems

In this female Xin Metal example, the 7 Killings Star (represented by Ding Fire) is located in the Year Stem, away from the Day Master. Not only is the Spouse Star not next to the Day Master, but it is a secondary Spouse Star. Accordingly, this is not considered a circumstance where it is favourable to have the Spouse Star appear only on the Stem.

However, there is a disadvantage as well to having the Spouse Star appear only in the Stem. If there is a Companion Element (Rob Wealth or Friend Star) right next to the Spouse Star, then the advantage immediately evaporates, especially if the Companion Element combines with the Spouse Star. In such a circumstance, the man of course will not find it hard to meet a member of the opposite sex, but may find that if he slips up or doesn't pay enough attention to her, his other half will be easily and successfully courted by another man. A woman will find that her husband or Other Half similarly, is easily enticed away by others in such circumstances.

時 Hour	日 Day	月 Month	年 Year	
傷官 HO 癸 Gui Yin Water	日元 DM 庚 Geng Yang Metal	正財 DW 乙 Yi Yin Wood	比肩 F 庚 Geng Yang Metal	天干 Heavenly Stems
未 Wei **Goat** Yin Earth	子 Zi **Rat** Yang Water	酉 You **Rooster** Yin Metal	申 Shen **Monkey** Yang Metal	地支 Earthly Branches
乙 Yi - Wood 財 DW; 己 Ji - Earth 印 DR; 丁 Ding - Fire 官 DO	癸 Gui - Water 傷 HO	辛 Xin - Metal 劫 RW	戊 Wu + Earth 卩 IR; 庚 Geng + Metal 比 F; 壬 Ren + Water 食 EG	藏干 Hidden Stems

In this male Geng Metal example, the Direct Wealth Star, represented by Yi Wood, is located on the Stem and is next to the Day Master. However, there is also a Friend Star is located right next to the Direct Wealth Star. As you will recall from the Stem Combinations, Geng and Yi is a Combination. Here, the Yi Wood has a choice of combining with either the Day Master or the Friend Star located in the Year Stem, a situation sometimes referred to as 'fighting to combine' in BaZi. This is an example of an instance where the Spouse Star appearing in the Stem is disadvantageous because a Companion Element also appears in the Stem and is likely to Combine with the Spouse Star. This situation denotes a man who may easily lose his Spouse or significant other to another man.

時 Hour	日 Day	月 Month	年 Year	
正印 DR 壬 Ren Yang Water	日元 DM 乙 Yi Yin Wood	正官 DO 庚 Geng Yang Metal	比肩 F 乙 Yi Yin Wood	天干 Heavenly Stems
午 Wu Horse Yang Fire	巳 Si Snake Yin Fire	辰 Chen Dragon Yang Earth	未 Wei Goat Yin Earth	地支 Earthly Branches
丁 Ding - Fire 食 EG; 己 Ji - Earth 才 IW	庚 Geng + Metal 官 DO; 丙 Bing + Fire 傷 HO; 戊 Wu + Earth 財 DW	癸 Gui - Water 卩 IR; 戊 Wu + Earth 財 DW; 乙 Yi - Wood 比 F	乙 Yi - Wood 比 F; 己 Ji - Earth 才 IW; 丁 Ding - Fire 食 EG	藏干 Hidden Stems

In this female Yi Wood example, the Direct Officer Star, represented by Geng Metal, is located on the Stem and is next to the Day Master. However, there is also a Friend Star is located right next to the Direct Officer Star. As you will recall from the Stem Combinations, Geng and Yi is a Combination. Here, the Geng Metal has a choice of combining with either the Day Master or the Friend Star located in the Year Stem, a situation sometimes referred to as 'fighting to combine' in BaZi. This is an example of an instance where the Spouse Star appearing in the Stem is disadvantageous because a Companion Element also appears in the Stem and is likely to Combine with the Spouse Star. This situation produces a similar outcome to the one above – the woman must fight off other women for her Spouse OR her spouse is easily enticed away by other women.

Where the chart only contains Secondary Spouse Stars (ie: either 7 Killings or Indirect Wealth Stars) and the Secondary Spouse Stars are present ONLY on the Stems, the interpretation changes. Typically this denotes the person easily pairs up with the opposite sex or has no difficulty with casual relationships but will find marriage or a serious long-term relationship elusive.

時 Hour	日 Day	月 Month	年 Year	
七殺 7K 丁 *Ding* Yin Fire	日元 DM 辛 *Xin* Yin Metal	正印 DR 戊 *Wu* Yang Earth	正財 DW 甲 *Jia* Yang Wood	天干 Heavenly Stems
酉 *You* **Rooster** Yin Metal	卯 *Mao* **Rabbit** Yin Wood	辰 *Chen* **Dragon** Yang Earth	子 *Zi* **Rat** Yang Water	地支 Earthly Branches
辛 *Xin* - Metal 比 F	乙 *Yi* - Wood 才 IW	癸 *Gui* - Water 食 EG; 戊 *Wu* + Earth 印 DR; 乙 *Yi* - Wood 才 IW	癸 *Gui* - Water 食 EG	藏干 Hidden Stems

In this female Xin Metal example, there is no Direct Officer Star and only a 7 Killings Star is present in the Hour Stem. Where only the Secondary Spouse Star is present in the chart, there is no advantage conferred in having it on the Stem next to the Day Master.

時 Hour	日 Day	月 Month	年 Year	
食神 EG 戊 Wu Yang Earth	日元 DM 丙 Bing Yang Fire	傷官 HO 己 Ji Yin Earth	偏財 IW 庚 Geng Yang Metal	天干 Heavenly Stems
子 Zi **Rat** Yang Water	寅 Yin **Tiger** Yang Wood	卯 Mao **Rabbit** Yin Wood	辰 Chen **Dragon** Yang Earth	地支 Earthly Branches
癸 Gui - Water 官 DO	戊 Wu + Earth 食 EG; 甲 Jia + Wood 卩 IR; 丙 Bing + Fire 比 F	乙 Yi - Wood 印 DR	癸 Gui - Water 官 DO; 戊 Wu + Earth 食 EG; 乙 Yi - Wood 印 DR	藏干 Hidden Stems

In this male Bing Fire example, there is no Direct Wealth Star and only a Indirect Wealth Star is present in the Year Stem. This chart has two disadvantageous when it comes to relationship matters – not only is the only Spouse Star present a Secondary Spouse Star, but the Star is not even located close to the Day Master. This is an example of a situation where having the Spouse Star appear on the Stem confers no advantage.

Spouse Stars appear only in the Branch.

In Chapter 9 of *The Destiny Code*, you were introduced to the concept of the Spouse Palace. The Spouse Palace refers to the Earthly Branch that is located directly underneath the Day Master.

時 Hour	日 Day	月 Month	年 Year	
				天干 Heavenly Stems
	Spouse Palace			地支 Earthly Branches
				藏干 Hidden Stems

If the Spouse Star is to appear in the Branch, then ideally, it should appear in the Spouse Palace and preferably *only* appear in the Spouse Palace as the Main Qi. In BaZi, too many Spouse Stars, be it for men or women, is usually a recipe for disaster or at least, a very expensive exercise called divorce and alimony. In any case, when it comes to any of the Elements, the rule is that quantity doesn't matter as much as quality.

Thus, we don't want to see multiple Spouse Stars in the Earthly Branches if the objective is a quality marriage and good, harmonious relationship. One Spouse Star in the Main Qi of the Earthly Branch within the Spouse Palace is all you really need, for both males and females.

A person with the Spouse Star in the Spouse Palace is likely to have a better quality marriage or have better quality relationships.

So what happens if your Spouse Star appears in the Branches but does not appear in the Spouse Palace? What if you have multiple Spouse Stars and a mix of Primary and Secondary Spouse Stars? Or what if you don't have the Primary Spouse Star in the Branches and only have the Secondary Spouse Star?

The simple conclusion is that if your chart falls into any of the above possibilities, then marriage or relationships will not be as easy or as smooth for you, compared to someone who only has the Spouse Star in the Spouse Palace. It's that simple. A person with the Spouse Star in the Spouse Palace is likely to have a better quality marriage or have better quality relationships.

Of course, there is more dimension to the interpretation than merely the statement that marriage is not going to be easy or smooth. Obviously, how hard or how challenging marriage or relationships will be depends on a number of factors. For example, the location of the Spouse Star in proximity to the Spouse Palace and whether or not the Spouse Star or Spouse Palace is affected by any chart interactions. What 10 God reside in the Spouse Palace will also have an effect, as it will denote the person's priorities and outlook when it comes to marriage and relationships.

In essence, the absence of the Spouse Star in the appropriate Spouse Palace typically denotes a need to work a little harder at the matrimonial game. This does not necessarily mean it is hard for you to meet someone but it may denote ups and downs or challenges with regards the marital relationship.

The Spouse Star Gold Standard: Stem or Branch or Rooted?

When it comes to the Spouse Star, the conventional rules vary slightly between men and women when it comes to the ideal positioning of the Spouse Star for good quality relationships. Bear in mind that this gold standard was developed with a more traditional viewpoint of marriage and relationships, and in many respects, is more Asian-centric. It may not constitute everyone's idea of an ideal relationship or marriage.

For men, it is regarded as ideal if the Spouse Star appears in the Spouse Palace and does not appear anywhere else. This indicates a high likelihood of marrying a wife who is a homemaker or a homebody and doesn't go off gallivanting whilst the man is at work! It is also not regarded as necessary for the Spouse Star to be rooted, although this is advantageous for non-relationship related reasons.

For women on the other hand, the Spouse Star should ideally appear on the Month Stem next to the Day Master and be rooted in the Month Branch. This denotes marrying a capable husband, but also ensures that the husband is clearly present in the woman's life and clearly seen by others around her to be her Spouse. If a woman's Spouse Star appears in the Spouse Palace alone and does not appear in the Stems, this denotes marrying a husband who is loving and is always at home but who may not necessarily be a high-flyer from a career standpoint (after all, if he's always at home, that means he's not at work!). People may not even know she is married!

This is because women continue to a large degree to be defined by their husbands (although admittedly, this is changing) and the quality of their husband. The fact is that it's not broadly acceptable for a woman to be seen in public without her spouse, but men can appear in public without the spouses all the time. In short, husbands need to be shown off and seen, but wives don't have to be!

時 Hour	日 Day	月 Month	年 Year	
偏財 IW 戊 Wu Yang Earth	日元 DM 甲 Jia Yang Wood	正官 DO 辛 Xin Yin Metal	正印 DR 癸 Gui Yin Water	天干 Heavenly Stems
辰 Chen **Dragon** Yang Earth	寅 Yin **Tiger** Yang Wood	酉 You **Rooster** Yin Metal	卯 Mao **Rabbit** Yin Wood	地支 Earthly Branches
癸 Gui - Water 印 DR; 戊 Wu + Earth 才 IW; 乙 Yi - Wood 劫 RW	戊 Wu + Earth 才 IW; 甲 Jia + Wood 比 F; 丙 Bing + Fire 食 EG	辛 Xin - Metal 官 DO	乙 Yi - Wood 劫 RW	藏干 Hidden Stems

This female Jia Wood's chart has some positive features when it comes to relationships. The Primary Spouse Star, namely the Direct Officer Star, represented by Xin Metal, is present in the chart, and close to the Day Master. This denotes relative ease with marriage. Whilst the Direct Officer Star is not present in the Spouse Palace, it is rooted, denoting that her husband is someone who she is seen with and who is known to be her spouse, but also that he is a capable man who likely has a good career. Of course, the chart is not without minus points either, notably the presence of the Friend Star in the Spouse Palace and the preponderance of Rob Wealth Star. As such, it would not be regarded as an exceptionally good chart from a marriage or relationship standpoint, but would not be regarded as poor either.

時 Hour	日 Day	月 Month	年 Year	
正印 DR 辛 *Xin* Yin Metal	日元 DM 壬 *Ren* Yang Water	偏印 IR 庚 *Geng* Yang Metal	劫財 RW 癸 *Gui* Yin Water	天干 Heavenly Stems
丑 *Chou* **Ox** Yin Earth	午 *Wu* **Horse** Yang Fire	申 *Shen* **Monkey** Yang Metal	丑 *Chou* **Ox** Yin Earth	地支 Earthly Branches
辛 *Xin* - Metal 印 DR; 己 *Ji* - Earth 官 DO; 癸 *Gui* - Water 劫 RW	丁 *Ding* - Fire 財 DW; 己 *Ji* - Earth 官 DO	戊 *Wu* + Earth 殺 7K; 庚 *Geng* + Metal 卩 IR; 壬 *Ren* + Water 比 F	辛 *Xin* - Metal 印 DR; 己 *Ji* - Earth 官 DO; 癸 *Gui* - Water 劫 RW	藏干 Hidden Stems

In this male Ren Water example, the Direct Wealth Star, represented by Ding Fire, is located in the Spouse Palace. This is the only Direct Wealth Star in the entire chart. This male chart would be considered an example of a chart that exemplifies the Gold Standard when it comes to relationships and marriage. This denotes the man marries a wife who is a homemaker or a homebody and who takes care of the family. Significantly, the Direct Wealth element in this chart is also a favourable element, which denotes an especially positive marital relationship.

時 Hour	日 Day	月 Month	年 Year	
傷官 HO 壬 *Ren* Yang Water	日元 DM 辛 *Xin* Yin Metal	正官 DO 丙 *Bing* Yang Fire	偏印 IR 己 *Ji* Yin Earth	天干 Heavenly Stems
辰 *Chen* **Dragon** Yang Earth	丑 *Chou* **Ox** Yin Earth	寅 *Yin* **Tiger** Yang Wood	卯 *Mao* **Rabbit** Yin Wood	地支 Earthly Branches
癸 *Gui* - Water 食 EG; 戊 *Wu* + Earth 印 DR; 乙 *Yi* - Wood 才 IW	辛 *Xin* - Metal 比 F; 己 *Ji* - Earth 卩 IR; 癸 *Gui* - Water 食 EG	戊 *Wu* + Earth 印 DR; 甲 *Jia* + Wood 財 DW; 丙 *Bing* + Fire 官 DO	乙 *Yi* - Wood 才 IW	藏干 Hidden Stems

In this female Xin Metal example, the Direct Officer Star, represented by Bing Fire, is present in the Month Stem and rooted in the Month Branch. Bing and Xin are also a Stem Combination. This female chart would be regarded as exemplifies the Gold Standard when it comes relationships and marriage. This denotes a woman who has a loving and close relationship with her spouse (as a result of the Combination in the Stem) and who is married to someone who is capable and has a good career (owing to the rooted nature of the Direct Officer Star and its location in the Month).

At this point, you're probably looking at your chart and starting to get nervous or worried.

DO NOT PRESS THE PANIC BUTTON.

Not everyone can achieve the BaZi gold standard of marriage, namely, the Spouse Star in the Spouse Palace for men and the Spouse Star appearing in the Month Stem, whilst rooted in the Month Branch, and in Combination with the Day Master for women. It is called a gold standard for a reason. Having everything when it comes to relationships is not easy.

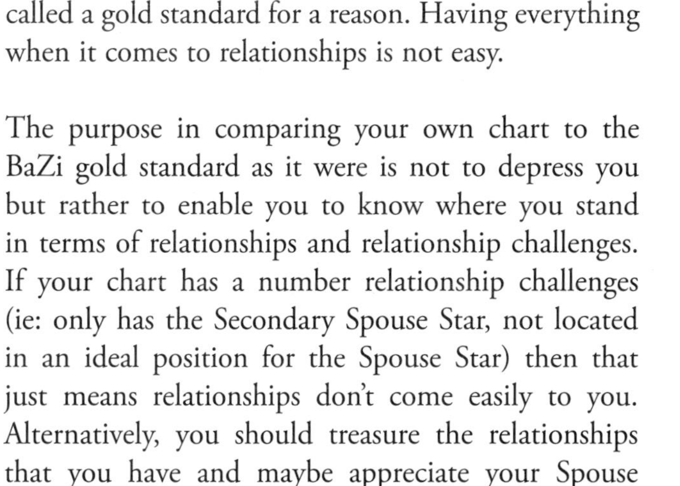

The purpose in comparing your own chart to the BaZi gold standard as it were is not to depress you but rather to enable you to know where you stand in terms of relationships and relationship challenges. If your chart has a number relationship challenges (ie: only has the Secondary Spouse Star, not located in an ideal position for the Spouse Star) then that just means relationships don't come easily to you. Alternatively, you should treasure the relationships that you have and maybe appreciate your Spouse more (hey, they have to put up with someone with a so-so chart when it comes to relationships). Finally, work hard at your marriage or relationships because it doesn't come easily or naturally to you.

The Relationship and Character Connection

How does character influence a person's capacity for relationships? Last I checked, very few men or women were happy to be married to a person of unsavoury character. Would you like to be married to a miser? Or a man who is unable to provide for his family? Or a man who has no honour? Or a man who is a loser? How about a woman who is a nag? Or a woman who is suspicious minded? Character problems account for great deal of the challenges that both male and females face when it comes to relationships. I'm not going to run through the whole gamut of possibilities here because there simply are too many permutations and possibilities. I will however elaborate on two specific circumstances where a specific character can have a negative effect on a relationship or marriage for women, and one in particular for men.

When it comes to looking at the connection between relationship and character, the approach varies for men and for women. This is natural because the challenges that women face in relationships and the challenges men face in relationships are different.

With women, one of the main sources of relationship obstacles is a strong character or a domineering personality. In most instances, this problem is caused by the Hurting Officer Star being a Dominant Characteristic in the chart.

When a woman has the Hurting Officer Star as a Dominant Characteristic, this denotes the Hurting Officer Star is prominent, indicating a woman of high intelligence, great capability and ambition. Such a woman will expect her Spouse accordingly to be able to match her in terms of intelligence, capability and ambition. She also expects her man to share her sense of ambition and aspirations for success and advancement. Hence, when the Hurting Officer Star is present as a Dominant Characteristic in a woman's chart, this is a woman with high standards when it comes to her Spouse or partner in life. This is not a woman who will settle down with any old chap nor will this be a woman content to marry someone who is happy to live off fresh air and sunshine.

The Hurting Officer Dominant Characteristic denotes a woman who expects her man to share her sense of ambition and who wants to succeed as much as she does.

From a technical standpoint, the Hurting Officer Star is always in elemental opposition to the Direct Officer Star, which is the Spouse Star for females. This is where the Hurting Officer Star gets its name – the element that represents the Hurting Officer Star always clashes (thus 'hurts') the Direct Officer Star. It is also for this reason that women with Hurting Officer Star as a Dominant Characteristic tend to have relationship problems. The table overleaf illustrates how the Hurting Officer Star is always the elemental opposite of the Direct Officer Star.

日元 Day Master	傷官星 Hurting Officer Star	正官星 Direct Officer Star
甲 *Jia* Yang Wood	丁 *Ding* Yin Fire	辛 *Xin* Yin Metal
乙 *Yi* Yin Wood	丙 *Bing* Yang Fire	庚 *Geng* Yang Metal
丙 *Bing* Yang Fire	己 *Ji* Yin Earth	癸 *Gui* Yin Water
丁 *Ding* Yin Fire	戊 *Wu* Yang Earth	壬 *Ren* Yang Water
戊 *Wu* Yang Earth	辛 *Xin* Yin Metal	乙 *Yi* Yin Wood
己 *Ji* Yin Earth	庚 *Geng* Yang Metal	甲 *Jia* Yang Wood
庚 *Geng* Yang Metal	癸 *Gui* Yin Water	丁 *Ding* Yin Fire
辛 *Xin* Yin Metal	壬 *Ren* Yang Water	丙 *Bing* Yang Fire
壬 *Ren* Yang Water	乙 *Yi* Yin Wood	己 *Ji* Yin Earth
癸 *Gui* Yin Water	甲 *Jia* Yang Wood	戊 *Wu* Yang Earth

BaZi is not about judgment but about the facts. If a woman has high standards or expectations, then the pool of eligible husbands naturally is smaller. Further, not every man is equipped to handle a woman of high intelligence nor does every man want an ambitious wife. With these in mind, a woman with the Hurting Officer Star as part of her Dominant Characteristics needs to be conscious of the fact that she may well be making life difficult for herself in a romantic relationship or marriage by having high expectations.

Of course, this does not mean that if you have the Hurting Officer Star as a Dominant Characteristic and you are female, that marriage is impossible. Rather, it denotes that you may find it a little harder to meet Mr Right or that you may have to put more effort into keeping your marriage harmonious and happy. Some re-examination of values and standards may be warranted and you may want to re-look your own behaviour in your relationship or marriage. Are you needlessly argumentative? Do you pick a fight at every chance and thrive on scoring points in the debates with your spouse? Do you insist on being right all the time? (sometimes even when you're right, marriage is about being able to say you're wrong). Do you have needlessly high expectations of your spouse? Are you holding out for a Prince Charming who does not exist?

The Hurting Officer Dominant Characteristic denotes a woman who expects her man to share her sense of ambition and who wants to succeed as much as she does.

In this age of the independent single woman, marriage is increasingly seen as optional since most working women don't need a man to provide for them any more. But if you happen to have the Hurting Officer Star as a Dominant Characteristic and you are having difficulties when it comes to relationships or marriage, then some self-reflection might well be in order.

So what of men? What kind of character makes a man less than suited for relationships or poses challenges to successful relationships? If the Hurting Officer Star is the female species Achilles heel when it comes to relationships, then the male equivalent is the Rob Wealth Star. Typically, a man whose chart has the Rob Wealth Star as a dominant characteristic will usually encounter difficulties with relationships or marriage.

Why the Rob Wealth Star? From a technical standpoint, the Rob Wealth Star is always the elemental counterpoint of the Direct Wealth Star (see the table on the next page). Recall the Direct Wealth Star is the Spouse Star for males.

日元 Day Master	正財星 Direct Wealth Star	劫財星 Rob Wealth Star
甲 *Jia* Yang Wood	己 *Ji* Yin Earth	乙 *Yi* Yin Wood
乙 *Yi* Yin Wood	戊 *Wu* Yang Earth	甲 *Jia* Yang Wood
丙 *Bing* Yang Fire	辛 *Xin* Yin Metal	丁 *Ding* Yin Fire
丁 *Ding* Yin Fire	庚 *Geng* Yang Metal	丙 *Bing* Yang Fire
戊 *Wu* Yang Earth	癸 *Gui* Yin Water	己 *Ji* Yin Earth
己 *Ji* Yin Earth	壬 *Ren* Yang Water	戊 *Wu* Yang Earth
庚 *Geng* Yang Metal	乙 *Yi* Yin Wood	辛 *Xin* Yin Metal
辛 *Xin* Yin Metal	甲 *Jia* Yang Wood	庚 *Geng* Yang Metal
壬 *Ren* Yang Water	丁 *Ding* Yin Fire	癸 *Gui* Yin Water
癸 *Gui* Yin Water	丙 *Bing* Yang Fire	壬 *Ren* Yang Water

From a practical level, a man who has the Rob Wealth Star as his Dominant Characteristic will be the kind of man who puts his friends before his Spouse. This is because the Rob Wealth Star, when it comes to persons and people, represents an individual's friends and buddies. Such a man's relationships will suffer because

A man who has the Rob Wealth Star as his Dominant Characteristic will be the kind of man who puts his friends before his Spouse.

rather than going home to his wife or spending time with his wife, he would rather be out drinking or golfing with his friends. Such a man will also tend to react when his friends are in trouble, but lack a sense of urgency when his wife is having a problem. In short, when a man has the Rob Wealth Star as his Dominant Characteristic, he's probably not very good at taking care of his wife and family and may even be irresponsible because he's not concerned about their needs.

時 Hour	日 Day	月 Month	年 Year	
劫財 RW 乙 Yi Yin Wood	日元 DM 甲 Jia Yang Wood	偏財 IW 戊 Wu Yang Earth	傷官 HO 丁 Ding Yin Fire	天干 Heavenly Stems
丑 Chou **Ox** Yin Earth	午 Wu **Horse** Yang Fire	申 Shen **Monkey** Yang Metal	卯 Mao **Rabbit** Yin Wood	地支 Earthly Branches
辛 Xin - Metal 官 DO; 己 Ji - Earth 財 DW; 癸 Gui - Water 印 DR	丁 Ding - Fire 傷 HO; 己 Ji - Earth 財 DW	戊 Wu + Earth 才 IW; 庚 Geng + Metal 殺 7K; 壬 Ren + Water 卩 IR	乙 Yi - Wood 劫 RW	藏干 Hidden Stems

In this male Jia Wood Day Master's chart, the Rob Wealth Star, represented by Yi Wood, is a Dominant Characteristic as Yi Wood is rooted in the Rabbit (Mao).

A man who has the Rob Wealth Star as his dominant characteristic will usually also not have much money or worse, be someone who lives off debt. This is because the presence of the Rob Wealth Star as a Dominant Characteristic denotes a spendthrift character. From a technical standpoint, having the Rob Wealth Star as a Dominant Characteristic potentially means the Wealth Star is either weak or compromised in some manner, depending on the quality of the Rob Wealth Star. Since the Wealth Star represents a man's Spouse, when the Wealth Star is weak or compromised in some manner, the man's relationships will doubtlessly be affected in some manner of form, depending on how the Rob Wealth Star, Day Master and Wealth Stars interact in the chart.

Take a look at the examples below which help to illustrate the point above.

時 Hour	日 Day	月 Month	年 Year	
正印 DR 甲 Jia Yang Wood	日元 DM 丁 Ding Yin Fire	劫財 RW 丙 Bing Yang Fire	正官 DO 壬 Ren Yang Water	天干 Heavenly Stems
辰 Chen **Dragon** Yang Earth	丑 Chou **Ox** Yin Earth	午 Wu **Horse** Yang Fire	寅 Yin **Tiger** Yang Wood	地支 Earthly Branches
癸 Gui - Water 殺 7K; 戊 Wu + Earth 傷 HO; 乙 Yi - Wood 卩 IR	辛 Xin - Metal 才 IW; 己 Ji - Earth 食 EG; 癸 Gui - Water 殺 7K	丁 Ding - Fire 比 F; 己 Ji - Earth 食 EG	戊 Wu + Earth 傷 HO; 甲 Jia + Wood 印 DR; 丙 Bing + Fire 劫 RW	藏干 Hidden Stems

In this chart of a male Ding Fire, the Rob Wealth Star, represented by Bing Fire, is clearly a Dominant Characteristic. However, as the Rob Wealth Star is further rooted in the Tiger (Yin), supported by the season of birth, which is Summer, and further supported by a partial Fire Frame Three Harmony Combination of Tiger and Horse, this Rob Wealth Star can be considered not just a Dominant Characteristic, but excessively Dominant. The Wealth Element in this chart, which is the element of Metal, is appropriately, very weak. It does not have seasonal support – Metal is considered Trapped in the Summer months. Whilst it is located in the Ox (Chou) Earthly Branch, it is only one of the Sub-Qi elements and accordingly is not that strong. This chart illustrates how when the Rob Wealth Star is a Dominant Characteristic and is also supported by the season of birth, the Wealth Star will be weak. Accordingly, this is an individual who has a hard time saving money or accumulating wealth, and thus potentially a candidate for problematic relationships because he is either too poor to get married, or lacks the kind of financial stability needed to provide for a family. This is also a man who puts his friends before his family, due to the Dominant nature of the Rob Wealth Star, which is another problem that puts pressure on his relationships.

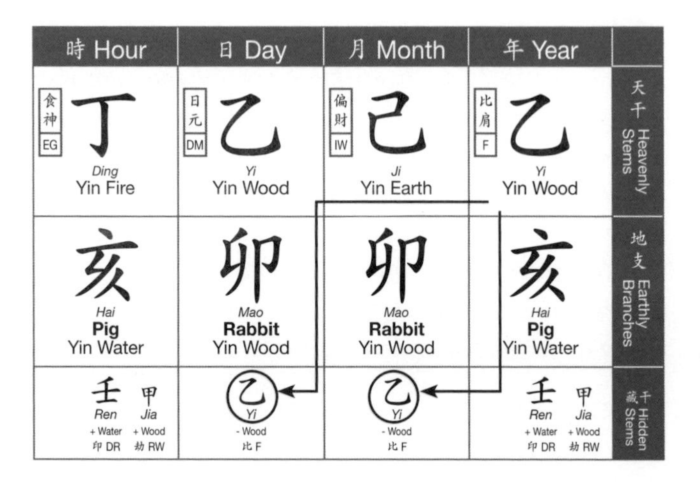

This male Yi Wood chart is another example of how the presence of a strong Companion Element often results in a weak Wealth Element or a compromised Wealth Element. Here, the Friend Star, represented by Yi Wood, is clearly a Dominant Characteristic by virtue of being rooted. The Rob Wealth Star, represented by Jia Wood, is considered Dominant here eventhough it is not rooted. As you will discover in the next Power of X book, an element can be Dominant through other ways aside from rooting. Here, Jia Wood is supported by the season of birth, which is Spring, when Wood is strongest. Further, Jia Wood in this chart is located in Pig (Hai), which is known as the Growth Star for Wood. Thus, we can say that in this chart, the Companion Element (comprising the Friend and Rob Wealth Stars) is clearly strong.

The Wealth Element, represented by the element of Earth, is by contrast, clearly Weak. The singular Wealth Star is located on the Stem only and is not rooted. It is also not supported by the season of birth, as Earth is only strong in the Summer season. If we look at this chart from a pictoral standpoint, it is a case of many shrubs (Yi Wood) and a few trees (Jia Wood) fighting for the same small patch of earth to grow upon. When we translate that imagery into reality, it denotes essentially a man who has to compete very hard to find a spouse.

時 Hour	日 Day	月 Month	年 Year	
正印 DR 戊 Wu Yang Earth	日元 DM 辛 Xin Yin Metal	偏印 IR 己 Ji Yin Earth	劫財 RW 庚 Geng Yang Metal	天干 Heavenly Stems
子 Zi **Rat** Yang Water	未 Wei **Goat** Yin Earth	卯 Mao **Rabbit** Yin Wood	申 Shen **Monkey** Yang Metal	地支 Earthly Branches
癸 Gui - Water 食 EG	乙 Yi - Wood 才 IW; 己 Ji - Earth 卩 IR; 丁 Ding - Fire 殺 7K	乙 Yi - Wood 才 IW	戊 Wu + Earth 印 DR; 庚 Geng + Metal 劫 RW; 壬 Ren + Water 傷 HO	藏干 Hidden Stems

In this male Xin Metal example, the Rob Wealth Star would be considered a Dominant Characteristic because it is rooted in the Monkey (Shen) in the Year Branch. However, the Wealth Element in this chart, represented by Wood, cannot be said to be weak, since it is supported by the season of birth, which is the Spring season, when Wood is strongest. However, this is still a chart where relationships problems are highly likely because although the Wealth Element is not weak, the Wealth Element is compromised or affected in some manner by the Rob Wealth Star.

Firstly, the Rob Wealth Star is a favourable Star in this chart, as the Day Master is weak. Remember a Weak Day Master favours the Companion and Resource Elements and does not favour the Wealth Element. As such, this man will prefer to spend time with his buddies

(as you will learn in later Power of X books, the Rob Wealth Star denotes one's friends) and having a good time with his friends, rather than his wife. Secondly, the Spouse Star in this chart (which is not the true Spouse Star, but the Secondary Spouse Star) actually prefers the Rob Wealth Star to the Day Master. Recall that Yi and Geng are a combination, whilst Xin and Yi would be regarded as more akin to a clash. This denotes the possibility of third party problems, suggesting the man easily loses his wife or partners to other men because he doesn't give her enough attention.

There are also a few other features in this chart which point at the conclusion of relationship issues. You will notice that this chart does not contain the Direct Wealth Star, which is the true Spouse Star for Xin Metal. This chart only contains the Indirect Wealth Star. Accordingly, the quality of relationships that this person will have is already questionable because there is no true Spouse Star. Further, the presence of only the Indirect Wealth Star tells us that this person does not have the temperament and character for marriage or long-term relationships – this is because the Indirect Wealth Star denotes a playboy and also a man who typically does not have the ability to focus or stay interested in any one thing for long. Indeed, playboys do have a tendency to have commitment issues.

When the Rob Wealth Star is a Dominant Characteristic, relationships are a challenge because the man is either too poor to wine and dine members of the opposite sex (or even take them to the movies) or he can't afford to get married because buying a home may not be within his reach. Alternatively, his relationship suffers because he's not paying his spouse enough attention. In some instances, the man may not have trouble attracting female attention and may even manage to get married – this is because the Rob Wealth Star makes a person popular and very appealing to be around. But the relationship will certainly suffer the minute it becomes apparent that he's living from hand to mouth, living off debt or not willing to put time at home with his wife and family.

I'll say it again: BaZi is about the facts and not about judgment, and might I add, I don't make the rules on how the game of love is played. You can be the nicest man in the world and if you have the Rob Wealth Star, then chances are you are a pretty smooth operator, a man with a convivial personality, who is pretty popular with everyone, not just the ladies. But if you can't afford to upkeep your family, pay the household bills or if you can't save money and provide for your children, or if you can't put your family before your friends, then this is going to put pressure on your relationship and marriage.

The 10 Gods and Wealth Matters

In this section, I will show you how to utilise the information about the Wealth Stars from Chapter 3 and combine it with the analysis methods discussed in Chapter 4 to gain certain some insights into a person's wealth capacity and their ability to achieve financial success. Let me just say at the onset - this section isn't about telling you how you to get rich. But it will give you some indicators as to why you might be having trouble achieving your financial goals in life.

Wealth Stars only on the Stem

By and large, the Direct Wealth and Indirect Wealth Stars appearing only on the Heavenly Stems is not regarded as ideal when it comes to wealth matters. As you will recall from Chapter 4, the Heavenly Stems represent surface Qi. Accordingly, when the Wealth Stars appear only on the Stem, this denotes superficial wealth only. In other words, the person only 'appears' to be wealthy but in reality, is probably just doing moderately well financially.

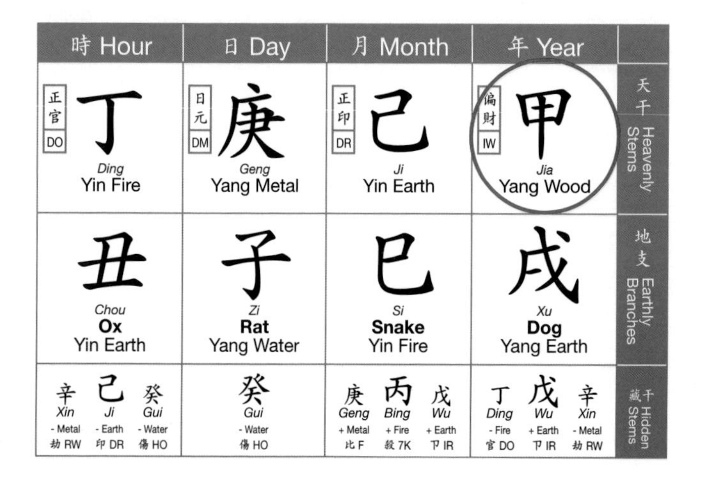

時 Hour	日 Day	月 Month	年 Year	
正官 DO 丁 Ding Yin Fire	日元 DM 庚 Geng Yang Metal	正印 DR 己 Ji Yin Earth	偏財 IW 甲 Jia Yang Wood	天干 Heavenly Stems
丑 Chou **Ox** Yin Earth	子 Zi **Rat** Yang Water	巳 Si **Snake** Yin Fire	戌 Xu **Dog** Yang Earth	地支 Earthly Branches
辛 Xin - Metal 劫 RW; 己 Ji - Earth 印 DR; 癸 Gui - Water 傷 HO	癸 Gui - Water 傷 HO	庚 Geng + Metal 比 F; 丙 Bing + Fire 殺 7K; 戊 Wu + Earth 卩 IR	丁 Ding - Fire 官 DO; 戊 Wu + Earth 卩 IR; 辛 Xin - Metal 劫 RW	藏干 Hidden Stems

In this chart, the only Wealth Star present is the Indirect Wealth Star on the Year Stem. Thus denotes a person who seems to make money easily and quickly through perhaps wheeling and dealing or hustling, and who appears to be the picture of the 'wealthy businessman', flashing money and spending lavishly but in fact may not be that wealthy in reality and possibly even living on credit!

The presence of Wealth Stars on the Heavenly Stems alone is regarded as unfavourable also because it denotes exposed wealth, meaning, wealth that is easily lost. This is because if the Wealth Stars are located on the Heavenly Stems, the arrival of a Rob Wealth Star in the Heavenly Stems of a Year Pillar or Month Pillar or Luck Pillar will result in the loss of Wealth, especially if the Rob Wealth Star combines with the Wealth Star.

時 Hour	日 Day	月 Month	年 Year	
正官 DO 壬 Ren Yang Water	日元 DM 丁 Ding Yin Fire	偏財 IW 辛 Xin Yin Metal	劫財 RW 丙 Bing Yang Fire	天干 Heavenly Stems
子 Zi **Rat** Yang Water	卯 Mao **Rabbit** Yin Wood	卯 Mao **Rabbit** Yin Wood	寅 Yin **Tiger** Yang Wood	地支 Earthly Branches
癸 Gui - Water 殺 7K	乙 Yi - Wood 卩 IR	乙 Yi - Wood 卩 IR	戊 Wu + Earth 傷 HO; 甲 Jia + Wood 印 DR; 丙 Bing + Fire 劫 RW	藏干 Hidden Stems

In this Ding Fire example, the only Wealth Star present is the Indirect Wealth Star (represented by Xin Metal) located in the Month Stem. This Indirect Wealth Star accordingly is vulnerable and exposed to being combined away by the Companion Stars. Right next to the Xin Metal Stem is Bing Fire. Bing Fire is the Rob Wealth Star of Ding Fire. Bing-Xin is a Stem Combination. Accordingly, the exposed Indirect Wealth Star here, which is the ONLY Wealth Star in the entire chart, has combined with the Rob Wealth Star. Thus, this person who we know is only superficially wealthy, is actually someone who loses more money than he actually makes.

You might be wondering what is the value of knowing this information – isn't it unduly nosy or even in bad form to snoop into someone's financial affairs? Well ask yourself the question of whether or not you want to do business with someone who talks the talk, but unfortunately hasn't got the cashflow or even the money to walk the walk. Do you want to be a salesman attempting to sell a big ticket item (like a house or a business) to a person who is only seemingly wealthy? Why waste time chasing this lead when there might be someone with a more definitive likelihood of being able to afford what you are selling?

And whilst this is going to sound shallow, the fact is that no woman wants to be married to a man who exaggerates his financial worth and turns out to be up to his eyeballs in credit card debt in order to wine and dine her. Imagine being married to a man who turns out to be unable afford to upkeep you in the lifestyle which you *thought* he could?

What if you are one of those people who only has Wealth Stars only in the Heavenly Stems? Essentially, you now will be aware that you are very vulnerable to loss of wealth and are likely to be an easy mark for people looking to borrow money or worse, pull a fast one on you. Accordingly, you may want to try to 'dress down' things a little and flash less of the cash. If you think about it, you really can't afford to throw it around that much anyway. Instead, focus your attention on wealth preservation as much as possible, and using good old-fashioned methods of prudence and enforced savings to improve your financial track-record.

Wealth Stars in the Branches

Wealth Stars in the Branches only are regarded as more advantageous compared to Wealth Stars in the Stems only. This means that the Wealth Stars in your chart ONLY appear in the Earthly Branches.

時 Hour	日 Day	月 Month	年 Year	
正官 DO 癸 Gui Yin Water	日元 DM 丙 Bing Yang Fire	食神 EG 戊 Wu Yang Earth	七殺 7K 壬 Ren Yang Water	天干 Heavenly Stems
巳 Si **Snake** Yin Fire	戌 Xu **Dog** Yang Earth	申 Shen **Monkey** Yang Metal	戌 Xu **Dog** Yang Earth	地支 Earthly Branches
庚 Geng + Metal 才 IW; 丙 Bing + Fire 比 F; 戊 Wu + Earth 食 EG	丁 Ding - Fire 劫 RW; 戊 Wu + Earth 食 EG; 辛 Xin - Metal 財 DW	戊 Wu + Earth 食 EG; 庚 Geng + Metal 才 IW; 壬 Ren + Water 殺 7K	丁 Ding - Fire 劫 RW; 戊 Wu + Earth 食 EG; 辛 Xin - Metal 財 DW	藏干 Hidden Stems

In this chart, the Wealth Stars are all in the Earthly Branches – the Direct Wealth Stars (represented by Xin Metal) in the Dog (Xu) and the Indirect Wealth Star (represented by Geng Metal) in the Monkey (Shen).

When the Wealth Stars are hidden inside the Earthly Branches and do not appear in the Stems, this denotes a person who is stealthily wealthy. In other words, they do not appear to be wealthy to the outside world and the extent of their wealth is not obvious, except to those who know them very well or close family members. A person with Wealth Stars that appear only in the Earthly Branches *definitely* has wealth and assets, unlike the person with Wealth Stars that appear only in the Heavenly Stems. This is because Qi in the Earthly Branches is regarded as having more staying power and endurance compared to Qi on the Heavenly Stems. In BaZi, it is said, one in Branch is worth three in Stem. Accordingly, a singular Wealth Star located in the Earthly Branches carries greater weight than three Wealth Stars on the Heavenly Stems.

Wealth Stars that only appear inside the Earthly Branches may also denote a person who is asset rich and cash rich, depending on which of the Earthly Branches the Wealth Star appears within, and whether it is the Direct Wealth Star or Indirect Wealth Star that appears within specific Earthly Branches. The great advantage of Wealth Stars that appear only in the Earthly Branches is that the Stars are not exposed, and thus, less vulnerable to the Rob Wealth Star or being combined away. Thus, such individuals are less likely to lose money easily or be duped to parting with their wealth. This is why as a general principle, it is considered acceptable, indeed favourable, for the Wealth Stars not to appear on the Stems and remain in the Branches.

The Wealth and Character Connection

If you have read any of the numerous books on the subject of generating wealth or creating greater wealth, you may have noticed that the overwhelming majority of these books (particularly *Rich Dad, Poor Dad* by Robert Kiyosaki) point to the importance of having the right mindset for wealth generation and wealth creation. When it comes to wealth matters in BaZi, there are some people who have a greater inclination towards generating wealth or creating wealth than others simply because their character (which you will recall, is a composite of not just your skills, talents, virtues and flaws, but mindset, attitude and perception) is inherently inclined that way. Equally, some people have a greater proclivity for losing money or struggling with Wealth matters for the same reasons.

By this point, you probably would have figured out already that individuals who have the Wealth Stars as part of their Dominant Characteristics have an overall higher likelihood of achieving financial success or generating and creating wealth. After all, the two Wealth Stars (Direct Wealth and Indirect Wealth) are the most closely connected to financial matters and materialistic endeavours so it makes sense that having either of these Stars as one's Dominant Characteristics increases the likelihood of the person achieving financial success or creating wealth for themselves. After all, you have to be focused on wanting to achieve financial success or create wealth in order to actually be pro-active and take the requisite steps or action needed to do so. Since individuals with Wealth Stars as their Dominant Characteristics will tend to think about making money and ways to make money MORE than individual who do not have Wealth Stars as their Dominant Characteristics, it is only natural that such individuals start with an inherent advantage.

So what if you don't have the Wealth Stars as part of your Dominant Characteristics? Does this mean that financial success or wealth generation are out of your hands? Of course, it is not the Wealth Stars alone that are responsible for financial success or wealth creation. There is a saying in BaZi: 食傷生財 which literally translates as, "*Eating [God] Hurting [Officer] Produces Wealth*".

If you look back at Chapter 2 and study the individual diagrams on how the 10 Gods are derived for each of the 10 Day Masters, you will notice that the Output Element produces the Wealth Element in every one of the 10 Day Masters.

There is a saying in BaZi: 食傷生財 which literally translates as, "Eating [God] Hurting [Officer] Produces Wealth".

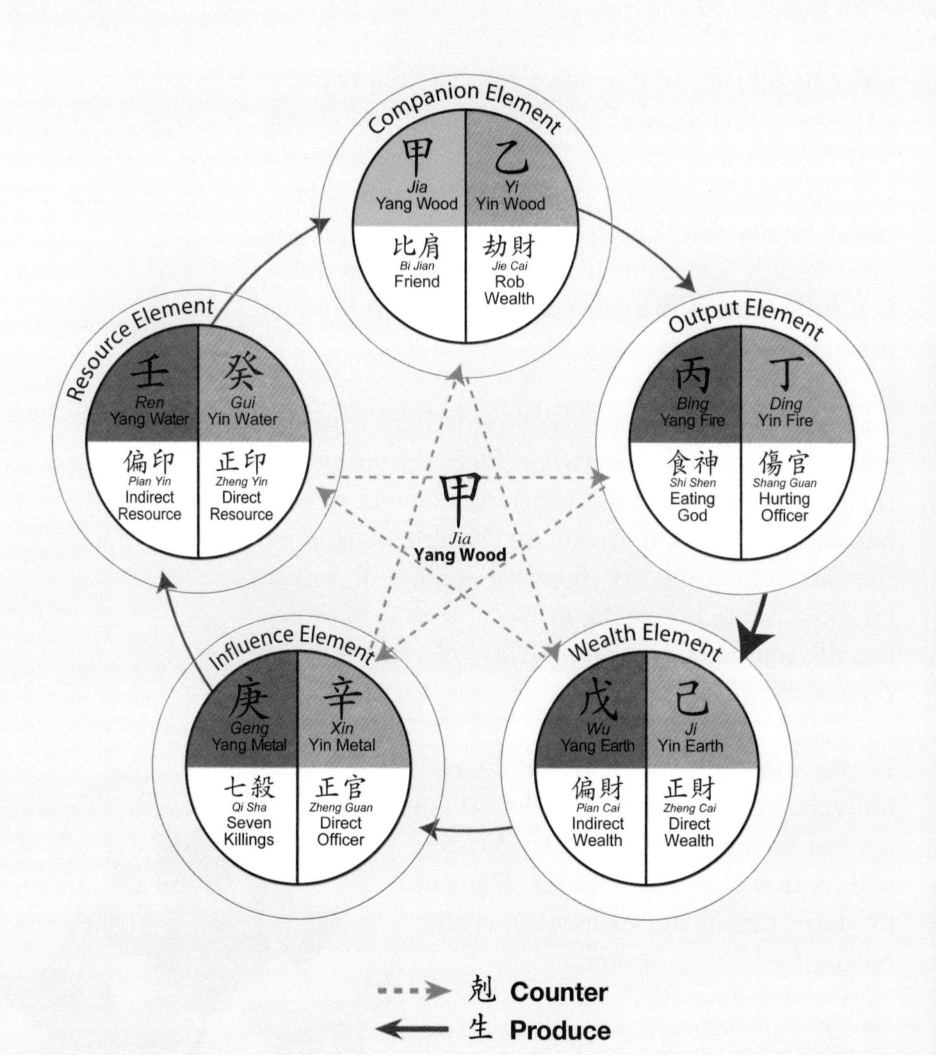
Companion Element
甲
Jia
Yang Wood
乙
Yi
Yin Wood
比肩
Bi Jian
Friend
劫財
Jie Cai
Rob Wealth
Output Element
丙
Bing
Yang Fire
丁
Ding
Yin Fire
食神
Shi Shen
Eating God
傷官
Shang Guan
Hurting Officer
Wealth Element
戊
Wu
Yang Earth
己
Ji
Yin Earth
偏財
Pian Cai
Indirect Wealth
正財
Zheng Cai
Direct Wealth
Influence Element
庚
Geng
Yang Metal
辛
Xin
Yin Metal
七殺
Qi Sha
Seven Killings
正官
Zheng Guan
Direct Officer
Resource Element
壬
Ren
Yang Water
癸
Gui
Yin Water
偏印
Pian Yin
Indirect Resource
正印
Zheng Yin
Direct Resource
甲
Jia
Yang Wood
剋 Counter
生 Produce

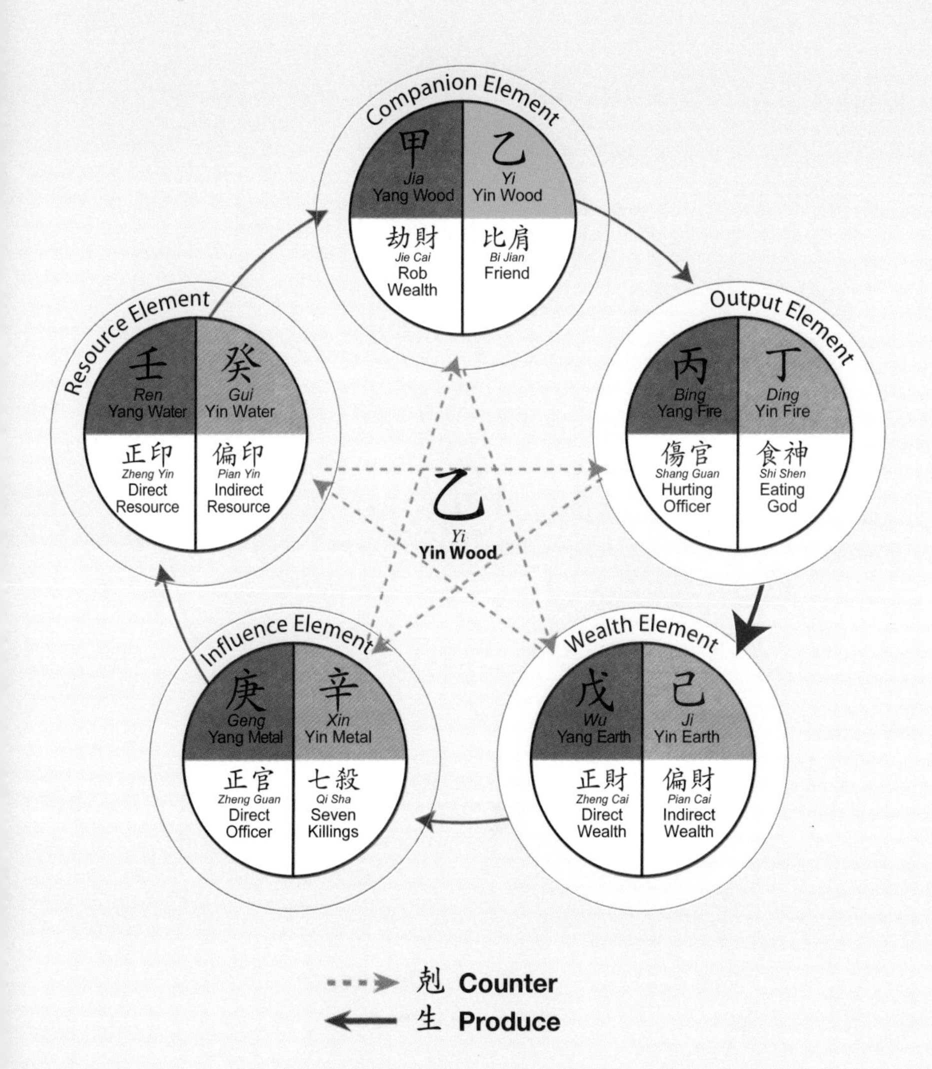
Companion Element
甲
Jia
Yang Wood
乙
Yi
Yin Wood
劫財
Jie Cai
Rob Wealth
比肩
Bi Jian
Friend
Output Element
丙
Bing
Yang Fire
丁
Ding
Yin Fire
傷官
Shang Guan
Hurting Officer
食神
Shi Shen
Eating God
Wealth Element
戊
Wu
Yang Earth
己
Ji
Yin Earth
正財
Zheng Cai
Direct Wealth
偏財
Pian Cai
Indirect Wealth
Influence Element
庚
Geng
Yang Metal
辛
Xin
Yin Metal
正官
Zheng Guan
Direct Officer
七殺
Qi Sha
Seven Killings
Resource Element
壬
Ren
Yang Water
癸
Gui
Yin Water
正印
Zheng Yin
Direct Resource
偏印
Pian Yin
Indirect Resource
乙
Yi
Yin Wood
剋 Counter
生 Produce

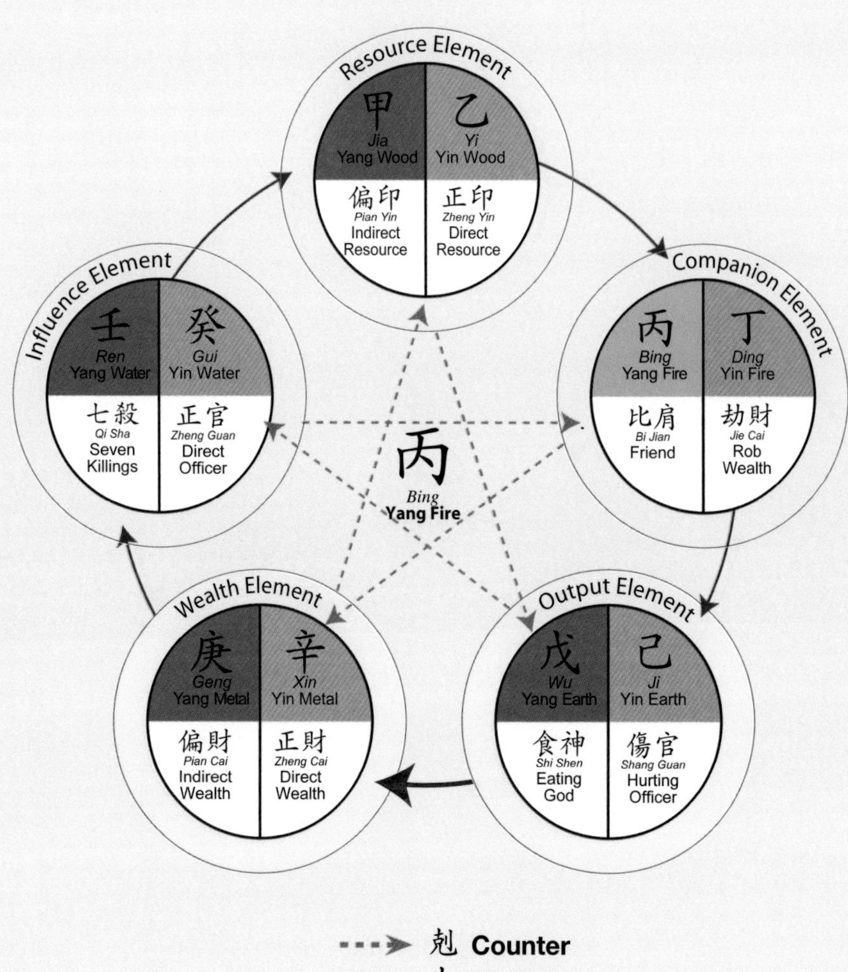
Resource Element
甲
Jia
Yang Wood
乙
Yi
Yin Wood
偏印
Pian Yin
Indirect Resource
正印
Zheng Yin
Direct Resource
Companion Element
丙
Bing
Yang Fire
丁
Ding
Yin Fire
比肩
Bi Jian
Friend
劫財
Jie Cai
Rob Wealth
Output Element
戊
Wu
Yang Earth
己
Ji
Yin Earth
食神
Shi Shen
Eating God
傷官
Shang Guan
Hurting Officer
Wealth Element
庚
Geng
Yang Metal
辛
Xin
Yin Metal
偏財
Pian Cai
Indirect Wealth
正財
Zheng Cai
Direct Wealth
Influence Element
壬
Ren
Yang Water
癸
Gui
Yin Water
七殺
Qi Sha
Seven Killings
正官
Zheng Guan
Direct Officer
丙
Bing
Yang Fire
剋 Counter
生 Produce

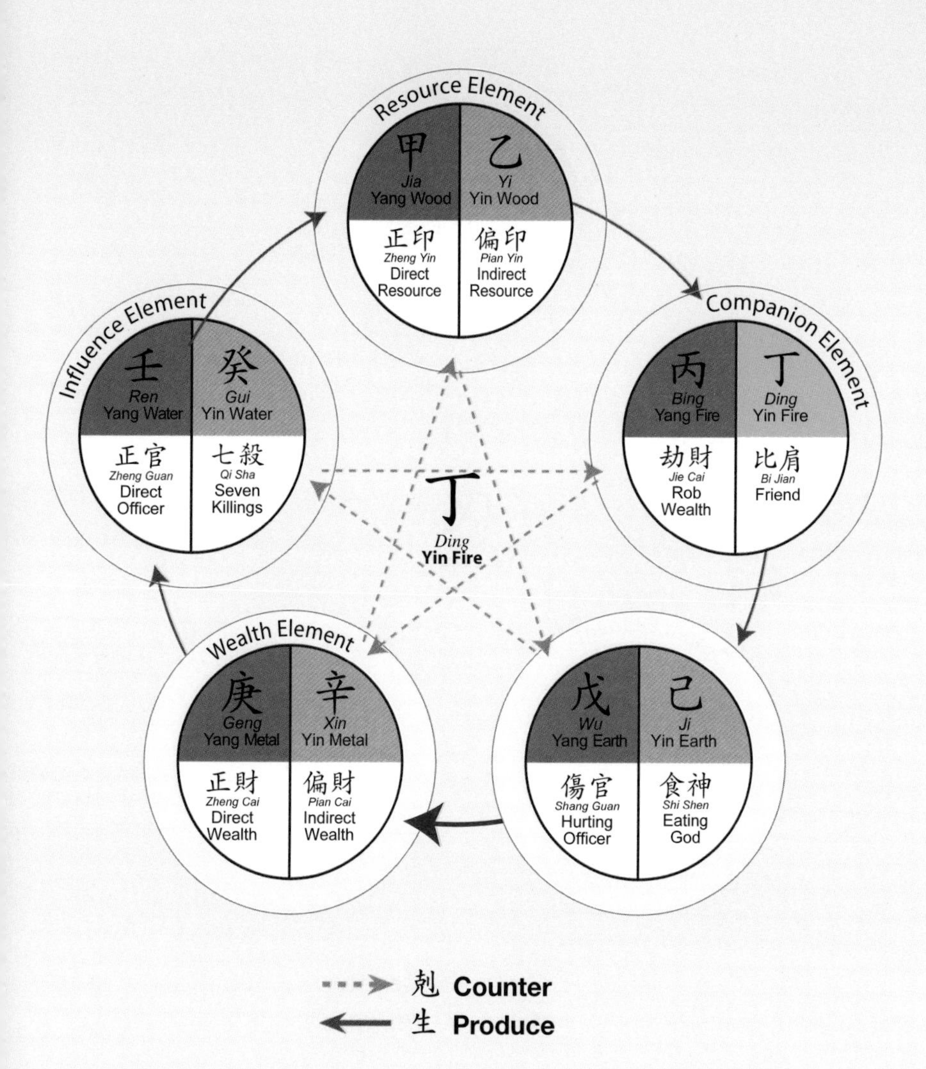
Resource Element
甲
Jia
Yang Wood
乙
Yi
Yin Wood
正印
Zheng Yin
Direct Resource
偏印
Pian Yin
Indirect Resource
Companion Element
丙
Bing
Yang Fire
丁
Ding
Yin Fire
劫財
Jie Cai
Rob Wealth
比肩
Bi Jian
Friend
Influence Element
壬
Ren
Yang Water
癸
Gui
Yin Water
正官
Zheng Guan
Direct Officer
七殺
Qi Sha
Seven Killings
丁
Ding
Yin Fire
Wealth Element
庚
Geng
Yang Metal
辛
Xin
Yin Metal
正財
Zheng Cai
Direct Wealth
偏財
Pian Cai
Indirect Wealth
戊
Wu
Yang Earth
己
Ji
Yin Earth
傷官
Shang Guan
Hurting Officer
食神
Shi Shen
Eating God
剋 Counter
生 Produce

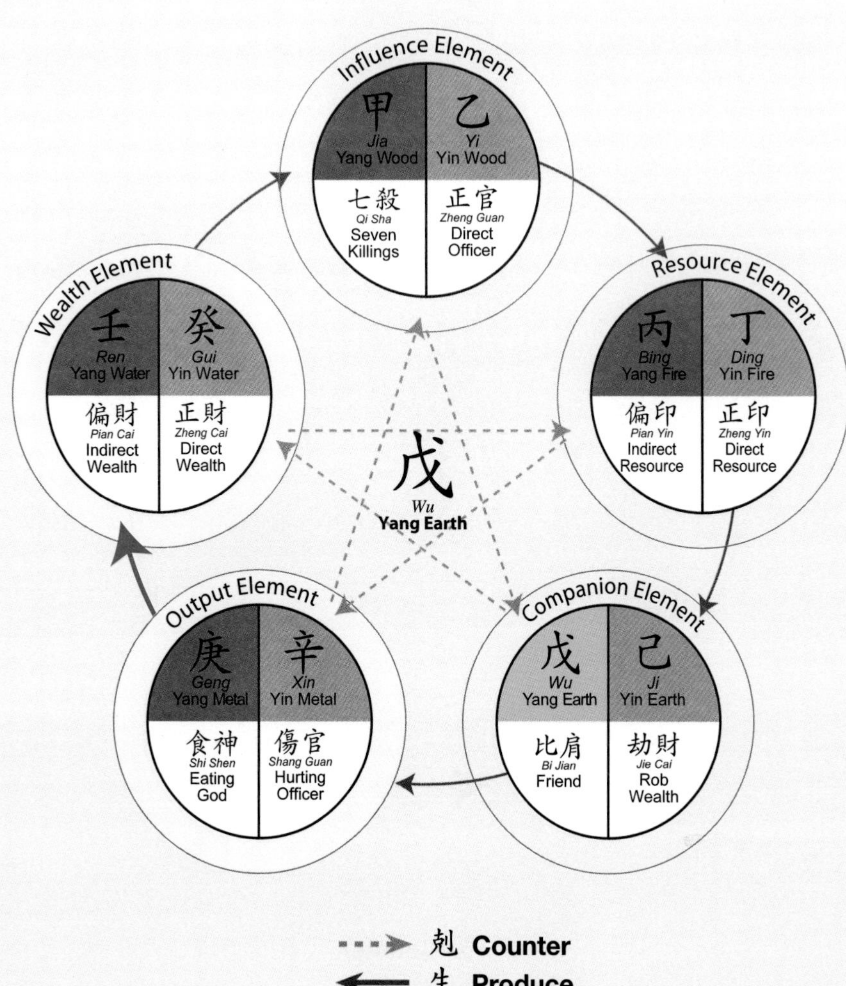
Influence Element
甲 Jia Yang Wood
乙 Yi Yin Wood
七殺 Qi Sha Seven Killings
正官 Zheng Guan Direct Officer
Resource Element
丙 Bing Yang Fire
丁 Ding Yin Fire
偏印 Pian Yin Indirect Resource
正印 Zheng Yin Direct Resource
Companion Element
戊 Wu Yang Earth
己 Ji Yin Earth
比肩 Bi Jian Friend
劫財 Jie Cai Rob Wealth
Output Element
庚 Geng Yang Metal
辛 Xin Yin Metal
食神 Shi Shen Eating God
傷官 Shang Guan Hurting Officer
Wealth Element
壬 Ren Yang Water
癸 Gui Yin Water
偏財 Pian Cai Indirect Wealth
正財 Zheng Cai Direct Wealth
戊 Wu Yang Earth
剋 Counter
生 Produce

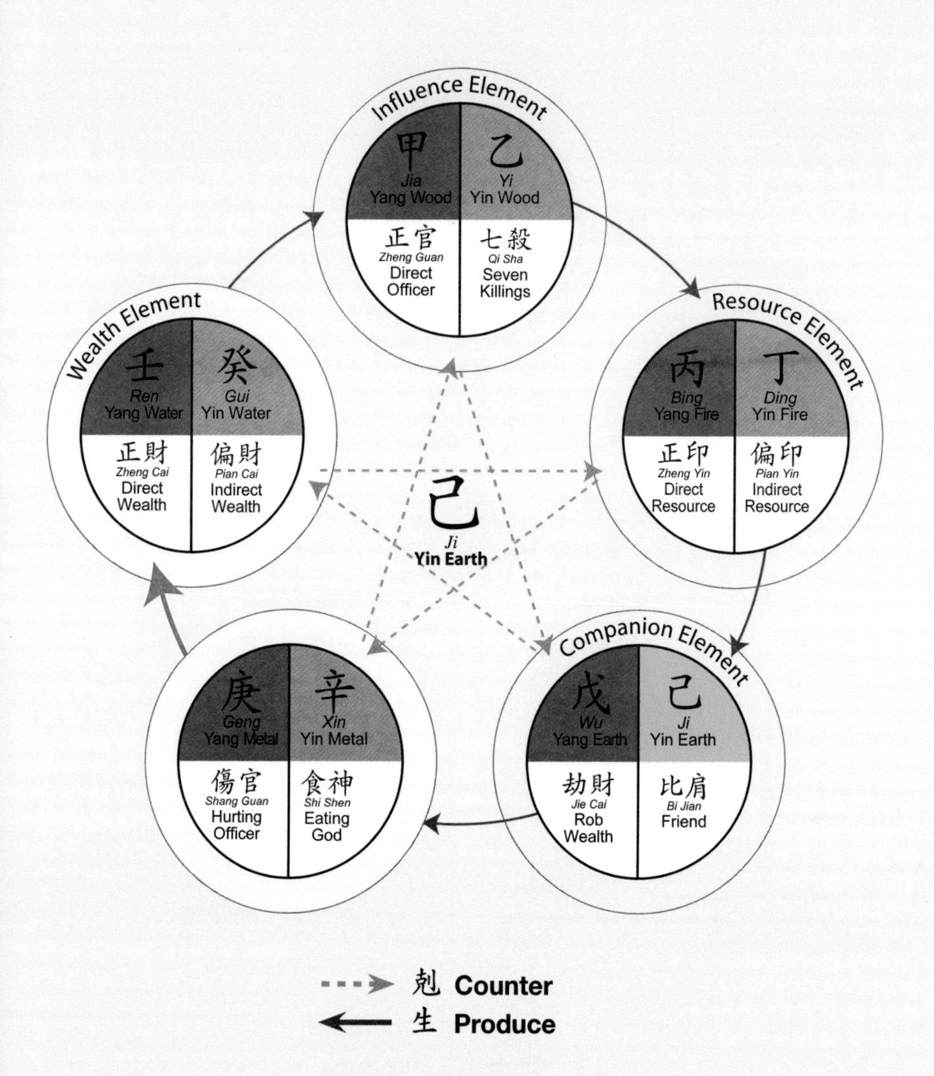
Influence Element
甲
Jia
Yang Wood
乙
Yi
Yin Wood
正官
Zheng Guan
Direct Officer
七殺
Qi Sha
Seven Killings
Resource Element
丙
Bing
Yang Fire
丁
Ding
Yin Fire
正印
Zheng Yin
Direct Resource
偏印
Pian Yin
Indirect Resource
Companion Element
戊
Wu
Yang Earth
己
Ji
Yin Earth
劫財
Jie Cai
Rob Wealth
比肩
Bi Jian
Friend
庚
Geng
Yang Metal
辛
Xin
Yin Metal
傷官
Shang Guan
Hurting Officer
食神
Shi Shen
Eating God
Wealth Element
壬
Ren
Yang Water
癸
Gui
Yin Water
正財
Zheng Cai
Direct Wealth
偏財
Pian Cai
Indirect Wealth
己
Ji
Yin Earth
剋 Counter
生 Produce

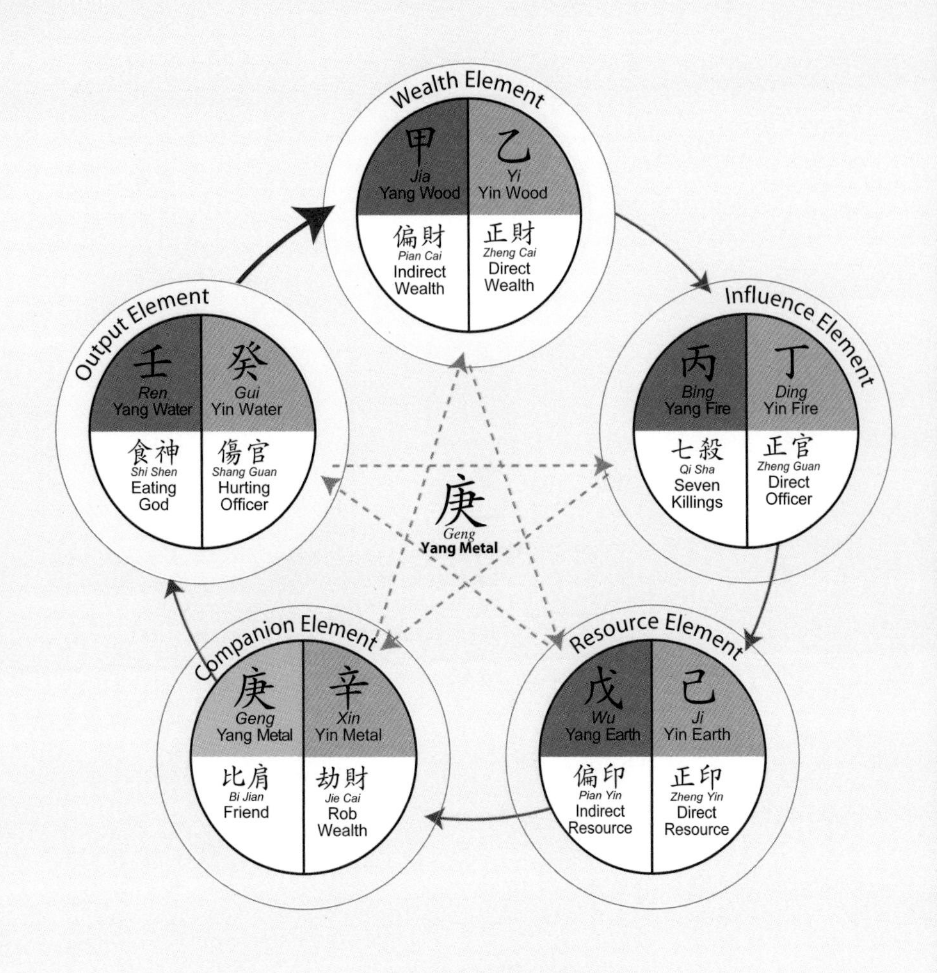
Wealth Element
甲
Jia
Yang Wood
乙
Yi
Yin Wood
偏財
Pian Cai
Indirect Wealth
正財
Zheng Cai
Direct Wealth
Influence Element
丙
Bing
Yang Fire
丁
Ding
Yin Fire
七殺
Qi Sha
Seven Killings
正官
Zheng Guan
Direct Officer
Resource Element
戊
Wu
Yang Earth
己
Ji
Yin Earth
偏印
Pian Yin
Indirect Resource
正印
Zheng Yin
Direct Resource
Companion Element
庚
Geng
Yang Metal
辛
Xin
Yin Metal
比肩
Bi Jian
Friend
劫財
Jie Cai
Rob Wealth
Output Element
壬
Ren
Yang Water
癸
Gui
Yin Water
食神
Shi Shen
Eating God
傷官
Shang Guan
Hurting Officer
庚
Geng
Yang Metal
剋 Counter
生 Produce

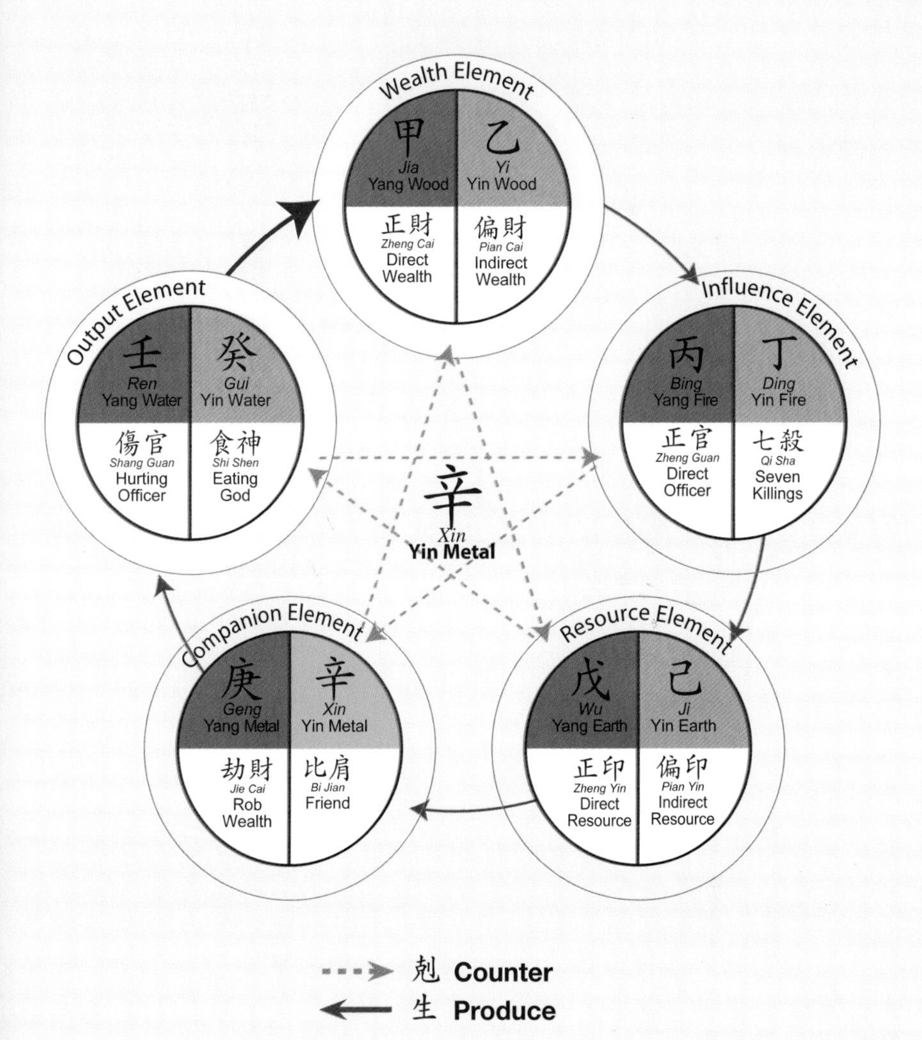
Wealth Element
甲
Jia
Yang Wood
乙
Yi
Yin Wood
正財
Zheng Cai
Direct Wealth
偏財
Pian Cai
Indirect Wealth
Influence Element
丙
Bing
Yang Fire
丁
Ding
Yin Fire
正官
Zheng Guan
Direct Officer
七殺
Qi Sha
Seven Killings
Resource Element
戊
Wu
Yang Earth
己
Ji
Yin Earth
正印
Zheng Yin
Direct Resource
偏印
Pian Yin
Indirect Resource
Companion Element
庚
Geng
Yang Metal
辛
Xin
Yin Metal
劫財
Jie Cai
Rob Wealth
比肩
Bi Jian
Friend
Output Element
壬
Ren
Yang Water
癸
Gui
Yin Water
傷官
Shang Guan
Hurting Officer
食神
Shi Shen
Eating God
辛
Xin
Yin Metal
剋 Counter
生 Produce

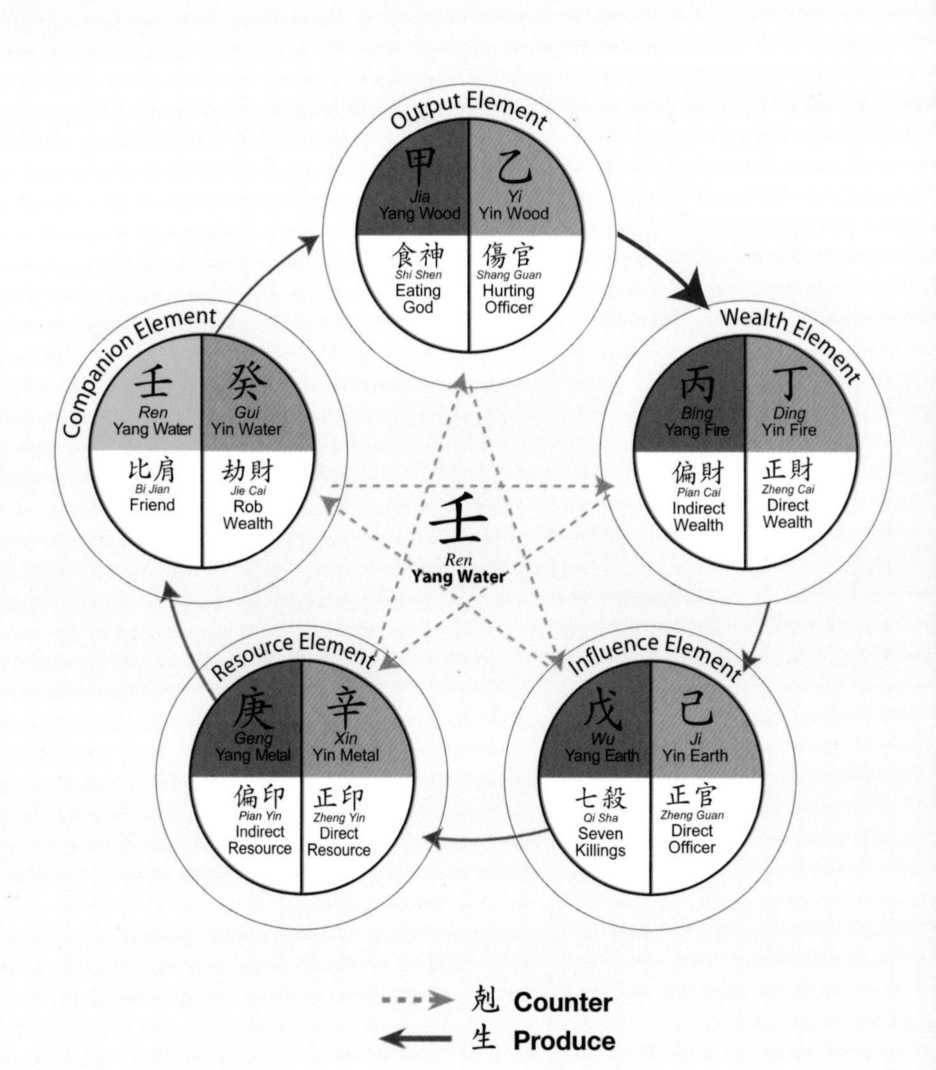
Output Element
甲
Jia
Yang Wood
乙
Yi
Yin Wood
食神
Shi Shen
Eating God
傷官
Shang Guan
Hurting Officer
Wealth Element
丙
Bing
Yang Fire
丁
Ding
Yin Fire
偏財
Pian Cai
Indirect Wealth
正財
Zheng Cai
Direct Wealth
Influence Element
戊
Wu
Yang Earth
己
Ji
Yin Earth
七殺
Qi Sha
Seven Killings
正官
Zheng Guan
Direct Officer
Resource Element
庚
Geng
Yang Metal
辛
Xin
Yin Metal
偏印
Pian Yin
Indirect Resource
正印
Zheng Yin
Direct Resource
Companion Element
壬
Ren
Yang Water
癸
Gui
Yin Water
比肩
Bi Jian
Friend
劫財
Jie Cai
Rob Wealth
壬
Ren
Yang Water
剋 Counter
生 Produce

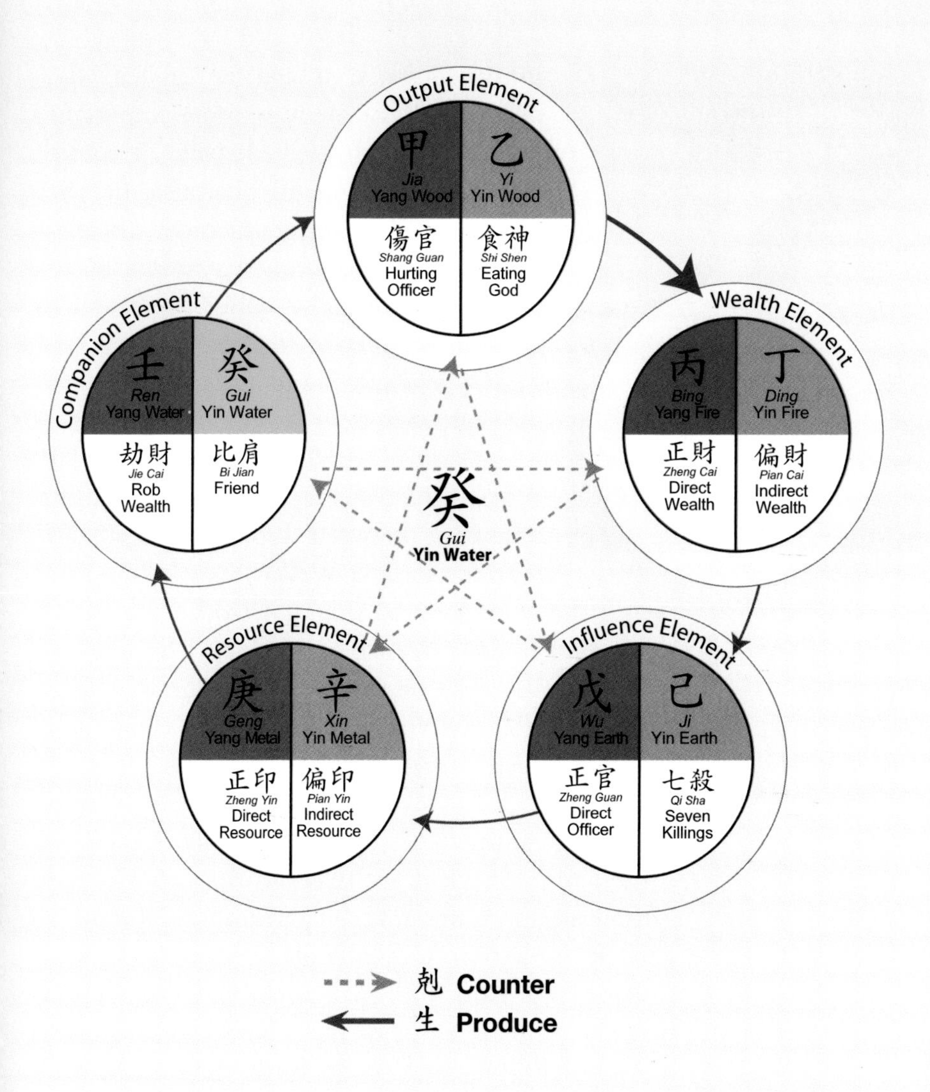
Output Element
甲
Jia
Yang Wood
乙
Yi
Yin Wood
傷官
Shang Guan
Hurting Officer
食神
Shi Shen
Eating God
Wealth Element
丙
Bing
Yang Fire
丁
Ding
Yin Fire
正財
Zheng Cai
Direct Wealth
偏財
Pian Cai
Indirect Wealth
Influence Element
戊
Wu
Yang Earth
己
Ji
Yin Earth
正官
Zheng Guan
Direct Officer
七殺
Qi Sha
Seven Killings
Resource Element
庚
Geng
Yang Metal
辛
Xin
Yin Metal
正印
Zheng Yin
Direct Resource
偏印
Pian Yin
Indirect Resource
Companion Element
壬
Ren
Yang Water
癸
Gui
Yin Water
劫財
Jie Cai
Rob Wealth
比肩
Bi Jian
Friend
癸
Gui
Yin Water
剋 Counter
生 Produce

The Wealth Stars imbue in a person the willingness to slog and work hard in order to achieve success. The Output Stars by contrast imbue a person with creativity and a desire to create and innovate, which indirectly, results in wealth.

In this respect, it can be argued that the Output Element is more important than the Wealth Element when it comes to matters of wealth because in the absence of the Output Element, there is no capacity for continuous generation of wealth. Accordingly, whilst the Wealth Stars are important for financial success, wealth generation and creation, requires the Output Stars.

What is the difference? Think of it as the difference between industriousness and innovation. The Wealth Stars imbue in a person the willingness to slog and work hard (or in the case of Indirect Wealth, work smart) in order to achieve success. The Output Stars by contrast imbue a person with creativity and a desire to create and innovate, which indirectly, results in wealth.

Of course, ultimately success in many ways is a combination of talent and hard work or as Thomas Edison succinctly declared, 99 percent perspiration, 1 percent inspiration. It doesn't matter if it's talent that comes first or hard work that comes first, the point is that one must have one or the other. And of course, one must be prepared to **do both**. Thus, it is not the case that those with Output Stars (Eating God or Hurting Officer) or Wealth Stars (Direct Wealth or Indirect Wealth) will be guaranteed financial success – creative individuals still need to put in the slog time and hard work, whilst those willing to put in the hard work should focus on better developing their innovation skills to reduce the need for hard work alone.

What then if neither the Wealth Stars or Output Stars are the Dominant Characteristics in your chart? Does that mean financial success is truly unattainable? The correct perception towards this is to look at it from the standpoint that your financial success is likely to be attained through working for someone rather than on your own. Asians tend to over-rate entrepreneurialism and under-rate professional careers in the employ of others.

If the Influence Stars are your Dominant Characteristics, you may be better served climbing the corporate ladder and focusing on management. If the Resource Stars are your Dominant Characteristics, you would be better off working for someone in a service-centric industry or something that requires soft skills or has an academic bent to it such as research and development. If the Companion Stars are your Dominant Characteristics, working for a large organisation where you are tasked with relationship building or managing relationships or deal-making is more likely your path to success, and accordingly financial success.

Stop trying to do what you're NOT good at doing and focus instead on what you are good at doing.

Ultimately, financial success is essentially a reward for being good at what you do so if you stop trying to do what you're NOT good at doing and focus instead on what you are good at doing, it's half the financial battle won.

Piecing Together the Destiny Code Puzzle

Readers who have perused *The Destiny Code* and *The Destiny Code Revealed* may be wondering how they reconcile the information about relationships, career and wealth that they have garnered from those books, with the information that they have obtained about Relationships, Career and Wealth in this book. The fact is that attempting to put all the information you have obtained from this book and the previous two books about your chart together will be difficult and confusing at this point. Thus, as tempting as it is, it is best to keep the conclusions that you have arrived at about your chart from the previous two books and this book, separate for now. Don't try to throw everything into the pot and make sense of it because it will simply stir more confusion.

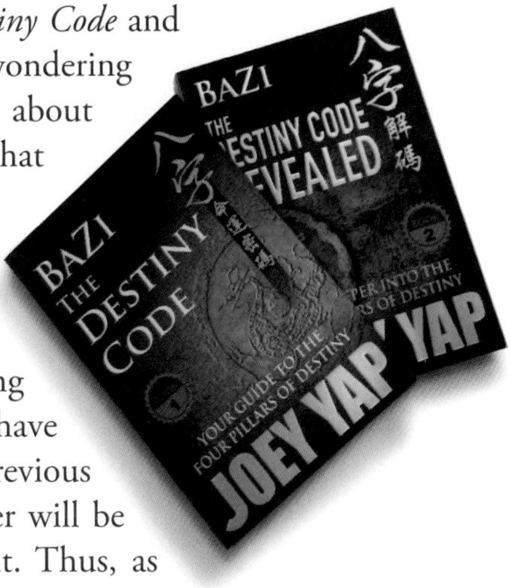

Whatever you have learned about yourself, your career, your relationships and your wealth matters from *The Destiny Code* and the *Destiny Code Revealed* remains useful and valid. The observations that you have about the interactions (Clash, Combination, Harm, Punishment, Destruction) going on in your chart remain valid, as do the insights regarding your Favourable and Unfavourable Elements. Whatever you learn and ascertain about yourself from this book simply adds a different layer (or even new insights) onto your previous understanding and knowledge of yourself and your BaZi chart.

Not all of you may be able to put everything together, whilst some of you (those with Indirect Resource inclinations) may already be able to see some measure of a composite picture emerging. For example, if your Wealth Star only appears on the Stems, and it is Clashed, clearly, this tells you that making money isn't going to come easy for you in this life. Or if your Spouse Palace appears in the Spouse Palace, suggesting good marriage BUT that Spouse Palace has a Harm, Destruction or Punishment affecting it, the positive implication of a good marriage may have to be downgraded somewhat.

If your Spouse Palace appears in the Spouse Palace, suggesting good marriage BUT ...

But if you are unable to put together the whole picture, do not be too concerned. Now is not the time to attempt to put the whole picture together yet because the pieces you possess are not quite yet complete. The trick however is not to be paralysed by what you don't know or obsessed with the notion that the answers will only emerge when you have all the theories and knowledge at your fingertips. Too many students of BaZi assume that knowing more necessarily means they are able to help themselves (or the people whom they are reading the chart for) in a more meaningful way. That is not always true. Sometimes, the most profound answers are the simplest ones. Work with what you have. Focus on what you now know from analysing your chart using the 10 Gods. Act upon that knowledge.

Knowing without acting upon the knowledge is as good as not knowing at all.

Now that you have awareness, it is imperative that you act upon that awareness by **committing** to implementing change. It doesn't matter if that change you make is small or big, as long as you commit emotionally to the idea that nothing will change in your life and destiny by itself. You have to be the one to create that change, by changing your mindset, adjusting your perceptions, improving your attitude, interacting effectively with people, making smart decisions and doing things differently.

Rest assured, as you learn more about how to evaluate and read the 10 Gods through out the *Power of X* series, these discrete puzzle pieces will eventually start to fit together to give you a more complete picture. And as your understanding of BaZi deepens, so new layers of understanding will unfurl about your chart and new ideas about how you can improve yourself will come to the fore. At that point, you will begin to understand how the information that you have from the initial *Destiny Code* books, such as Favourable and Unfavourable Elements, as well as Clashes, Combinations, Harms, Destructions and Punishments is utilised *together with* the 10 Gods.

But we're not there yet!

Do not be disheartened for BaZi is a subject that one must mature into and as you continue down this road, your knowledge and understanding can only deepen.

For now, your aim should not be not to figure out the Grand Scheme of All Things BaZi. Focus on getting comfortable with using the 10 Gods as the core of your BaZi analysis. Get comfortable with thinking in terms of the 10 Gods whenever you look at a BaZi chart. It's time to think about things in the specific and precise manner as demanded by the 10 Gods rather than the very broad approach permitted by the methods discussed in *The Destiny Code* and the *Destiny Code Revealed.*

Going Forward

What I have done here in the first of the *Power of X* series is to give you a broad-based introduction to the 10 Gods. By know, you know the attributes of each of the 10 Gods and have some simple analysis methods at your disposal to gain a snapshot of a person's character. You also know that each 10 God has positive and negative attributes. However, in which circumstances will the negative attributes be more prominent and which circumstances the negative attributes will be less prominent? How do you gauge the quality of a particular 10 God in a BaZi chart and what is the value of being able to gauge the quality of a particular 10 God? These are some of the questions that will be addressed and explored in the next book in the *Power of X* series.

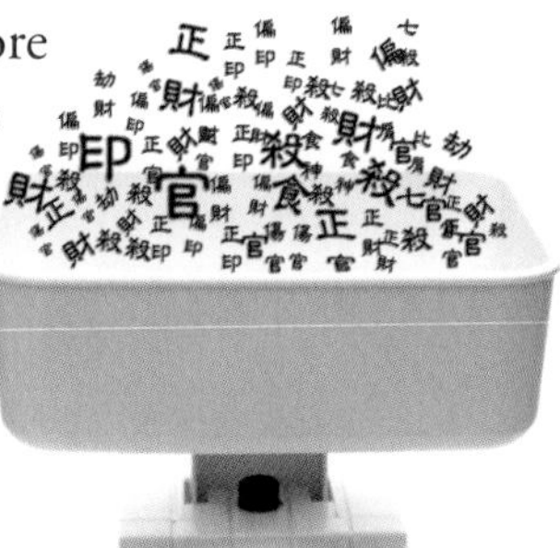

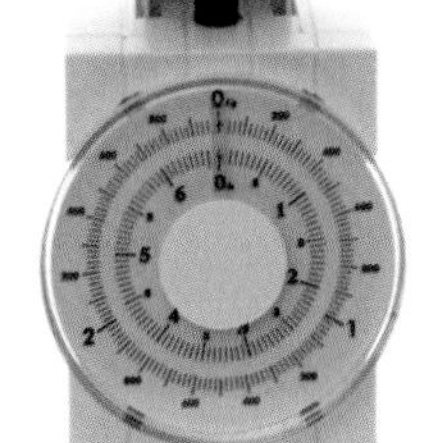

Ultimately, a complete and thorough analysis of a person's Destiny Code involves looking at more than one 10 God at a given time, whilst taking into account the various interactions (Clash, Combination, Harm, Destruction, Punishment) that are going on in the chart, which all then has to be related back to the Day Master. Some the 10 Gods share overlapping or similar traits – what is the significance of such a feature in the chart? How do the 10 Gods interact with each other in the chart?

These and more are the questions that I plan to explore with you further through the *Power of X* series. In each book, I will also show you how to gain deeper and more accurate insight into issues of wealth, career and relationships. Each of these topics will be revisited as you advance your knowledge and understanding of the 10 Gods.

As you attain a greater understanding of the 10 Gods and in turn, deepen and expand your knowledge of BaZi, you will be gaining greater insights into yourself as a person whilst unlocking valuable understanding of your potential.

But it doesn't end there.

With the knowledge you have and will gain, you will also be able to analyse the BaZi charts of people around you who matter and those who you will meet along the way in the journey of life. You'll be know how to better interact and communicate with these people as well as collaborate or handle them more effectively because you actually truly understand how they think, why they think that way and most importantly, what motivates their actions or inaction as well as their decisions and choices.

Finally, there's the predictive power of BaZi, which you'll gradually be able to harness as your understanding of the 10 Gods and chart interactions advances. By understanding how the 10 Gods in the Ten Year Luck Pillar and Annual Luck Pillars interact with the 10 Gods in a given BaZi chart, you are able to anticipate challenges, risk-manage and capitalise strategically upon opportunities. You will be able to drive your destiny in the truest manner possible, and in so doing, prime yourself to be victorious in the game of life.

Work Sheets

Five Factors	Element	Yin 陰	Yang 陽
Output *(EG 食, HO 傷)*			
Wealth *(IW 才, DW 財)*			
Influence *(7K 殺, DO 官)*			
Resource *(IR 卩, DR 印)*			
Companion *(F 比, RW 劫)*			

正財星 Direct Wealth Star	
偏財星 Indirect Wealth Star	
正官星 Direct Officer Star	
七殺星 7 Killings Star	
正印星 Direct Resource Star	
偏印星 Indirect Resource Star	
傷官星 Hurting Officer Star	
食神星 Eating God Star	
比肩星 Friend Star	
劫財星 Rob Wealth Star	

10 Gods Checklist	
Hurting Officer Star	
Eating God Star	
Direct Wealth Star	
Indirect Wealth Star	
Direct Officer Star	
7 Killings Star	
Direct Resource Star	
Indirect Resource Star	
Rob Wealth Star	
Friend Star	

Hour Stem 10 God	Day Master	Month Stem 10 God	Year Stem 10 God
Hour Branch 10 God (Main Qi)	Day Branch 10 God (Main Qi)	Month Branch 10 God (Main Qi)	Year Branch 10 God (Main Qi)
Hour Branch 10 God (Sub-Qi)	Day Branch 10 God (Sub- Qi)	Month Branch 10 God (Sub-Qi)	Year Branch 10 God (Sub-Qi)

What's Next for Me?
Simple. Be A Better You!

Now that you've read the Destiny Code series of books and understood your chart, there are further avenues to explore towards becoming a Better You and improving your Destiny.

Take up a course in BaZi:

1. Attend a Class

Joey Yap's Mastery Academy offers two options for genuine students and enthusiasts of Chinese Astrology. There are **Live Courses** scheduled regularly at the Academy or at selected cities around the world. Please visit our website, **www.masteryacademy.com** for our full Academic Calendar and Events details.

2. Study from Home

Joey Yap's Home Study Courses provides the convenience to those who prefer to study at their own pace and the convenience of their own home.

Course	Live	Home Study
Design Your Destiny This is a three-day program with a focus on the DRT™ (Decision Referential Technology) method, a tool that helps you make better decisions based on your BaZi Personality Profile Type. It's an ideal entry level program for anyone looking for the most effective and easiest way to study BaZi. This program introduces you to the *least resistant way to transform your life.* **www.masteryacademy.com/DRT**	✓	

Course		
BaZi Mastery: Module One **Mapping Your Life** This is the foundation course designed to introduce you to the essential theories and application techniques of BaZi. Learn how to Map Your Life and decode your destiny in terms of Wealth, Health and Relationships. Ideal for beginners and those who are interested to practice BaZi professionally. **www.bazimastery.com**	✓	✓
BaZi Mastery: Module Two **Mastering Your Future** This module provides an in-depth, comprehensive knowledge on the tools and methods required to practice BaZi professionally. Joey Yap designed this class to be EASY for anyone to learn and understand with a structured and comprehensive workbook (more than 400 pages worth of information) and teaching method. This course brings you deeper into understanding your chart and more importantly, what corrective measures one can take to improve one's destiny. **www.bazimastery.com**	✓	✓
BaZi Mastery: Module Three **Advanced Practitioners Course** This course is structured to give serious students an advanced-level understanding of the principal concepts of BaZi. Its emphasis on BaZi assessment methods, that depart from the more theoretical slant of the previous modules, to emphasize modes of reading and evaluation that go a long way toward building the skills of BaZi practitioners. You will learn how to predict outcomes and improve one's destiny.	✓	
BaZi Mastery: Module Four **Master Course in BaZi** This module sharpens the students' critical and structural reading skills while building up proficiency in theories and principles to perform more sophisticated analyses using classical methodologies, as well specific BaZi Date Selection methods. This program covers in-depth explanation of various ancient texts of BaZi, revealing closely guarded secrets of famous Ming and Qing Dynasty masters of this art.	✓	

About Joey Yap

Joey Yap first began learning about Chinese Metaphysics from masters in the field when he was fifteen.

Despite having graduated with a Commerce degree in Accounting, Joey never became an accountant. Instead, he began to give seminars, talks and professional Chinese Metaphysic consultations in Malaysia, Singapore, India, Australia, Canada, England, Germany and the United States, becoming a household name in the field.

By the age of twenty-six, Joey became a self-made millionaire and in 2008, he was listed in The Malaysian Tatler as the Top 300 Most Influential People in Malaysia and Prestige's Top 40 Under 40.

His practical and result-driven take on Feng Shui and BaZi sets him apart from other older, traditional masters and practitioners in the field. He shows people how the ancient teachings can be utilized for tangible REAL world benefits. The success he and his clients enjoy, thanks to his advice, is positive proof that Feng Shui and BaZi Astrology works, whether everyone believes in it or not!

Today, Joey has helped and worked with governments and the wealthiest people in Singapore, Hong Kong, China, Malaysia and Japan. His clients include multinationals, developers, tycoons and royalties. On Bloomberg, he is featured on-air as a regular guest on the subject of Feng Shui annual forecasts. He is retained by twenty-five top Malaysian property developers to help determine suitable candidates to take top management, change their space and Feng Shui mechanism, the way they make decisions, and understand the natural cosmic energies that can influence their decision-making.

Joey is devoted to using his success to advance the field he works within.

The Joey Yap Consulting Group is the world's largest and first specialized metaphysics consultation firm. His consultancy, and professional speaking and training engagements with Microsoft, HP, Bloomberg, Citibank, HSBC and many more have seen the benefits of Classical Feng Shui and BaZi find their way into corporate environment and culture. Celebrities, property developers and other large organizations turn to Joey when they need the best.

After years of field-testing and fine-tuning his teachings, he has put together a team in the form of Joey Yap Research International. The objective of this Research Team is to scientifically track and verify the positive impact of Feng Shui and BaZi on subjects and ultimately to assist more people in achieving their life goals.

The Mastery Academy of Chinese Metaphysics which Joey founded teaches thousands of students from all around the world about Classical Feng Shui, Chinese Astrology and Face Reading. Many graduates have gone on to become successful in their own right, becoming sought after consultants, setting up their own consultancy businesses or even becoming educators, passing on Chinese Metaphysics knowledge to others.

Joey has also created the Decision Referential Technology™, offering decision reformation training on how to make better decisions in business and in personal life. He has led his team of highly trained consultants to help clients create more positive change in corporate boardrooms and increase production in their companies, helping people see their business outlook for each year so they may anticipate, plan and execute their strategies successfully.

Joey's work has been featured regularly in various popular global publications and networks like Time, Forbes, the International Herald Tribune and Bloomberg. He has also written columns for The New Straits Times, The Star and The Edge – Malaysia's leading newspapers. He has achieved bestselling author status with over sixty-five books, which have sold more than three million copies to-date.

It is safe to say that Joey Yap is a world leader in the field of Chinese Metaphysics.

His success is not limited to matters of Feng Shui and BaZi. Although his success is a product of them, he is also a successful entrepreneur, leading his own companies and property investment portfolio. When not teaching metaphysics or consulting around the world, Joey is a Naruto-fan, avid snowboarder and is crazy for fruits de mer.

Author's personal website :

www.joeyyap.com

Joey Yap on Facebook:

www.facebook.com/JoeyYapFB

MASTERY ACADEMY
OF CHINESE METAPHYSICS

Your **Preferred** Choice to the Art & Science of Classical Chinese Metaphysics Studies

Bringing **innovative** techniques and **creative** teaching methods to an ancient study.

Mastery Academy of Chinese Metaphysics was established by Joey Yap to play the role o disseminating this Eastern knowledge to the modern world with the belief that this valuable knowledg should be accessible to anyone, anywhere.

Its goal is to enrich people's lives through accurate, professional teaching and practice of Chines Metaphysics knowledge globally. It is the first academic institution of its kind in the world to adopt th tradition of Western institutions of higher learning - where students are encourage to explore, questio and challenge themselves and to respect different fields and branches of study - with the appreciation an respect of classical ideas and applications that have stood the test of time.

The art and science of Chinese Metaphysics studies – be it Feng Shui, BaZi (Astrology), Mian Xiang (Fac Reading), ZeRi (Date Selection) or Yi Jing – is no longer a field shrouded with mystery and superstitior In light of new technology, fresher interpretations and innovative methods as well as modern teachin tools like the Internet, interactive learning, e-learning and distance learning, anyone from virtually an corner of the globe, who is keen to master these disciplines can do so with ease and confidence under th guidance and support of the Academy.

It has indeed proven to be a center of educational excellence for thousands of students from over thirt countries across the world; many of whom have moved on to practice classical Chinese Metaphysic professionally in their home countries.

At the Academy, we believe in enriching people's lives by empowering their destinies through th disciplines of Chinese Metaphysics. Learning is not an option - it's a way of life!

MASTERY ACADEMY
OF CHINESE METAPHYSICS™

MALAYSIA
19-3, The Boulevard, Mid Valley City, 59200 Kuala Lumpur, Malaysia
Tel : +603-2284 8080 | Fax : +603-2284 1218
Email : info@masteryacademy.com
Website : www.masteryacademy.com

Australia, Austria, Canada, China, Croatia, Cyprus, Czech Republic, Denmark, France, Germany, Greece, Hungary, India, Italy, Kazakhstan, Malaysia, Netherlands (Holland), New Zealand, Philippines, Poland, Russian Federation, Singapore, Slovenia, South Africa, Switzerland, Turkey, U.S.A., Ukraine, United Kingdom

www.masteryacademy.com | +603 - 2284 8080

Mastery Academy around the world

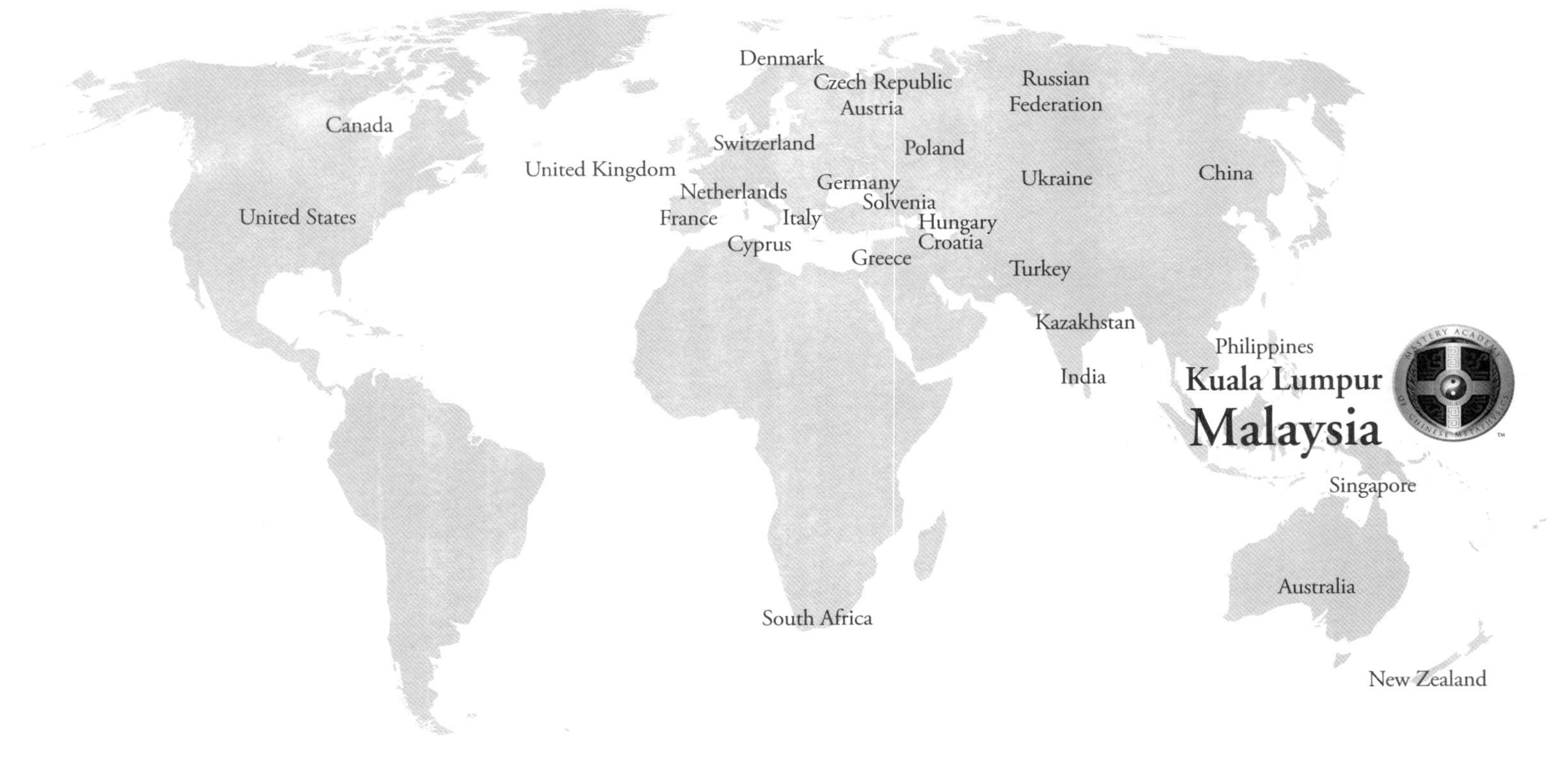

JOEY YAP CONSULTING GROUP

Pioneering Metaphysics - Centric Personal Coaching and Corporate Consulting

The Joey Yap Consulting Group is the world's first specialised metaphysics consultation firm. Founded in 2002 by renown international Feng Shui and BaZi consultant, author and trainer Joey Yap, the Joey Yap Consulting Group is a pioneer in the provision of metaphysics-driven coaching and consultation services for individuals and corporations.

The Group's core consultation practice areas are Feng Shui and BaZi, which are complimented by ancillary services like Date Selection, Face Reading and Yi Jing Divination. The Group's team of highly-trained professional consultants are led by Principal Consultant Joey Yap. The Joey Yap Consulting Group is the firm of choice for corporate captains, entrepreneurs, celebrities and property developers when it comes to Feng Shui and BaZi-related advisory and knowledge.

Across Industries: Our Portfolio of Clients

Our diverse portfolio of both corporate and individual clients from all around the world bears testimony to our experience and capabilities.

Joey Yap Consulting Group is the firm of choice for many of Asia's leading multi-national corporations, listed entities, conglomerates and top-tier property developers when it comes to Feng Shui and corporate BaZi.

Our services also engaged by professionals, prominent business personalities, celebrities, high-profile politicians and people from all walks of life.

JOEY YAP CONSULTING GROUP

Name (Mr./Mrs./Ms.):____________________

Contact Details

Tel:______________ Fax:______________

Mobile :____________________

E-mail:____________________

What Type of Consultation Are You Interested In?

☐ Feng Shui ☐ BaZi ☐ Date Selection ☐ Corporate Events

Please tick if applicable:

☐ Are you a Property Developer looking to engage Joey Yap Consulting Group?

☐ Are you a Property Investor looking for tailor-made packages to suit your investment requirements?

Please attach your name card here.

Thank you for completing this form. Please fax it back to us at:

Malaysia & the rest of the world
Fax : +603-2284 2213 Tel : +603-2284 1213

www.joeyyap.com

Feng Shui Consultations

For Residential Properties
- Initial Land/Property Assessment
- Residential Feng Shui Consultations
- Residential Land Selection
- End-to-End Residential Consultation

For Commercial Properties
- Initial Land/Property Assessment
- Commercial Feng Shui Consultations
- Commercial Land Selection
- End-to-End Commercial Consultation

For Property Developers
- End-to-End Consultation
- Post-Consultation Advisory Services
- Panel Feng Shui Consultant

For Property Investors
- Your Personal Feng Shui Consultant
- Tailor-Made Packages

For Memorial Parks & Burial Sites
- Yin House Feng Shui

BaZi Consultations

Personal Destiny Analysis
- Personal Destiny Analysis for Individuals
- Children's BaZi Analysis
- Family BaZi Analysis

Strategic Analysis for Corporate Organizations
- Corporate BaZi Consultations
- BaZi Analysis for Human Resource Management

Entrepreneurs & Business Owners
- BaZi Analysis for Entrepreneurs

Career Pursuits
- BaZi Career Analysis

Relationships
- Marriage and Compatibility Analysis
- Partnership Analysis

For Everyone
- Annual BaZi Forecast
- Your Personal BaZi Coach

Date Selection Consultations

- **Marriage Date Selection**
- **Caesarean Birth Date Selection**
- **House-Moving Date Selection**
- **Renovation & Groundbreaking Dates**
- **Signing of Contracts**
- **Official Openings**
- **Product Launches**

Corporate Events

Many reputable organizations and instituitions have worked closely with Joey Yap Consulting Group to build a synergistic business relationship by engaging our team of consultants, led by Joey Yap, as speakers at their corporate events.

We tailor our seminars and talks to suit the anticipated or pertinent group of audience. Be it department, subsidiary, your clients or even the entire corporation, we aim to fit your requirements in delivering the intended message(s).

Chinese Metaphysics Reference Series

The Chinese Metaphysics Reference Series is a collection of reference texts, source material, and educational textbooks to be used as supplementary guides by scholars, students, researchers, teachers and practitioners of Chinese Metaphysics.

These comprehensive and structured books provide fast, easy reference to aid in the study and practice of various Chinese Metaphysics subjects including Feng Shui, BaZi, Yi Jing, Zi Wei, Liu Ren, Ze Ri, Ta Yi, Qi Men and Mian Xiang.

The Chinese Metaphysics Compendium

At over 1,000 pages, the *Chinese Metaphysics Compendium* is a unique one-volume reference book that compiles all the formulas relating to Feng Shui, BaZi (Four Pillars of Destiny), Zi Wei (Purple Star Astrology), Yi Jing (I-Ching), Qi Men (Mystical Doorways), Ze Ri (Date Selection), Mian Xiang (Face Reading) and other sources of Chinese Metaphysics.

It is presented in the form of easy-to-read tables, diagrams and reference charts, all of which are compiled into one handy book. This first-of-its-kind compendium is presented in both English and the original Chinese, so that none of the meanings and contexts of the technical terminologies are lost.

The only essential and comprehensive reference on Chinese Metaphysics, and an absolute must-have for all students, scholars, and practitioners of Chinese Metaphysics.

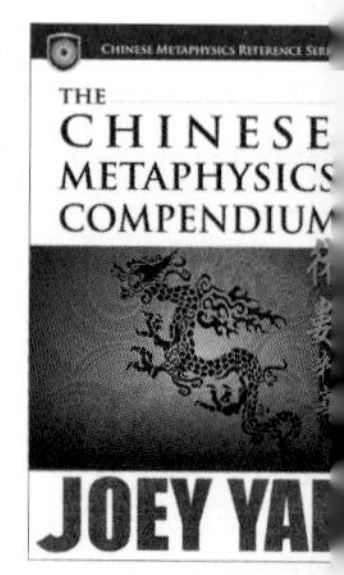

The Ten Thousand Year Calendar (Pocket Edition)

The Ten Thousand Year Calendar

Dong Gong Date Selection

The Date Selection Compendium

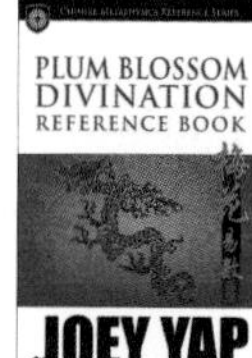

Plum Blossoms Divination Reference Book

San Yuan Dragon Gate Eight Formations Water Method

Xuan Ko Gua Ten T Year Cal

Bazi Hour Pillar Useful Gods - Wood

Bazi Hour Pillar Useful Gods - Fire

Bazi Hour Pillar Useful Gods - Earth

Bazi Hour Pillar Useful Gods - Metal

Bazi Hour Pillar Useful Gods - Water

Xuan Kong Da Gua Structures Reference Book

Xuan Kong I Gua Transfo Analy

Bazi Structures and Structural Useful Gods - Wood

Bazi Structures and Structural Useful Gods - Fire

Bazi Structures and Structural Useful Gods - Earth

Bazi Structures and Structural Useful Gods - Metal

Bazi Structures and Structural Useful Gods - Water

Xuan Kong Purple White Script

Earth S Discern Second E

Joey Yap's BaZi Profiling System

hree Levels of BaZi Profiling (English & Chinese versions)

BaZi Profiling, there are three levels that reflect three different stages of a person's personal ature and character structure.

Level 1 – The Day Master

he Day Master in a nutshell is the BASIC YOU. The inborn personality. It is your essential character. t answers the basic question "WHO AM I". There are ten basic personality profiles – the TEN Day Masters – each with its unique set of personality traits, likes and dislikes.

Level 2 – The Structure

he Structure is your behavior and attitude – in other words, how you use your personality. It xpands on the Day Master (Level 1). The structure reveals your natural tendencies in life – are you nore controlling, more of a creator, supporter, thinker or connector? Each of the Ten Day Masters xpress themselves differently through the FIVE Structures. Why do we do the things we do? Why do we like the things we like? – The answers are in our BaZi STRUCTURE.

Level 3 – The Profile

he Profile reveals your unique abilities and skills, the masks that you consciously and unconsciously put on" as you approach and navigate the world. Your Profile speaks of your ROLES in life. There re TEN roles – or Ten BaZi Profiles. Everyone plays a different role.

Vhat makes you happy and what does success mean to you is different to somebody else. Your ense of achievement and sense of purpose in life is unique to your Profile. Your Profile will reveal our unique style.

he path of least resistence to your success and wealth can only be accessed once you get into our "flow." Your BaZi Profile reveals how you can get FLOW. It will show you your patterns in vork, relationship and social settings. Being AWARE of these patterns is your first step to positive ife Transformation.

BaZi Collections

Leading Chinese Astrology Master Trainer Joey Yap makes it easy to learn how to unlock your Destin through your BaZi with these books. BaZi or Four Pillars of Destiny is an ancient Chinese science whic enables individuals to understand their personality, hidden talents and abilities as well as their luck cycl simply by examining the information contained within their birth data.

Understand and appreciate more about this astoundingly accurate ancient Chinese Metaphysical scienc with this BaZi Collection.

Feng Shui Collection

Must-Haves for Property Analysis!

For homeowners, those looking to build their own home or even investors who are looking to apply Fe Shui to their homes, these series of books provides valuable information from the classical Feng Sh therioes and applications.

In his trademark straight-to-the-point manner, Joey shares with you the Feng Shui do's and dont's wh it comes to finding a property with favorable Feng Shui, which is condusive for home living.

Stories & Lessons on Feng Shui Series

All in all, this series is a delightful chronicle of Joey's articles, thoughts and vast experience - as a profession Feng Shui consultant and instructor - that have been purposely refined, edited and expanded upon make for a light-hearted, interesting yet educational read. And with Feng Shui, BaZi, Mian Xiang and Jing all thrown into this one dish, there's something for everyone.

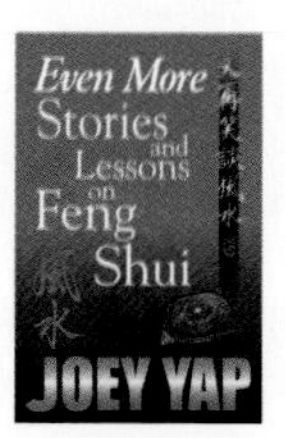

Continue Your Journey with Joey Yap Books in Feng Shui

Pure Feng Shui

Pure Feng Shui is Joey Yap's debut with an international publisher, CICO Books, and is a refreshing and elegant look at the intricacies of Classical Feng Shui – now compiled in a useful manner for modern-day readers. This book is a comprehensive introduction to all the important precepts and techniques of Feng Shui practice.

Your Aquarium Here

This book is the first in Fengshuilogy Series, a series of matter-in-fact and useful Feng Shui books designed for the person who wants to do a fuss-free Feng Shui.

Xuan Kong Flying Stars

This book is an essential introductory book to the subject of Xuan Kong Fei Xing, a well-known and popular system of Feng Shui. Learn 'tricks of the trade' and 'trade secrets' to enhance and maximize Qi in your home or office.

Walking the Dragons

Compiled in one book for the first time from Joey Yap's Feng Shui Mastery Excursion Series, the book highlights China's extensive, vibrant history with astute observations on the Feng Shui of important sites and places. Learn the landform formations of Yin Houses (tombs and burial places), as well as mountains, temples, castles, and villages.

The Art of Date Selection: Personal Date Selection

With the *Art of Date Selection: Personal Date Selection*, learn simple, practical methods you can employ to select not just good dates, but personalized good dates. Whether it's a personal activity such as a marriage or professional endeavor such as launching a business, signing a contract or even acquiring assets, this book will show you how to pick the good dates and tailor them to suit the activity in question, as well as avoid the negative ones too!

Face Reading Collection

Discover Face Reding (English & Chinese versions)

This is a comprehensive book on all areas of Face Reading, covering some of the most important facial features, including the forehead, mouth, ears and even philtrum above your lips. This book eill help you analyse not just your Destiny but help you achieve your full potential and achieve life fulfillment.

Joey Yap's Art of Face Reading

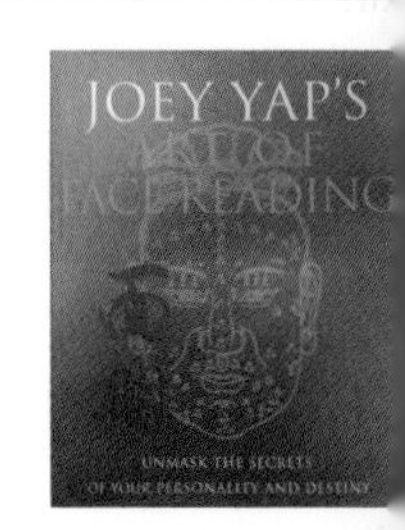

The Art of Face Reading is Joey Yap's second effort with CICO Books, and takes a lighter, more practical approach to Face Reading. This book does not so much focus on the individual features as it does on reading the entire face. It is about identifying common personality types and characters.

Easy Guide on Face Reading (English & Chinese versions)

The Face Reading Essentials series of books comprises 5 individual books on the key features of the fac – Eyes, Eyebrows, Ears, Nose, and Mouth. Each book provides a detailed illustration and a simple ye descriptive explanation on the individual types of the features.

The books are equally useful and effective for beginners, enthusiasts, and the curious. The series is designe to enable people who are new to Face Reading to make the most of first impressions and learn to appl Face Reading skills to understand the personality and character of friends, family, co-workers, and eve business associates.

Annual Releases

2011 Annual Outlook & Tong Shu

Chinese Astrology for 2011

Feng Shui for 2011

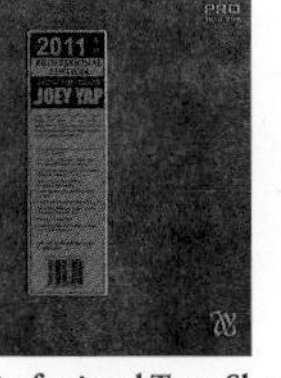

Tong Shu Desktop Calendar 2011

Professional Tong Shu Diary 2011

Tong Shu Monthly Planner 2011

Weekly Ton Diary 20

Educational Tools and Software

Xuan Kong Flying Stars Feng Shui Software

The Essential Application for Enthusiasts and Professionals

The Xuan Kong Flying Stars Feng Shui Software will assist you in the practice of Xuan Kong Feng Shui with minimum fuss and maximum effectiveness. Superimpose the Flying Stars charts over your house plans (or those of your clients) to clearly demarcate the 9 Palaces. Use it to help you create fast and sophisticated chart drawings and presentations, as well as to assist professional practitioners in the report-writing process before presenting the final reports for your clients. Students can use it to practice their Xuan Kong Feng Shui skills and knowledge, and it can even be used by designers and architects!

BaZi Ming Pan Software Version 2.0

Professional Four Pillars Calculator for Destiny Analysis

The BaZi Ming Pan Version 2.0 Professional Four Pillars Calculator for Destiny Analysis is the most technically advanced software of its kind in the world today. It allows even those without any knowledge of BaZi to generate their own BaZi Charts, and provides virtually every detail required to undertake a comprehensive Destiny Analysis.

This Professional Four Pillars Calculator allows you to even undertake a day-to-day analysis of your Destiny. What's more, all BaZi Charts generated by this software are fully printable and configurable! Designed for both enthusiasts and professional practitioners, this state-of-the-art software blends details with simplicity, and is capable of generating 4 different types of BaZi charts: **BaZi Professional Charts, BaZi Annual Analysis Charts, BaZi Pillar Analysis Charts and BaZi Family Relationship Charts.**

Joey Yap Feng Shui Template Set

Directions are the cornerstone of any successful Feng Shui audit or application. The **Joey Yap Feng Shui Template Set** is a set of three templates to simplify the process of taking directions and determining locations and positions, whether it's for a building, a house, or an open area such as a plot of land, all with just a floor plan or area map.

The Set comprises 3 basic templates: The Basic Feng Shui Template, 8 Mansions Feng Shui Template, and the Flying Stars Feng Shui Template.

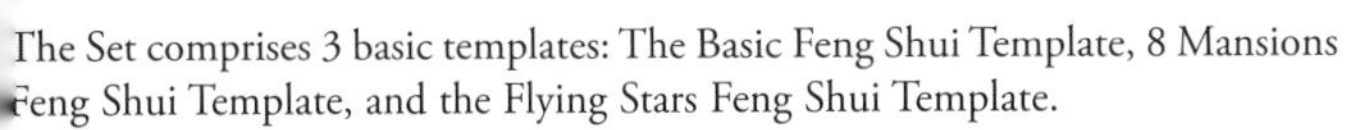

Mini Feng Shui Compass

The Mini Feng Shui Compass is a self-aligning compass that is not only light at 100gms but also built sturdily to ensure it will be convenient to use anywhere. The rings on the Mini Feng Shui Compass are bi-lingual and incorporate the 24 Mountain Rings that is used in your traditional Luo Pan.

The comprehensive booklet included will guide you in applying the 24 Mountain Directions on your Mini Feng Shui Compass effectively and the 8 Mansions Feng Shui to locate the most auspicious locations within your home, office and surroundings. You can also use the Mini Feng Shui Compass when measuring the direction of your property for the purpose of applying Flying Stars Feng Shui.

Educational Tools and Software

Xuan Kong Vol.1
An Advanced Feng Shui Home Study Course

Learn the Xuan Kong Flying Star Feng Shui system in just 20 lessons! Joey Yap's specialised notes and course work have been written to enable distance learning without compromising on the breadth or quality of the syllabus. Learn at your own pace with the same material students in a live class would use. The most comprehensive distance learning course on Xuan Kong Flying Star Feng Shui in the market. Xuan Kong Flying Star Vol.1 comes complete with a special binder for all your course notes.

Feng Shui for Period 8 - (DVD)

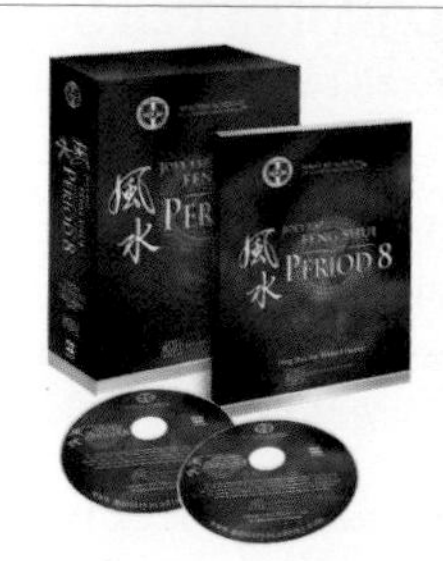

Don't miss the Feng Shui Event of the next 20 years! Catch Joey Yap LIVE and find out just what Period 8 is all about. This DVD boxed set zips you through the fundamentals of Feng Shui and the impact of this important change in the Feng Shui calendar. Joey's entertaining, conversational style walks you through the key changes that Period 8 will bring and how to tap into Wealth Qi and Good Feng Shui for the next 20 years.

Xuan Kong Flying Stars Beginners Workshop - (DVD)

Take a front row seat in Joey Yap's Xuan Kong Flying Stars workshop with this unique LIVE RECORDING of Joey Yap's Xuan Kong Flying Stars Feng Shui workshop, attended by over 500 people. This DVD program provides an effective and quick introduction of Xuan Kong Feng Shui essentials for those who are just starting out in their study of classical Feng Shui. Learn to plot your own Flying Star chart in just 3 hours. Learn 'trade secret' methods, remedies and cures for Flying Stars Feng Shui. This boxed set contains 3 DVDs and 1 workbook with notes and charts for reference.

BaZi Four Pillars of Destiny Beginners Workshop - (DVD)

Ever wondered what Destiny has in store for you? Or curious to know how you can learn more about your personality and inner talents? BaZi or Four Pillars of Destiny is an ancient Chinese science that enables us to understand a person's hidden talent, inner potential, personality, health and wealth luck from just their birth data. This specially compiled DVD set of Joey Yap's BaZi Beginners Workshop provides a thorough and comprehensive introduction to BaZi. Learn how to read your own chart and understand your own luck cycle. This boxed set contains 3 DVDs and 1 workbook with notes and reference charts.

DVD Series

oey Yap's Face Reading Revealed DVD Series

Aian Xiang, the Chinese art of Face Reading, is an ancient form of physiognomy and entails the use of the face nd facial characteristics to evaluate key aspects of a person's life, luck and destiny. In his Face Reading DVDs eries, Joey Yap shows you how the facial features reveal a wealth of information about a person's luck, destiny nd personality.

Aian Xiang also tell us the talents, quirks and personality of an individual. Do you know that just by looking at person's face, you can ascertain his or her health, wealth, relationships and career? Let Joey Yap show you how he 12 Palaces can be utilised to reveal a person's inner talents, characteristics and much more.

eng Shui for Homebuyers DVD Series

n these DVDs, you will also learn how to identify properties with good Feng Shui features that will help ou promote a fulfilling life and achieve your full potential. Discover how to avoid properties with negative eng Shui that can bring about detrimental effects to your health, wealth and relationships.

oey will also elaborate on how to fix the various aspects of your home that may have an impact on the Feng hui of your property and give pointers on how to tap into the positive energies to support your goals.

Discover Feng Shui with Joey Yap: Set of 4 DVDs

nformative and entertaining, classical Feng Shui comes alive in *Discover Feng Shui with Joey Yap!*

ou have the questions. Now let Joey personally answer them in this 4-set DVD ompilation! Learn how to ensure the viability of your residence or workplace, eng Shui-wise, without having to convert it into a Chinese antiques' shop. Classical Feng Shui is about harnessing the natural power of your environment o improve quality of life. It's a systematic and subtle metaphysical science.

Walking the Dragons with Joey Yap (The TV Series)

This DVD set features eight episodes, covering various landform Feng Shui nalyses and applications from Joey Yap as he and his co-hosts travel through China. It includes case studies of both modern and historical sites with a focus n Yin House (burial places) Feng Shui and the tombs of the Qing Dynasty mperors.

The series was partly filmed on-location in mainland China, and the state of elangor, Malaysia.

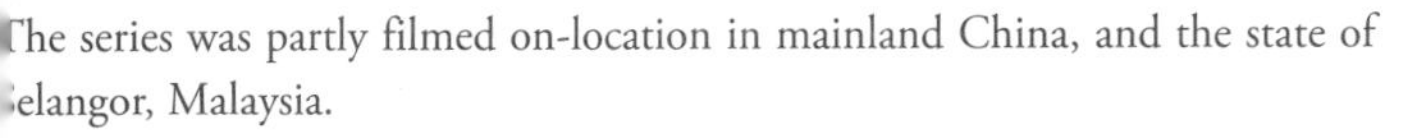

Home Study Courses

Gain Valuable Knowledge from the Comfort of Your Home

Now, armed with your trusty computer or laptop and Internet access, knowledge of Chinese Metaphysic is just a click away!

3 easy steps to activate your Home Study Course:

Step 1:
Go to the URL as indicated on the Activation Card, and key in your Activation Code

Step 2:
At the Registration page, fill in the details accordingly to enable us to generate your Student Identification (Student ID).

Step 3:
Upon successful registration, you may begin your lessons immediately.

Joey Yap's Feng Shui Mastery HomeStudy Course

Module 1: **Empowering Your Home**
Module 2: **Master Practitioner Program**
Learn how easy it is to harness the power of the environment to promote health, wealth and prosperity in your life. The knowledge and applications of Feng Shui will no more be a mystery but a valuable tool you can master on your own.

Joey Yap's BaZi Mastery HomeStudy Course

Module 1: **Mapping Your Life**
Module 2: **Mastering Your Future**
Discover your path of least resistance to success with insights about your personality and capabilities, and what strengths you can tap on to maximize your potential for success and happiness by mastering BaZi (Chinese Astrology). This course will teach you all the essentials you need to interpret a BaZi chart and more.

Joey Yap's Mian Xiang Mastery HomeStudy Course

Module 1: **Face Reading**
Module 2: **Advanced Face Reading**
A face can reveal so much about a person. Now, you can learn the art and science of Mian Xiang (Chinese Face Reading) to understand a person's character based on his or her facial features with ease and confidence.

Mian Xiang Mastery Series™
LIVE COURSES (MODULES ONE AND TWO)

The Mian Xiang Mastery Series™ comprises of Mian Xiang Mastery Modules 1 and 2 to allow students to learn this ancient art in a thorough, detailed manner. Each module has a carefully-developed syllabus that allows students to get acquainted with the fundamentals of Mian Xiang before moving on to the more intricate theories and principles that will enable them to practice Mian Xiang with greater depth and complexity.

Module One:
Basic Face Reading

Module Two:
Practical Face Reading

Yi Jing Mastery Series™
LIVE COURSES (MODULES ONE AND TWO)

The Yi Jing Mastery Series™ comprises Modules 1 and 2. Both Modules aim to give casual and serious Yi Jing enthusiasts a serious insight into one of the most important philosophical treatises in ancient Chinese thought. Yi Jing uses sophisticated formulas and calculations to derive the answers to questions we pose. It is a science of divination, and in our classes there is a heavy emphasis on the scientific aspect of it. It bears no religious or superstitious affiliation.

Module One:
Traditional Yi Jing

Module Two:
Plum Blossom Numerology

Ze Ri Mastery Series™
LIVE COURSES (MODULES ONE AND TWO)

The ZeRi Mastery Series™ consists of ZeRi Mastery Modules 1 and 2. This program provides students with a thorough introduction to the art of Date Selection both for Personal and Feng Shui purposes. Our ZeRi Mastery Series™ aims to provide a thorough and comprehensive program on the art of Date Selection, covering everything from Personal and Feng Shui Date Selection to Xuan Kong Da Gua Date Selection.

Module One:
Personal and Feng Shui Date Selection

Module Two:
Xuan Kong Da Gua Date Selection

Feng Shui for Life

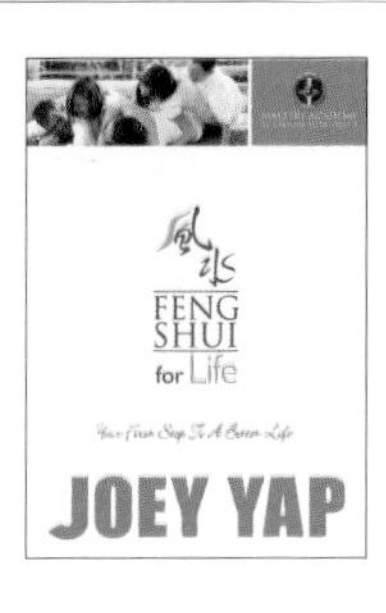

This is an entry-level five-day course designed for the Feng Shui beginner to learn the application of practical Feng Shui in day-to-day living. Lessons include quick tips on analyzing the BaZi chart, simple Feng Shui solutions for the home, basic Date Selection, useful Face Reading techniques and practical Water formulas. A great introduction course on Chinese Metaphysics studies for beginners.

Joey Yap's
Design Your Destiny

This is a three-day life transformation program designed to inspire awareness and action for you to create a better quality of life. It introduces the DRT™ (Decision Referential Technology) method, which utilizes the BaZi Personality Profiling system to determine the right version of you, and serves as a tool to help you make better decisions and achieve a better life in the least resistant way possible based on your Personality Profile Type.

Walk the Mountains! Learn Feng Shui in a Practical and Hands-on Program

Feng Shui Mastery Excursion™

Learn landform (Luan Tou) Feng Shui by walking the mountains and chasing the Dragon's vein in China. This Program takes the students in a study tour to examine notable Feng Shui landmarks, mountains, hills, valleys, ancient palaces, famous mansions, houses and tombs in China. The Excursion is a 'practical' hands-on course where students are shown to perform readings using the formulas they've learnt and to recognize and read Feng Shui Landform (Luan Tou) formations.

Read about China Excursion here:
http://www.fengshuiexcursion.com

Mastery Academy courses are conducted around the world. Find out when will Joey Yap be in your area by visiting **www.masteryacademy.com** or call our office at **+603-2284 8080**.